SONS OF GOD

Michael

Bless you in

eternal

Zen Garcia

Zen Garcia
SONS OF GOD

Who We Are, Why We Are Here

TATE PUBLISHING
AND ENTERPRISES, LLC

Published by Tate Publishing & Enterprises, LLC
127 E. Trade Center Terrace | Mustang, Oklahoma 73064 USA
1.888.361.9473 | www.tatepublishing.com

Tate Publishing is committed to excellence in the publishing industry. The company reflects the philosophy established by the founders, based on Psalm 68:11,
"The Lord gave the word and great was the company of those who published it."

Book design copyright © 2012 by Tate Publishing, LLC. All rights reserved.
Cover design by Rodrigo Adolfo
Interior design by Nathan Harmony

Published in the United States of America

ISBN: 978-1-62295-011-9
1. Religion / Christian Theology / Angelology & Demonology
2. Religion / Christian Theology / General
12.10.22

DEDICATION

As always first honor to the Holy Trinity (Great Mystery): YHWH Father Creator, Yahushuah, only begotten Son, and Barbelo the Holy Spirit, for all life and being, chance and opportunity. I lovingly dedicate this book to those seekers of lost paradise who dedicate self to serving Yahushuah Savior Messiah, who pick up the cross of salvation and, displaying it proudly, wear it as a badge of honor. I honor you for associating self to the only truth and way that leads to everlasting life and escape from the evils of this world and the flesh. The overcomers will be rewarded with a return to our first estate and restoration of our original bright natured immortal status as ministering spirits under the Morningstar administration of Christ Yahushuah. Those not written into the Book of Life will suffer a similar fate as the rebel angels or fallen watchers that both rebelled against the Lord so long ago, and for their evil will be wiped from reality as if they had never existed.

I also dedicate this book to my mother, Myong Hwa Shin Garcia, my father, Manuel Pedro Garcia, my son, Justin James Garcia, and his mother, Stacy Painter Wilson. I can never thank you, Lord, enough for the blessing of incredible family. I would be among the lost and wayward now if it weren't for their unconditional love and persistent forgiveness. I pray, Lord, that you keep them and the rest of us under your wing of protection and guide us in the discernment you would have us share with one another in awakening each other to the realities of what we face here on this planet as angels trapped in a fallen state, imprisoned on a fallen world and bound under the influence of demonic forces we are only now beginning to comprehend. I pray this book awaken you to who you are and why we are here on this planet and at this special time.

ACKNOWLEDGEMENTS

I would like to honor my friends, listeners, and viewers whom have, over the course of many years, supported me in my work to awaken others to the strangeness of our current life reality.

I would especially like to thank Dr. Joye Jeffries Pugh, Professor Truth, John the Baptist, Jonathan Kleck, Kenneth Beer, Roman White, and Alexander Bachman, among others, whose friendship has sustained and confirmed my own discernment on so many esoteric aspects of scripture. Truly out of the mouths of two or three witnesses shall the truth be established.

TABLE OF CONTENTS

The Lord possessed me in the beginning of his way, before his works of old. I was set up from everlasting, from the beginning, or ever the earth was. When there were no depths, I was brought forth; when there were no fountains abounding with water. Before the mountains were settled, before the hills was I brought forth: While as yet he had not made the earth, nor the fields, nor the highest part of the dust of the world. When he prepared the heavens, I was there: when he set a compass upon the face of the depth: When he established the clouds above: when he strengthened the fountains of the deep: When he gave to the sea his decree, that the waters should not pass his commandment: when he appointed the foundations of the earth: Then I was by him, as one brought up with him: and I was daily his delight, rejoicing always before him; Rejoicing in the habitable part of his earth; and my delights were with the sons of men.

Proverbs 8:22-31

FOREWORD

Back in the seventies I listened to Jack Van Impe on my record player at the age of nine. I had recently received the Baptism of the Holy Spirit and was overwhelmed with a hunger to learn about our Heavenly Father and Jesus Christ (Yahushua), His son, my King. After decades of so-called *advanced* Bible teaching from traditional theologians educated by the Tavistock Institute, it wasn't until approximately thirty-seven years later I would really begin to understand the Bible's deeper mysteries. Through a series of supernatural coincidences, I was led to our brother Zen Garcia and have been deeply blessed by our developing friendship and continuously unfolding revelations.

> For nothing is secret that will not be revealed, nor anything hidden that will not be known and come to light. Therefore take heed how you hear. For whoever has, to him more will be given; and whoever does not have, even what he seems to have will be taken from him.
>
> Luke 8:17-18 (NKJV)

There are twenty-two books mentioned in the sixty-six-book canon of the common Holy Bible of today that do not appear in the Bible. Some are lost (or so they say). Some were simply rejected by an appointed committee. If Jesus had to rebuke Satan while talking to his own apostle Peter (Mark 16:23, get thee behind me Satan!), how much more so have our post Nicean Council canon committees been infiltrated by the works of the dark side?

As I sit here in my office writing this on October 27, 2011 (supposedly the eve of the end of the Mayan long-count calendar), I am expecting at any moment a war to break out. Never mind the ominous approaching date of 11/11/11 and the pending threats of the Hoover Dam being destroyed by the Serpent. So the serpent spewed water out of his mouth like a flood after the woman, that he might cause her to be carried away by the flood (Revelation 12:15, KJV).

Given the date of this writing, one might expect that the above-mentioned war to be with the country of Iran. The real threat to humanity is not coming from Russia or China; it's coming from afar on the wings of chariots that are carried as the wind upon the earth. In 1611 the original King James Bible was written and assembled. It contained a series of inspired writings from the prophet Esdras. Since then, those books have been pillaged from our hands by the forces of evil. Revealed in those prophecies are mysteries of our current day. It contains warnings from one of our Heavenly Father's greatest prophets that have been intentionally hidden from our view. Indeed as the prophet Esdras warned us, the dragons of Arabia come to war—one that will take place here on Earth.

2 Esdras 15:29 says, "Where the nations of the dragons of Arabia shall come out with many chariots, and the multitude of them shall be carried as the wind upon earth, that all they which hear them may fear and tremble."

As the author of over 350 articles published on the website www.tribulation-now.org, over the years I have struggled intensely with accepting all things esoteric. We all suffer from the sin of unbelief. The devil's army has not only pillaged our scripture, but it has infiltrated our churches, ensuring that anyone searching for the truth outside the sixty-six-book canon be labeled a heretic. If you dare mention an Erich von Daniken book within the earshot of a fellow brother, you're certain to hear, "That's of the devil!" Not only are we restricted to the itchy ears, milky doctrine of the tax-free, 501 c-3 bound IRS churches, we are blinded by our ignorance to the eventual demise and damnation of many fellow brothers and sisters—particularly those lost in the dimension of the New Age. When God (YHWH, our Heavenly Father and Most High God) says he will send a strong delusion (2 Thesselonians 2:11) this matter cannot be taken lightly.

When I started writing articles for *Tribulation Now*, I didn't even believe in UFOs, let alone fallen angels. To the detriment of my marriage, and at the expense of hundreds of hours of intense research, I began my quest for the truth behind this New World Order. Using what I refer to as the Venn Diagram method of research, I created overlapping ovals on a white board. Each oval represented an area of necessary study. The dots had to be connected. I instinctively knew there was a common element to the evil cabal attempting to overthrow the world. Somehow this mystery had to include aliens. Somehow the Bible had to explain fallen angels and UFOs. And indeed it does.

Through a series of supernatural *coincidences* and a research path laden with astonishment and tears, I frequently cried out to our Heavenly Father, asking for understanding. While studying the horrors associated with alien abductions and the hybridization of mankind through the intentional manipulation of the mind and human genome, the question *why* kept surfacing. Along this pathway of metaphorical broken glass, I struggled to understand who we are as humans in the universe of extraterrestrial beings. This glorious revelation will not only excite you about who you are in the universe of life-forms but can save the souls of those hijacked by Lucifer and New Age Ashtar Command minions.

I am excited about this book. God has deeply blessed us with brother Zen Garcia's ability to deep dive through endless and diverse subject matter to uncover the deepest mysteries of our existence and measure the efficacy of the findings against the accepted canon. This is a gift from the Holy Spirit that only the most open minded and humble can accept with grace and revelation.

Be careful *how* you hear. May God bless you mightily. May you stand blameless before the Son of Man.

Yahushua Jesus Christ the King of Kings

John Seitzinger aka John the Baptist

www.tribulation-now.org.

INTRODUCTION

I've been asked by many readers, listeners, and viewers to provide resources for why I believe we are the Sons of God who were once part of the Elohim that served in the Celestial Morningstar council of Yahweh/Yahushuah's administration prior to this incarnation as modern-day human beings. To help establish this premise and unravel the paradigm which, in my opinion, is the most incredibly profound tale that one could ever imagine possible, a story which will retrace the fall and elevation of humanity from paradise to the earth in explaining who we truly are, why we are here, and what this life is really all about. Hopefully, once conveyed, this book will help one comprehend the profound nature of who we are so that all of us can then awaken to remembrance of self that affects world in positivity.

I believe the whole reason why the Lord aspired us to know self is because this revelation can explain, for those whom embrace it, why we are here as fallen angels trapped in the armor of flesh on a prison planet overrun by devils and demons. Unless one awakens to who you are and why you/we are here, one would not understand why the Lord had to come into flesh to redeem us from body, strange vessel of soul, as we live out one lifetime in the immortal journey of spirit.

Because of the controversial nature of my previous works, I decided in 2010 to splinter this information off from the book that I was then publishing, *Lucifer: Father of Cain*. I did not want this information tainted by the focus of that book as the title alone has solicited what I feel undeserved condemnation, and so held it back for publication at a later date. I still do not feel that many people will be able to understand the profound nature of this revelation and that I will probably be much maligned for it, yet I have decided to go ahead with its release due to the lateness of the hour.

Many people consider my work contentious simply because I quote extensively from a wide variety of sources which include the Nag Hammadi codices, Dead Sea Scrolls, apocryphal, pseudepigraphal, Sumerian, Babylonian, Masonic, Satanic, Luciferian, Egyptian, Celtic, Mayan as well as Old Testament, New Testament, and extra biblical sources. The reason I provide such extensive citation is so the reader can verify for himself or herself the sources used in tying and piecing together the story that I will unfold here.

When it comes to truth, do not trust any mortal opinion—the preachers, the bully pulpits, the doublespeak politicians, or the talking bobble heads on TV. We must individually do one's own research when determining truth as far as one's worldview, for how can anyone judge anything without having first investigated the relevancy of its message or the profoundness of its content? Doubt everything brought before you, believe nothing, do one's own homework, and know truth.

> A society whose citizens refuse to see and investigate the facts, who refuse to believe that their government and their media will routinely lie to them and fabricate a reality contrary to verifiable facts, is a society that chooses and deserves the Police State Dictatorship it's going to get.
>
> —Ian Williams Goddard

> Condemnation without investigation is the height of ignorance.
>
> —Albert Einstein

During the course of this book I will bring forth many quotations from the biblical canon, which, unless explained this way, cannot make sense in a paradigm that unifies the totality of scripture with what is available to us as world history, mythology, religion, and fantasy. This knowledge can unify all the aspects of what would seem to be individualized and disparate pieces of unconnected truth in presenting a cohesive pattern, which ties together creature creation and Creator.

> When the pearl is cast down into the mud, it becomes greatly despised, nor if it is anointed with balsam oil will it become more precious. But it always has value in the eyes of its owner. Compare the Sons of God: wherever they may be, they still have value in the eyes of their Father.
>
> Gospel of Philip

Books, like people, should not be judged based on cover alone. It's my contention that should one be able to suspend one's belief system and embrace the possibilities of this book that it has the potential to help one wake up to the remembrance of who you are, why we are here, and what this world is all about.

I realize also that probably not many will be ready for this information and that only a few will get it and yet I believe the world is now ripe for the release of this knowledge. My hope is that many of you will find long sought for secrets within these pages. Knowledge which will confirm those things that I have been stating for years in my radio work and on the www.fallenangels.tv website. The Father has testified in His word as to the desperate nature of the times we would be living in at the end of days and that unless the days were shortened there should be no flesh left. And though no man knows the day or the hour, we are called as children of the light to recognize the signs of the season. This teaching on the Sons of God, along with the revelation of the three Adams and the three World Ages, is, in my opinion, essential for understanding whom Yahushuah our savior messiah was, is, and will be. As the light of creation, the Word, and only begotten Son of Yahweh Elohim, the Father of us all, it was necessary for Him to come into the flesh on a DNA rescue mission to save us as fallen angels condemned to die the death of humanity. I will explain our condemnation, how it stemmed from the eating of the forbidden fruit, what that fruit was, how it led to original sin, and why we are in the fallen state of being we now find ourselves in.

Woven into the explanation is the story of why Lucifer was banished from the heavens and why he decided to rebel initially. I will also tie into this magnificent tale such cryptic and esoteric issues as pre-existence, incarnation, salvation, harvest, and judgment. I will summarize within these pages the fullness of our Father's plan for creation and how His Son, as the first Adam, would come later into flesh to defeat death and show by example that He is the author of eternal life and way to escape all those things prophesied to occur to the Earth which, according to the Word, will make men's hearts fail them.

I will also cover, in detail, the separate creations of the Genesis 1:26 Elohim-molded Primitive Worker, to the Holy Trinity-formed Genesis 2:7, sixth-day spirit-endowed hermaphroditic creation of Civilized Man, who we know as Adam of Paradise, who—having fallen—was transformed into flesh on the 8th day. One must make sense of the 3 World ages and 3 creations of Adam to understand our current world condition.

This third Adam was elevated once he and Eve lost their bright natures, and having fallen to this prison planet, found themselves surrounded by demons and devils bent on persecuting and oppressing themselves and their offspring. Most have never heard about the elevation of Adam and Eve once they were in a fallen state, and yet this teaching too is vital for opening up secrets hidden within the contents of not only the Bible but all other ancient and mostly forgotten books of wisdom, religion, and mythology.

Over the years I have spoken about these things in many books, and recorded many radio shows to expand upon the principles that the Lord has led me to in discerning truth. I believe that this book is the culmination of my plight to remember who I am in playing out my part in the grander scheme of creation, which is life. Everything I have learned, I have attempted to present to you in a way that is cohesive and easily understood.

I know that many things that I expound are very contentious indeed and that many will outright reject and probably never ever even look into the things that I will be writing about here, yet I also know that there are those out there that, like myself, must glean truth through the experience of one's own introspection and imaginative contemplation.

It is my intent that this information only further strengthens and confirms one's faith in our Lord Yahushuah Savior Messiah. With that singular goal in mind, I present this interpretation on the works of myriad apostles, prophets, historians, and traditions with hopes that it only further verifies for you the veracity of the Old and New Testament as books of law for a way of life. Also note that I do not read or study books written by others about gnosis or the interpretation of it. I simply utilize my own discernment in bringing forward the information found here. And like my other books I ask you to believe nothing I bring forth, but to do your own homework to further expound upon those things I have taught for years on my websites and through my video/radio work.

I ask you to go forward in your own relationship with the Most High and ask the Lord to confirm whether the things presented here are true or not for you. I am not worthy to judge, and I certainly am no authority in telling others what they should and should not read or believe in. It's my opinion that, in uncovering wisdom, we must exhaust every avenue of study in trying to put together the puzzles of truth underlying all belief systems everywhere.

—Zen Garcia, July 28, 2011

SONS OF GOD

TIMELINE FOR CREATION

DAY NONE

Everything exists within and as part of the invisible Holy Trinity; the Father, Son, and Holy Spirit are the Source for pre-existence for all forms of creation. Yahushuah as the Word, Light, Tree of Life, and embodiment of the Father unfolds the higher invisible realms and angelic hierarchy, which includes us as Sons of God, part of the Morningstar administration prior to the rebellion of Lucifer. Contrary to belief, there never was a beginning nor will there ever be an ending that surpasses coming judgment. The Holy Trinity as Great Mystery has, was, is, and always will be Alpha Omega and everything in between visible and unseen.

Jehovih said: Have I not declared Myself in the past; in My works have I not provided thousands of years in advance? As I have shown system in the corporeal worlds, know thou, O man, that system prevaileth in the firmament (Book of Jehovih).

In the beginning God created the heaven and the earth. And the earth was without form, and void; and darkness was upon the face of the deep. And the Spirit of God moved upon the face of the waters (Genesis 1, KJV).

DAY ONE

The Son is revealed to the sons of God as light of the universe; creation becomes visible. The angels shout for joy at the revealing of the Great Mystery. The invisible realms are unfolded in perfection and glory forming the foundation for Sophia (Matter) to replicate as a shadow mirror of visible physical worlds. Prior to the separation of light and darkness, the lower angels thought themselves pre-existent beings. Like us they were witness to Yahushuah being called forth by the voice of Father Creator in granting dominion to His Son.

> And God said, Let there be light: and there was light. And God saw the light, that it was good: and God divided the light from the darkness. And God called the light Day, and the darkness he called Night. And the evening and the morning were the first day.
>
> Genesis 1 (KJV)

> Where wast thou when I laid the foundations of the earth? Declare, if thou hast understanding. Who hath laid the measures thereof, if thou knowest? Or who hath stretched the line upon it? Whereupon are the foundations thereof fastened? Or who laid the corner stone thereof; When the morning stars sang together, and all the sons of God shouted for joy? Or who shut up the sea with doors, when it brake forth, as if it had issued out of the womb? When I made the cloud the garment thereof, and thick darkness a swaddlingband for it, And brake up for it my decreed place, and set bars and doors, And said, Hitherto shalt thou come, but no further: and here shall thy proud waves be stayed?
>
> Job 38:4-11 (KJV)

> In the beginning was the Word, and the Word was with God, and the Word was God. The same was in the beginning with God. All things were made by him; and without

him was not any thing made that was made. In him was life; and the life was the light of men. And the light shineth in darkness; and the darkness comprehended it not.

John 1 (KJV)

To the tree I gave life; to man I gave life and spirit also. And the spirit I made was separate from the corporeal life.

Book of Jehovih

DAY TWO

Lucifer (cherubim) contrives envy in his heart desires to be like the Most High, challenges the authority of Yahushuah and tempts one third of the (Seraphim) angels to rebel. War in heaven ensues, and Lucifer becomes Satan the adversary, accuser of the brethren, and is banished with his angels to the five lower heavens.

Niburu (their planet of habitation) is captured as part of our Solar System, bringing the fallen ones to this space, time, and aeon of the universe.

And God said, Let there be a firmament in the midst of the waters, and let it divide the waters from the waters. And God made the firmament, and divided the waters which were under the firmament from the waters which were above the firmament: and it was so. And God called the firmament Heaven. And the evening and the morning were the second day.

Genesis 1:6-8 (KJV)

The division of the firmaments, waters, and heavens above are reference to the ancient war between the Lord of Hosts and the dragon Tiamat as memorialized in the Enuma elish. The Lord would use Niburu to destroy Rahab, dividing the solar system into what became the division of the heavens into inner and outer planets. On Niburu's second orbit as the newest captured member of this solar system, it carried the still coalescing carcass of Tiamat, into what would be the new orbital position for Earth, or Ki, establishing the conditions necessary to harbor life. This was the pivotal moment of history for beings that would later occupy and evolve in what would be a world hospitable to the quick replication and foundation of what became the story of life here on Earth.

But now, O Adam, we will make known to you, what came over us through him, before his fall from heaven. He gathered together his hosts, and deceived them, promising to give them a great kingdom, a divine nature; and other promises he made them. His hosts believed that his word was true, so they yielded to him, and renounced the glory of God. He then sent for us—according to the orders in which we were—to come under his command, and to accept his vein promise. But we would not, and we did not take his advice.

Then after he had fought with God, and had dealt forwardly with Him, he gathered together his hosts, and made war with us. And if it had not been for God's strength that was with us, we could not have prevailed against him to hurl him from heaven. But when he fell from among us, there was great joy in heaven, because of his going down from us.

For if he had remained in heaven, nothing, not even one angel would have remained in it. But God in His mercy, drove him from among us to this dark earth; for he had become darkness itself and a worker of unrighteousness.

The First Book of Adam and Eve, 55

I have made a covenant with my chosen, I have sworn unto David my servant, Thy seed will I establish for ever, and build up thy throne to all generations. Selah. And the heavens shall praise thy wonders, O Lord: thy faithfulness also in the congregation of the saints. For who in the heaven can be compared unto the Lord? Who among the sons of the mighty can be likened unto the LORD. God is greatly to be feared in the assembly of the saints, and to be had in reverence of all them that are about him. O LORD God of hosts, who is a strong LORD like unto thee? Or to thy faithfulness round about thee? Thou rulest the raging of the sea: when the waves thereof arise, thou stillest them. Thou hast broken Rahab in pieces, as one that is slain; thou hast scattered thine enemies with thy strong arm. The heavens are thine, the earth also is thine: as for the world and the fulness thereof, thou hast founded them.

Psalms 89:3-10 (KJV)

Is there any thing whereof it may be said, 'See, this is new?' It hath been already of old time, which was before us (Eccl.1:10, KJV).

The previous quotations reference the prior times before the creation of this world and modern sixth-day humanity. It immortalizes the destruction of Tiamat, here referenced as Rahab, and the climactic events that led to the destruction and recreation of this solar system as portrayed by the ancient creation stories. The Lord even references the enmity between the two different seed-lines and how the line of David would be the blessed line that would lead to the birth of the Messiah.

DAY THREE

Father Creator allowed Niburu to be captured as part of the solar system so that He could utilize this interloper planet to repattern the number, arrangement, and orbits of all of the other planetary members. Niburu would split the heavens, firmaments, or waters into two main divisions, thus its name as the planet of the crossing. After the destruction of Tiamat, Ki, or the new Earth, was shifted from an orbit outside of to one inside of Mars, usurping it as the new third planet from the sun. This event was celebrated by the ancients as having resulted in the perfect circumstance for life to begin multiplying rapidly on what was the recreated planet Earth.

The Annunaki would target this planet in order to acquire the gold necessary to heal a breach in the atmosphere of their planet. Way stations were established by the fallen ones on the moon and Mars for the transportation of gold as both had less gravitational pull, making it possible to lift heavier loads for transport back to Niburu.

> And God said, Let the waters under the heaven be gathered together unto one place, and let the dry land appear: and it was so. And God called the dry land Earth; and the gathering together of the waters called he Seas: and God saw that it was good.
>
> Genesis 1 (KJV)

> The pillars of heaven are stunned at His rebuke. He quiets The sea with his power, and by his understanding He shatters, Rahab, by His spirit the heavens were beautiful; His hand forbids the fugitive snake.
>
> Job 26:11, KJV

> For the creation was not willingly subjected to vanity, but through Him subjecting it, on hope; that also the creation will be freed from the slavery of corruption to the freedom and the glory of the children of God. For we know that all the creation groans together and travails together until now.
>
> Romans 8:20 (KJV)

DAY FOUR

The solar system begins to resettle into new orbits and circuits. Niburu also normalizes into a counterclockwise orbit called a shar that, according to Sumerian calculations, is a period of 3,600 years. As all the planets of the solar system began to synchronize with their newly establish positions, the constellations, sun, moon, and stars also settle into what became a cycle of movement through the twelve houses of the zodiac, a period of 25,920 years. The Annunaki claim that they arrived here on Earth 120 shars ago, which totals 120 x 3600 = 432,000 or the period of time outlined by both Beroussus and the Sumerian King List as the time that the hybrid demigods were granted kingship by their fallen angel parents to rule as vicars upon the Earth. The Enuma elish cites Niburu as the planet of crossing because its orbit dissects the ecliptic exactly where the hammered bracelet or asteroid belt now is.

> And God said, Let the earth bring forth grass, the herb yielding seed, and the fruit tree yielding fruit after his kind, whose seed is in itself, upon the earth: and it was so. And the earth brought forth grass, and herb yielding seed after his kind, and the tree yielding fruit, whose seed was in itself, after his kind: and God saw that it was good. And the evening and the morning were the third day. And God said, Let there be lights in the firmament of the heaven to divide the day from the night; and let them be for signs, and for seasons, and for days, and years: And let them be for lights in the firmament of the heaven to give light upon the earth: and it was so. And God made two great lights; the greater light to rule the day, and the lesser light to rule the night: he made the stars also. And God set them in the firmament of the heaven to give light upon the earth, And to rule over the day and over the night, and to divide the light from the darkness: and God saw that it was good. And the evening and the morning were the fourth day.
>
> Genesis 1:14-19 (KJV)

> Observe ye everything that takes place in the heaven, how they do not change their orbits, and the luminaries which are in the heaven, how they all rise and set in order each in its season, and transgress not against their appointed order.
>
> The Book of Enoch 2:1

DAY FIVE

After the destruction of the First World Age and Tiamat, the fallen angels arrive some 457 to 439,000 years ago on the new earth (Ki) and establish Eridu as their first city and base of operations. It's my opinion that the Annunaki are neither gods nor immortal, and even though they have very long lifespans, they can be killed and die as referenced by Isaiah 14 and Ezekiel 28 on the fall of Lucifer and the destruction of his children.

They are now holding form as flesh-and-blood spirit men and can eat food, drink water, sleep, dream, and procreate much like modern-day humanity. This does not detract from their abilities as multi-dimensional reptilian dragon-like shape-shifting beings that can possess and hold form in all variety of bodies.

> But thou art cast out of thy grave like an abominable branch, and as the raiment of those that are slain, thrust through with a sword, that go down to the stones of the pit; as a carcase trodden under feet. Thou shalt not be joined with them in burial, because thou hast destroyed thy land, and slain thy people: the seed of evildoers shall never be renowned. Prepare slaughter for his children for the iniquity of their fathers; that they do not rise, nor possess the land, nor fill the face of the world with cities. For I will rise up against them, saith the LORD of hosts, and cut off from Babylon the name, and remnant, and son, and nephew, saith the LORD.
>
> Isaiah 14:19-22 (KJV)

> Because thou hast set thine heart as the heart of God; Behold, therefore I will bring strangers upon thee, the terrible of the nations: and they shall draw their swords against the beauty of thy wisdom, and they shall defile thy brightness. They shall bring thee down to the pit, and thou shalt die the deaths of them that are slain in the midst of the seas. Wilt thou yet say before him that slayeth thee,

I am God? But thou shalt be a man, and no God, in the hand of him that slayeth thee. Thou shalt die the deaths of the uncircumcised by the hand of strangers: for I have spoken it, saith the Lord GOD. Thine heart was lifted up because of thy beauty, thou hast corrupted thy wisdom by reason of thy brightness: I will cast thee to the ground, I will lay thee before kings, that they may behold thee. Thou hast defiled thy sanctuaries by the multitude of thine iniquities, by the iniquity of thy traffick; therefore will I bring forth a fire from the midst of thee, it shall devour thee, and I will bring thee to ashes upon the earth in the sight of all them that behold thee. All they that know thee among the people shall be astonished at thee: thou shalt be a terror, and never shalt thou be any more.

Ezekiel 28:6-10, 17-19 (KJV)

Alalu, an exiled Niburian king, landed on the Earth prior to Enki and another group of fifty Annunaki arriving from Niburu. They implement a plan to establish five cities for the monumental task of acquiring, refining, mining, and delivering gold to their own planet for help in combating the ecological disaster they were said to have been experiencing. According to Sumerian teachings they needed huge quantities of gold in order for them to be able to crush it into powder form and then suspend it into the atmosphere to refract the sun's rays. Not being particularly fond of work, they devise a plan to create a primitive worker to serve as slave and relieve them from the burden of labor.

Though this creature was capable of menial tasks, it was not able to understand the secrets of heaven. According to the Chaldean historian Berossus, it was during the early history of pre-adamic humanity that the Annunaki engage in direct bestiality, as well as genetic experimentation on all other animal and plant species available then on planet. It was during this time that an abundance of uniquely hybrid monstrosities came into being.

This creature was not the modern Yahweh Yahushuah-created sixth-day spirit-filled Adam of Genesis 3. The God spoken about in Genesis 1 and 2 is actually a plural term that represents the Elohim or the fallen ones and their genetic intervention upon this planet before modern humans were created.

> And God said, Let the waters bring forth abundantly the moving creature that hath life, and fowl that may fly above the earth in the open firmament of heaven. And God created great whales, and every living creature that moveth, which the waters brought forth abundantly, after their kind, and every winged fowl after his kind: and God saw that it was good. And God blessed them, saying, "Be fruitful, and multiply, and fill the waters in the seas, and let fowl multiply in the earth." And the evening and the morning were the fifth day. And God said, "Let the earth bring forth the living creature after his kind, cattle, and creeping thing, and beast of the earth after his kind": and it was so. And God made the beast of the earth after his kind, and cattle after their kind, and every thing that creepeth upon the earth after his kind: and God saw that it was good. And God said, Let us make man in our image, after our likeness: and let them have dominion over the fish of the sea, and over the fowl of the air, and over the cattle, and over all the earth, and over every creeping thing that creepeth upon the earth. So God created man in his own image, in the image of God created he him; male and female created he them. And God blessed them, and God said unto them, Be fruitful, and multiply, and replenish the earth, and subdue it: and have dominion over the fish of the sea, and over the fowl of the air, and over every living thing that moveth upon the earth. And God said, Behold, I have given you every herb bearing seed, which is upon the face of all the earth, and every tree, in which is the fruit of a tree yielding seed; to you it shall be for meat. And to every beast of the earth, and to every fowl of the air, and to

every thing that creepeth upon the earth, wherein there is life, I have given every green herb for meat: and it was so. And God saw every thing that he had made, and, behold, it was very good. And the evening and the morning were the sixth day.

Genesis 1:20-31 (KJV)

I looked over the wide heavens that I had made, and I saw countless millions of spirits of the dead that had lived and died on other corporeal worlds before the earth was made. I spake in the firmament, and My voice reached to the uttermost places. And there came in answer to the sounds of My voice, myriads of angels from the roadway in heaven, where the earth traveleth. I said to them, Behold! A new world have I created; come ye and enjoy it. Yea, ye shall learn from it how it was with other worlds in ages past. There alighted upon the new earth millions of angels from heaven; but many of them had never fulfilled a corporeal life, having died in infancy, and these angels comprehended not procreation nor corporeal life. And I said, go and deliver Asu from darkness, for he shall also rise in spirit to inherit my etherean worlds. And now was the earth in the latter days of se'mu, and the angels could readily take on corporeal bodies for themselves; out of the elements of the earth clothed they themselves, by force of their wills, with flesh and bones. By the side of the Asuans took they on corporeal forms. And I said: Go ye forth and partake of all that is on the earth; but partake ye not of the tree of life, lest in that labor ye become procreators and as if dead to the heavens whence ye came. But those who had never learned corporeal things, being imperfect in wisdom, comprehended not Jehovih's words, and they dwelt with the Asuans, and were tempted, and partook of the fruit of the tree of life; and lo and behold they saw their own nakedness. And there was born of the first race (Asu) a new race called man; and Jehovih took the earth out of the travail of se'mu and the angels gave up their

corporeal bodies. Jehovih said: Because ye have raised up
those that shall be joint heirs in heaven, ye shall tread the
earth with your feet, and walk by the sides of the new born,
being guardian angels over them, for they are of your own
flesh and kin. Fruit of your seed have I quickened with my
spirit, and man shall come forth with a birth-right to My
etherean worlds.

Book of JehovIh

DAY SIX: SEVEN THOUSAND YEARS AGO

What most don't realize is that not only were the fallen angels
already here before the creation of modern-day humanity, but pre-
adamic man was also already upon the world stage. It was this big
foot type creature that was utilized to create what the Annunaki
call the primitive worker. What's interesting about the Sumerian
stories is that they also cite the sudden appearance of the breath
filled modern-day creation of sixth-day humanity or civilized man.
The Elohim or Annunaki were upon the Earth before the creation
and advent of the seed of Adam. The Elohim were the originators
of the initial root race and civilization. They had established a global
empire, based on trade, that extended to all parts of the world before
pre-adamic humanity had gathered in tribes. It was these beings that
were initially manipulated by the Elohim to bring forth the primitive
worker. The legends of Poseidia, Atlantis, Mu, Lemuria, and Muror
are based on the reality of this original angelic culture and civiliza-
tion.It was during the time of this kingdom, or what the Egyptians
call Zep Tepi—the beginning time—that the hybrid demigods ruled
upon the Earth.In a book called *Mu Revealed*, ancient Mayan documents are cited, which discuss the priesthood of Atlantis specifically
a young priest named Kland as he is educated through the Temple
system. Kland discusses many things within the scope of this scroll,
giving us insight into Atlantis's legend and past. He documents war
and environmental destruction, which spanned a period of 50,000

Bc to 13,000 Bc, when the final destruction of Atlantis occurred with the drowning of the continent. One of the major disputes of that epoch is based on the rights and treatment of these primitive workers. Freedoms were not extended to those creatures and many were treated and used like economic slaves without intrinsic worth or value. Like the Emerald Tablets of Thoth, *Mu Revealed* describes some of the Annunaki as the sons of Belial or sons of darkness, as they begin delving into magic associated to star-gates and the opening of portals. It was during one of these experiments that the Lord brought judgment and destruction upon them, sinking the lands of Atlantis from memory and view. This destruction is described in Jeremiah 4:23.

> A wonder of wonders it is,
>> in the wilderness by themselves to have come about!
>> Indeed a wonder of wonders it is,
>> a new breed of Earthling on Earth has emerged,
>> A Civilized Man has the Earth itself brought forth,
>> Farming and shepherding, crafts and toolmaking he
> can be taught!
>> So was Enlil to Enki saying.
>> Let us of the new breed to Anu word send!
>> Of the new breed word to Anu on Nibiru was beamed.
>> Let seeds that can be sown, let ewes that sheep become,
>> to Earth be sent!
>> So did Enki and Enlil to Anu the suggestion make.
>> By Civilized Man let Anunnaki and Earthlings become
> satiated!
>> Anu the words heard, by the words he was amazed:
>> That by life essences one kind to another leads is not
> unheard of!
>> to them words back he sent.
>> That on Earth a Civilized Man from the Adamu so
> quickly appeared, that is unheard of!
>
> Lost Book of Enki

This sixth-day creation was elevated by Yahushuah as Adam of light and would be the creature tempted to fall from paradise by Lucifer Satan, or whom we come to know as the Sumerian Enki. He, as the nachash of Genesis 3, would tempt Eve to eat of the forbidden fruit once she was separated from Adam. The reason the Lord separated them and placed them in paradise was to actually protect them from the fallen ones. This is also why Lucifer had to sneak into paradise guised as a serpent just to be able to tempt the Lord's highest creatures. He would cause them to fall from paradise having eaten of the fruit of the tree of the knowledge of good and evil, whereupon losing their bright nature they would lose their protection in paradise and be banished to reside with the other fallen angels on the lower earth. After the Sabbath and day of rest, the Lord would reinstitute plans to redeem Adam and descendents while at the same time condemn the fallen angels for their perpetuation of evil in this world.

> For this cause, therefore, have I brought the keys of the mysteries of the kingdom of heaven; otherwise no flesh in the world would be saved. For without mysteries no one will enter into the Light-kingdom, be he a righteous or a sinner. For this cause, therefore, have I brought the keys of the mysteries into the world, that I may free the sinners who shall have faith in me and hearken unto me, so that I may free them from the bonds and the seals of the æons of the rulers and bind them to the seals and the vestures and the orders of the Light, in order that he whom I shall free in the world from the bonds and the seals of the æons of the rulers, may be freed in the Height from the bonds and seals of the æons of the rulers, and in order that he whom I shall bind in the world to the seals and the vestures and the orders of the Light, may be bound in the Light-land to the orders of the inheritances of the Light. For the sake of sinners, therefore, have I torn myself asunder at this time and have brought them the mysteries, that I may free them from the æons of the rulers and bind them to the inherit-

ances of the Light, and not only the sinners, but also the righteous, in order that I may give them the mysteries and that they may be taken into the Light, for without mysteries they cannot be taken into the Light.

Pistis Sophia

Thus the heavens and the earth were finished, and all the host of them. And on the seventh day God ended his work, which he had made; and he rested on the seventh day from all his work, which he had made. And God blessed the seventh day, and sanctified it: because that in it he had rested from all his work which God created and made.

Genesis 2:1-24 (KJV)

While Adam was listening to the speech of his Lord to him, and standing upon the place of Golgotha, all the creatures being gathered together that they might hear the conversation of God with him, lo! a cloud of light carried him and went with him to Paradise and the choirs of Angels sang before him, the cherubim among them blessing and the seraphim crying 'Holy!' until Adam came into Paradise. He entered it at the third hour on Friday, and the Lord, to Him be praise! gave him the commandment, and warned him against disobedience to it. Then the Lord, to Him be praise! threw upon Adam a form of sleep, and he slept a sweet sleep in Paradise. And God took a rib from his left side, and from it He created Eve. When he awoke and saw Eve he rejoiced over her and lived with her, and she was in the pleasant garden of Paradise. God clothed them with glory and splendour.

They outvied one another in the glory with which they were clothed, and the Lord crowned them for marriage, the Angels congratulated them, and there was joy there such as never has been the like and never will be till the day in which the people at the right hand shall hear the glorious voice from the Lord. Adam and Eve remained in Paradise for three hours… Then God planted the tree of life in the middle of Paradise and it was the form of the cross which was stretched upon it, and it was the tree of life and salvation. Satan remained in his envy to Adam and Eve for the favour which the Lord shewed them, and he contrived to enter into the serpent, which was the most beautiful of the animals, and its nature was above the nature of the camel. He carried it till he went with it in the air to the lower parts of Paradise. The reason for Iblis the cursed hiding himself in the serpent was his ugliness, for when he was deprived of his honour he got into the acme of uglincss, till none of the creatures could have borne the sight of him uncovered, and if Eve had seen him unveiled in the serpent, when she spoke to him, she would have run away from him, and neither cunning nor deceit would have availed him with her; but he contrived to hide himself in the serpent, the cunning creature, to teach the birds with round tongues the speech of men in Greek and such like...

But the cursed Devil, when he entered the serpent, came towards Eve, when she was alone in Paradise away from Adam, and called her by her name. She turned to him, and looked at her likeness behind a veil, and he talked to her, and she talked to him, and he led her astray by his speech, for woman's nature is weak, and she trusts in every word, and he lectured her about the forbidden tree in obedience to her desire, and described to her the goodness of its taste, and that when she should eat of it she should become a god; and she longed for what the cursed one made her long for, and she would not hear from the Lord, may His names be sanctified! what He had commanded Adam about the tree.

She hastened eagerly towards it, and seized some of its fruit in her mouth. Then she called Adam, and he hastened to her, and she gave him of the fruit, telling him that if he ate of it he would become a god. He listened to her advice because he should become a god as she said. When he and she ate the deadly fruit they were bereft of their glory, and their splendour was taken from them, and they were stripped of the light with which they had been clothed. When they looked at themselves, they were naked of the grace which they had worn, and their shame was manifest to them; they made to themselves aprons of fig-leaves, and covered themselves therewith, and they were in great sadness for three hours.

They did not manage to continue in the grace and the power with which the Lord had endued them before their rebellion for three hours, till it was taken from them and they were made to slip and fall down at the time of sun-set on that day, and they received the sentence of God in punishment. After the clothing of fig-leaves they put on clothing of skins, and that is the skin of which our bodies are made, being of the family of man, and it is a cloth-ing of pain. The entrance of Adam into Paradise was at the third hour. He and Eve passed through great power in three hours, they were naked for three hours, and in the ninth hour they went out from Paradise, unwillingly, with much grief, great weeping, mourning and sighing.

KITAB AL-MAGALL

The reason I cite this passage from the Books of Rolls is because it is one of those rare passages that actually describes sixty-day Adam's ini-tial creation as occurring between the physical Earth and the atmos-phere beneath paradise. Created in sight of the Annunaki before being taken up into paradise, where he was placed by the Creator in a protective type space or enclosure called the garden of the Lord, Adam was crowned King and given dominion of paradise on the same day of his creation. Much like Lucifer's refusal to bow before our Lord before the war in heaven, Satan here refuses to bow before sixth-day Adam, Adam of paradise. Jealous of his appointment, creation, and dominion, Satan decides to tempt the innocence of Adam and Eve after the Lord formed her from and of Adam. This text shows that before the temptation, Adam and Eve are bright natured, angelic type beings not yet transformed to flesh, and that eating of the fruit from the Tree of the Knowledge of Good and Evil resulted in their fall from grace and transformation into flesh form, whereby all the prophecies of Genesis 3 would then be fulfilled.

Now the serpent was more subtle than any beast of the field which the LORD God had made. And he said unto the woman, "Yea, hath God said, Ye shall not eat of every tree of the garden?" And the woman said unto the serpent, "We may eat of the fruit of the trees of the garden: But of the fruit of the tree which is in the midst of the garden, God hath said, 'Ye shall not eat of it, neither shall ye touch it, lest ye die.'" And the serpent said unto the woman, "Ye shall not surely die:

For God doth know that in the day ye eat thereof, then your eyes shall be opened, and ye shall be as gods, knowing good and evil." And when the woman saw that the tree was good for food, and that it was pleasant to the eyes, and a tree to be desired to make one wise, she took of the fruit thereof, and did eat, and gave also unto her husband with her; and he did eat. And the eyes of them both were opened, and they knew that they were naked; and they sewed fig leaves together, and made themselves aprons. And they heard the voice of the LORD God walking in the garden in the cool of the day: and Adam and his wife hid themselves from the presence of the LORD God amongst the trees of the garden. And the LORD God called unto Adam, and said unto him, "Where art thou?" And he said, "I heard thy voice in the garden, and I was afraid, because I was naked; and I hid myself." And he said, "Who told thee that thou wast naked? Hast thou eaten of the tree, whereof I commanded thee that thou shouldest not eat?" And the man said, "The woman whom thou gavest to be with me, she gave me of the tree, and I did eat."

And the LORD God said unto the woman, "What is this that thou hast done?" And the woman said, "The serpent beguiled me, and I did eat." And the LORD God said unto the serpent, "Because thou hast done this, thou art cursed above all cattle, and above every beast of the field; upon thy belly shalt thou go, and dust shalt thou eat all the days of thy life: And I will put enmity between thee and the woman, and between thy seed and her seed; it shall bruise thy head, and thou shalt bruise his heel." Unto the woman he said, "I will greatly multiply thy sorrow and thy conception; in sorrow thou shalt bring forth children; and thy desire shall be to thy husband, and he shall rule over thee."

And unto Adam he said, "Because thou hast hearkened unto the voice of thy wife, and hast eaten of the tree, of which I commanded thee, saying, 'Thou shalt not eat of it': cursed is the ground for thy sake; in sorrow shalt thou eat of it all the days of thy life; Thorns also and thistles shall it bring forth to thee; and thou shalt eat the herb of the field; In the sweat of thy face shalt thou eat bread, till thou return unto the ground; for out of it wast thou taken: for dust thou art, and unto dust shalt thou return."

And Adam called his wife's name Eve; because she was the mother of all living. Unto Adam also and to his wife did the LORD God make coats of skins, and clothed them. And the LORD God said, Behold, the man is become as one of us, to know good and evil: and now, lest he put forth his hand, and take also of the tree of life, and eat, and live for ever: Therefore the LORD God sent him forth from the garden of Eden, to till the ground from whence he was taken. So he drove out the man; and he placed at the east of the garden of Eden Cherubims, and a flaming sword which turned every way, to keep the way of the tree of life.

Genesis 3:1-24 (KJV)

DAY SEVEN

Rest and sabbath are appointed the Lord's holy day and signify completion of the higher and lower orders. In this day the Lord has all of the angels and creatures worship Him in honored remembrance as a token of Thanksgiving for their/our life and being. Saboath, or Sabbath, is sanctified as the holiest day of the week. The Lord would use this day to celebrate His unfolding creation, but because of the rebellion of Lucifer and fall of Adam and Eve, He would institute a plan for judgment, the redeeming of humanity through Yahushuah the Word and the condemnation of the fallen angels. His Son would enter flesh and defeat death, extending grace and salvation to those that believe on Him and in Him. The recreation of Adam and Eve into flesh bodies happens on the eighth day and is described in the Nag Hammadi codices as the elevation of the third creation of eighth-day dust Adam and Eve.

DAY EIGHT

Adam and Eve are re-created into bodies of flesh and find themselves living on the wilderness of the earth in a place called the Cave of Treasures. Having lost their bright nature they are transformed into flesh bodies which adhere to the laws of nature and physical rules of this third-dimensional universe. In this form they would fulfill all of the prophecies of Genesis 3 in that they would bring children into the world, have to work to feed them, and would eventually die.

The second world age would also be dominated by the enmity between the seed of the woman and the seed of the serpent. This enmity would begin with Eve as the mother of all living. She would be the womb through which her two blood lines, as well as peoples, would come into being; Satan's seed began with the birth of Cain and Adam's seed with Abel, who would be replaced with Seth because Cain would murder his brother. The Word Himself would end this war, being prophesized that He would be sacrificed on the cross where David had buried the skull of Goliath. When Yahushuah was sacrificed on the cross on the hill of Golgotha (which means Goliath of Gath), he actually fulfilled the prophecy of Genesis 3:15, "And I will put enmity between thee and the woman, and between thy seed and her seed; it shall bruise thy head, and thou shalt bruise his heel." Christ, as the seed of the woman, was—on the day of His crucifixion— crushing the skull of Goliath, whom as a hybrid giant was of the seed of the serpent, nipping at the heel of the Lord.

> Time no longer slept on the bosom of God, for now there was change where before all had been unchanging, and change is time. Now within the Universal Womb was heat, substance and life, and encompassing it was the Word which is the Law.
>
> Kolbrin Bible

YAHUSHUAH: LIGHT OF THE WORLD

Yahushuah, as the Son of Yahweh, would incarnate into the flesh, defeat death, and then by example show to the world what eternal life was and what salvation would mean for those that follow Him. Many are familiar with this aspect of His story and how He was the fulfillment of many centuries of prophecy predicting His incarnation into flesh exactly 5,500 years after the fall of humanity and beginning of what would be the Second World Age of flesh, and yet not much else is known about Yahushuah's role in the creation prior to entrance into flesh.

I will cover this little known story while also expounding on the Three World Ages, what each reflect, and why each came into being. Lucifer, since his banishment, has sought to corrupt, hide, and alter those doctrines that teach about the promised salvation that Yahushuah would and did bring to world. Most have never heard of the Three World Ages or how they parallel the three creations of Adam or what role Yahushuah played prior to incarnation as God manifest in flesh. Most have never heard of Yahushuah being the glory originally called forth by the voice of Yahweh in the moment when light was separated from darkness, imperishability from perishability. I will attempt to elucidate this hidden aspect of our Savior's story so that you, as reader, can understand who our

Lord was and is in ruling creation. The concept I am about to present is not well known and little understood, yet I consider it vital to piecing together the tale of why Lucifer was banished from the upper heavens and when.

The opening passage from the book of John, though cryptic in its wording, associates Yahushuah as being one with the Father. He is the verbal expression and physical embodiment of the Most High, and as the Word, He was the One who brought all things into being. This passage also verifies that it was the Son as light, who was given dominion to create and manifest all worlds. The reason that Yahushuah is called the Word is because the Father gave to Him the power to bring forth in instant manifestation anything spoken into being. It is said that He sang the universe into vibration by the power, authority of His voice, and focused intent. It's important to understand that the Son is the physical embodiment of the hidden Father and that they together are one.

> In the beginning was the Word, and the Word was with God, and the Word was God. The same was in the beginning with God. All things were made by him; and without him was not any thing made that was made. In him was life; and the life was the light of men. And the light shineth in darkness; and the darkness comprehended it not.
>
> John 1:15 (KJV)

An interesting account from the Kolbrin Bible like John 1 also describes authority being given to the Word, or Son of God, and how He as the spiritual embodiment of the Father utilized this power to create all that is visible from the invisible. And even though the Kolbrin Bible is written from the perspective of the Egyptian and Celtic priesthoods that deny Yahushuah as the Son of God, there is still much truth within it for those that have the eyes to see, ears to hear, and mind to understand.

There are no true beginnings on Earth, for here all is effect, the ultimate cause being elsewhere. For who among men can say which came first, the seed or the plant? Yet in truth it is neither, for something neither seed nor plant preceded both, and that thing was also preceded by something else. Always there are ancestors back to the beginning, and back beyond to there is only God. This, then, is how these things were told in The Great Book of The Sons of Fire.

The name which is uttered cannot be that of this Great Being who, remaining nameless, is the beginning and the end, beyond time, beyond the reach of mortals, and we in our simplicity call it God. He who preceded all existed alone in His strange abode of uncreated light, which remains ever unextinguishable, and no understandable eye can ever behold it. The pulsating draughts of the eternal life light in His keeping were not yet loosed. He knew Himself alone, He was uncontrasted, unable to manifest in nothingness, for all within His Being was unexpressed potential.

The Great Circles of Eternity were yet to be spun out, to be thrown forth as the endless ages of existence in substance. They were to begin with God and return to Him completed in infinite variety and expression. Earth was not yet in existence, there were no winds with the sky above them; high mountains were not raised, nor was the great river in its place. All was formless, without movement, calm, silent, void and dark. No name had been named and no destinies foreshadowed.

Eternal rest is intolerable, and unmanifested potential is frustration. Into the solitude of timelessness can Divine Loneliness and from this arose the desire to create, that He might know and express Himself, and this generated the Love of God. He took thought and brought into being within Himself the Universal Womb of Creation containing the everlasting essence of slumbering spirit.

The essence was quickened by a ripple from the mind of God and a creative thought was projected. This generated power which produced light, and this formed a substance like unto a mist of invisible dust. It divided into two forms of energy through being impregnated with The Spirit of God and, quickening the chaos of the void within the Universal Womb, became spun out into whirlpools of substance. From this activity, as sparks from a fire, came an infinite variety of spirit minds, each having creative powers within itself.

The activating word was spoken, its echoes vibrate still, and there was a stirring movement which caused instability. A command was given and this became the Everlasting Law. Henceforth, activity was controlled in harmonious rhythm and the initial inertia was overcome. The Law divided the materializing chaos from God and then established the boundaries of the Eternal Spheres.

Time no longer slept on the bosom of God, for now there was change where before all had been unchanging, and change is time. Now within the Universal Womb was heat, substance and life, and encompassing it was the Word which is the Law.

The command was given, Let the smallest of things form the greatest and that which lives but a flash form everlastingness. Thus the universe came into being as a condensation of God's thought, and as it did so it obscured Him from all enclosed within His solidifying creation. Henceforth, God was hidden, for He has always remained dimly reflected in His creation. He became veiled from all that came forth from Him. Creation does not explain itself, under the Law it cannot do so, its secrets have to be unraveled by the created.

All things are by nature finite, they have a beginning, a middle and an end. An unaccomplishable purpose would be eternal frustration and therefore, the universe being created purposefully it must have an objective. If it ended without anything else following, then the God existing must slumber indifferent to its activities. But He has made it a living work of greatness operating under the changeless Law.

The creating word had been spoken, now there was another command and the power going forth smote the sun so its face was lit, and it shone with a great radiance pouring warmth and light upon its sister Earth. Henceforth she would live within the protection of her brother's household, rejoicing in his benevolence and strength.

Kolbrin Bible

And the city had no need of the sun, neither of the moon, to shine in it: for the glory of God did lighten it, and the Lamb is the light thereof (Revelation 22:10-23).

The Nag Hammadi codices also confirm our Lord as the light of the universe that was called forth that brought the creation into visibility. Yahushuah is He that jewels creation with brightness, luster, and gloss, making objects visible to the naked eye. Without Him nothing could be seen, and much would not be understood as much is revealed through the light of day. Most do not associate Him as having a connection with the light as most have never studied the scriptures, which alludes to this veiled possibility. Take, for instance, this quote from a book called the Book of the Bee, a 12th century text written by a Syrian bishop named Solomon (Shelêmôn). Solomon's intent was to expound upon the full history of the Christian Dispensation according to the Nestorians, which led to the formation of the Church of the East. This text provides commentary and insight into what the early church elders thought of specific interpretation of the word and provides interesting introspection into the accepted belief systems of prior church elders.

When the holy angels were created on the evening of the first day, without voice, they understood not their creation, but thought within themselves that they were self-existent beings and not made. On the morning of the first day

God said in an audible and commanding voice, Let there be light, and immediately the effused light was created. When the angels saw the creation of light, they knew of a certainty that He who had made light had created them.

And they shouted with a loud voice, and praised Him, and marvelled at His creation of light, as the blessed teacher saith, When the Creator made that light, the angels marvelled thereat, etc.; and as it is said in Job, When I created the morning star, all my angels praised me.

The Book of Bee, 6

The effused light referred to here is the unveiling of Yahushuah Savior Messiah as the light of the universe. The moment all things became visible is the same moment when Yahweh had given dominion to His Son and the same moment when the angels, who were witness to the light being given dominion over the universe, became aware that He who called forth the light as the only begotten of the invisible Father, was He that was and is the Creator, Father of all. The passage from the *Book of the Bee* is similar in reference and esoteric concept to many of extra-biblical works associated with obscure collections of unconnected texts which also make mention of this seemingly arcane possibility.

And his will became a deed and it appeared with the mind; and the light glorified it. And the word followed the will. For because of the word, Christ the divine Autogenes created everything. And the eternal life <and> his will and the mind and the foreknowledge attended and glorified the invisible Spirit and Barbelo, for whose sake they had come into being. And the holy Spirit completed the divine Autogenes, his son, together with Barbelo, that he may attend the mighty and invisible, virginal Spirit as the divine Autogenes, the Christ whom he had honored with a mighty voice.

He came forth through the forethought. And the invisible, virginal Spirit placed the divine Autogenes of truth over everything. And he subjected to him every authority, and the truth which is in him, that he may know the All which had been called with a name exalted above every name. For that name will be mentioned to those who are worthy of it. For from the light, which is the Christ, and the indestructibility, through the gift of the Spirit the four lights (appeared) from the divine Autogenes.

The Sophia of Jesus Christ

Comprehending that Yahushuah was and is the light which made all things visible as called forth by the authoritative voice of Yahweh is essential for understanding the next part of the story, as associated to the war in heaven, and what lead to the banishment of Lucifer—and one third of the angels of Yahweh—from what were then the upper heavens.

It is he alone who came to be, that is, the Christ. And, as for me, I anointed him as the glory of the Invisible Spirit, with goodness. Now the Three, I established alone in eternal glory over the Aeons in the Living Water, that is, the glory that surrounds him who first came forth to the Light of those exalted Aeons, and it is in glorious Light that he firmly perseveres. And he stood in his own Light that surrounds him, that is, the Eye of the Light that gloriously shines on me.

Trimorphic Protennoia

Then the Son who is perfect in every respect — that is, the Word who originated through that Voice; who proceeded from the height; who has within him the Name; who is a Light — he revealed the everlasting things, and all the unknowns were known. And those things difficult to interpret and secret, he revealed. And as for those who dwell in Silence with the First Thought, he preached to them. And he revealed himself to those who dwell in darkness, and he showed himself to those who dwell in the abyss, and to those who dwell in the hidden treasuries, he told ineffable mysteries, and he taught unrepeatable doctrines to all those who became Sons of the Light.

Trimorphic Protennoia

In witnessing Yahweh call forth the Son, the Father had hoped that all of the angels would know that it was to His Son Yahushuah Savior Messiah, the light of the universe, that He had given dominion over all things and that they should praise Him as the Exalted One and only begotten of the Creator. We must remember that the plan of glory that is salvation has been carefully prepared for and laid out according to the will of the Father even before the foundations of this world. This plan has been known to Him since even before He brought all things into being through His Son, the light of the universe. The plan of salvation would serve as reward for those who choose to love and serve Him; it would also serve as a condemnation for the archons—fallen angels—and humans who would war against the seed of Adam. The loss of our bright natures and fall into the flesh would be redeemed by and through the blood of our Creator, who coming into the flesh would become Savior for all those seeking to escape this world.

> The Saviour answered and said unto Mary: Amen, I say unto you: All which is appointed unto every one through the Fate, whether all good or all sins,—in a word, all which is appointed them, cometh unto them. For this cause, therefore, have I brought the keys of the mysteries of the kingdom of heaven; otherwise no flesh in the world would be saved. For without mysteries no one will enter into the Light-kingdom, be he a righteous or a sinner.
>
> For this cause, therefore, have I brought the keys of the mysteries into the world, that I may free the sinners who shall have faith in me and hearken unto me, so that I may free them from the bonds and the seals of the æons of the rulers and bind them to the seals and the vestures and the orders of the Light, in order that he whom I shall free in

the world from the bonds and the seals of the æons of the rulers, may be freed in the Height from the bonds and seals of the æons of the rulers, and in order that he whom I shall bind in the world to the seals and the vestures and the orders of the Light, may be bound in the Light-land to the orders of the inheritances of the Light. For the sake of sinners, therefore, have I torn myself asunder at this time and have brought them the mysteries, that I may free them from the æons of the rulers and bind them to the inheritances of the Light, and not only the sinners, but also the righteous, in order that I may give them the mysteries and that they may be taken into the Light, for without mysteries they cannot be taken into the Light.

For this cause, therefore, I have not hidden it, but I have cried it aloud clearly. And I have not separated the sinners, but I have cried it aloud and said it unto all men, unto sinners and righteous, saying: 'Seek that ye may find, knock that it may be opened unto you; for every one who seeketh in truth, will find, and who knocketh, to him it will be opened.' For I have said unto all men: They are to seek the mysteries of the Light-kingdom which shall purify them and make them refined and lead them into the Light.

Pistis Sophia

The most amazing and awesome story about creation is that the Creator would become human in order to save the creature into which He breathed the spirit of life. His coming into the flesh would also trump the powers of the lower order, death, flesh, and mortality. It would be His power that would shame the rulers of darkness and the principalities who thought they could thwart salvation and judgment by preventing the birth of the Messiah and the redemption of Adam's seed. Our Lord, in His grace and in His mercy, would suffer with Adam and the rest of us, the limitations and condemnation of incarnation into flesh. In this form, we as well as He would experience the entire spectrum of pain, pleasure, and the duality of good and evil.

Once one studies all the world's mythologies, traditions, religions, belief systems, and forgotten lore, one finds that all of them reflect the same story and, even though names change from culture to culture, it's the same cast of characters woven throughout all mythologies and religion. When Yahushuah separated darkness from light and the visible world from the invisible, the angels were arranged according to class and distinction into a higher and lower order. The invisible Holy Elohim would serve the Morningstar administration of the Trinity in administering to creation and humanity while the lower order would serve under Lucifer as a fallen cherub.

The reason the Father allowed all of the angels to witness His creating all things through the Son, the Word, was so that they would know and understand their place within the kingdom of Yahweh, the I AM THAT I AM, and Alpha Omega. The Father had hoped to utilize the angels as standard bearers, witnesses to the human creatures He would bring forth later in likeness and image to inhabit the recreated lower world. Because humanity had not witnessed the Lord unfolding all things, humans would exceedingly stray from the commandments and knowledge of our Creator. As such it would be and is the duty of the higher angels to work with humanity to help us realize our place within the creation and to whom we should give praise and homage to the Creator, Most High, and Father of us all. We are sons of God, only in a fallen state, having been forced to drink of the cup of forgetfulness when incarnating into the flesh.

I have said, Ye are gods; and all of you are children of the most High. But ye shall die like men, and fall like one of the princes (Psalm 82:6-7, KJV).

> With each and every one of us is an angel of this group—called the guardian angel—who directs man from his conception until the general resurrection. The number of each one of these classes of angels is equal to the number of all mankind from Adam to the resurrection. Hence it is handed down that the number of people who are going

to enter the world is equal to the number of all the heavenly hosts; but some say that the number is equal to that of one of the classes only, that they may fill the place of those of them who have fallen through transgressing the law; because the demons fell from three classes (of angels), from each class a third part.

If then it is an acknowledged fact that there are three orders of angels, and in each order there are three classes, and in every class a number equivalent to that of all mankind, what is the total number of the angels? Some say that when the angels were created, and were arranged in six divisions—Cherubim, Seraphim, Thrones, Principalities, Archangels, and Angels—the three lower divisions reflected (saying), 'What is the reason that these are set above, and we below? for they have not previously done anything more than we, neither do we fall short of them.' On account of this reflection as a cause, according to the custom of the (divine) government, Justice took from both sides, and established three other middle classes of angels—Lords, Powers, and Rulers—that the upper might not be (unduly) exalted, nor the lower think themselves wronged.

The Book of Bee, 1

Once the spirits of the First World Age were separated into powers, principalities, and the rulers of light and darkness, confrontation would soon ensue as Lucifer and the rebel angels would attempt to usurp the throne of Yahweh and dominion of the Son.

For on the first day He created the heavens which are above and the earth and the waters and all the spirits which serve before him the angels of the presence, and the angels of sanctification, and the angels [of the spirit of fire and the angels] of the spirit of the winds, and the angels of the spirit of the clouds, and of darkness, and of snow and of hail and of hoar frost, and the angels of the voices and of the thunder and of the lightning, and the angels of the spirits of cold and of heat, and of winter and of spring and of autumn and of summer and of all the spirits of his creatures which are in the heavens and on the earth.

The Book of Jubilees, 2

The angels that were witness to Yahushuah, being called forth as the light of the universe, were meant to witness how the Trinity together brought the creation into being. They were supposed to be the perfect ministering spirits to what would be the coming creation and elevation of modern humanity—a creature not blessed to behold how all things were manifested. The angels were tasked with reminding us as the Most High's beloved creatures who the Trinity is and was in lording over the universe.

Yet rather than submit to serve, some angels rebelled against their positions, desiring elevated status. Lucifer arrogantly refused to subject himself to the authority of Yahushuah and imagined exalting himself above the throne of Yahweh. For entertaining such a thought, he was cast out of heaven on the second day of creation along with those angels that aligned themselves in allegiance to his transgression. The Lord allowed the fallen ones chance for self-rule and though many civilized cultures accepted them openly as gods or benevolent angels; the fallen ones corrupted and lead astray those cultures that followed their advice, often demanding of them blood or victim sacrifice.

> And he made a plan with his powers. *He sent his angels to the daughters of men, that they might take some of them for themselves and raise offspring for their enjoyment.* And at first they did not succeed. When they had no success, they gathered together again and they made a plan together. They created a counterfeit spirit, who resembles the Spirit who had descended, so as to pollute the souls through it. *And the angels changed themselves in their likeness into the likeness of their mates (the daughters of men), filling them with the spirit of darkness, which they 25 had mixed for them, and*

with evil. They brought gold and silver and a gift and copper and iron and metal and all kinds of things. And they steered the people who had followed them into great troubles, by leading them astray with many deceptions. They (the people) became old without having enjoyment. They died, not having found truth and without knowing the God of truth. And thus the whole creation became enslaved forever, from the foundation of the world until now. And they took women and begot children out of the darkness according to the likeness of their spirit. And they closed their hearts, and they hardened themselves through the hardness of the counterfeit spirit until now.

The Apocryphon of John

Now the first Adam, (Adam) of Light, is spirit-endowed and appeared on the first day. The second Adam is soul-endowed and appeared on the sixth day, which is called Aphrodite. The third Adam is a creature of the earth, that is, the man of the law, and he appeared on the eighth day […] the tranquility of poverty, which is called The Day of the Sun (Sunday). And the progeny of the earthly Adam became numerous and was completed, and produced within itself every kind of scientific information of the soul-endowed Adam. But all were in ignorance.

On the Origin of the World

SONS OF GOD

ADAM OF LIGHT
AND THE THREE
WORLD AGES

The passage about the three Adam's is key for unlocking the three world ages teaching as well as for understanding the various creations of Adam and how, why, and when each one came into being. The accompanying quote is what led me to understand that what was being described as the garden tale in the non-canonical sources was actually a different account for a different creation of Adam than what is talked about as the fall in the Old Testament Genesis 3. In fact the Genesis 3 Adam is a whole different being from the Genesis 2 creature molded by the Elohim prior to humanity's recreation on the eighth day as cited in the Nag Hammadi codices. It took me a long time to discern it this way, so please bear with me as I try to explain this teaching so that others can understand it without having to pour years of research into all of these seemingly unconnected esoteric passages.

I emphasize this quote from *On the Origin of the World* as it clarifies that there are various creation verses and garden teachings associated to each world age. It is important to understand that we are sixth-day modern humanity made in the image of our Lord, filled with the Holy Spirit, and that it is Yahushuah within us that is the temple that we must rebuild to be born again. He is the eternal part of us that surpasses death, inheriting the Father's promise of everlasting life and salvation from wrath. He who created humanity on day six is the part of us that is Adam of light, Yahushuah, within all things.

This sixth day Adam was separated from the fallen angels, protected, and placed in Paradise, the garden of the Lord located at the third heaven. This Adam was given assignment to tend the garden before Eve, his wife, was split off from him to bring both male and female genders into being. This Eve is the one that was seduced by Sammael, Satan, as the serpent in Paradise. This beguiling is what lead to the loss of their bright natures and fall from grace. In this chapter I will attempt to elucidate the Three World Ages and their association to this cryptic passage.

The Three World Ages parallel the three creations of Adam, and thus it is in my opinion essential to understand this quote to understand how each age fits in with those creations of Adam. This quote is essential to unlocking and understanding how the creation of Adam of Light revealed on the first day, a soul-endowed Adam revealed on the sixth day, and a flesh Adam revealed on the eighth day parallel the three world ages' teaching. The first Adam, Adam of light (Yahushuah), banished Lucifer and his angels from the heavens, the central theme for the First World Age. The second creation of Adam, Adam of Paradise, resulted in the separation of hermaphroditic angelic male and female natures, the creation of woman, loss of immortality, and fall from paradisiacal grace.

The eating of the fruit of the knowledge of good and evil, as promised by the Lord, led to incarnation in flesh on the eighth day where they would fulfill those prophecies as outlined by Genesis 3 and eventually succumb to death that the Lord said would overcome them. The forbidden fruit symbolically veiled incarnation, the blossoming of sexuality, impregnation of Eve by the archons once transformed into flesh bodies, and humanity's first awareness of their genitalia.

Unto the woman he said, I will greatly multiply thy sorrow and thy conception; in sorrow thou shalt bring forth children; and thy desire shall be to thy husband, and he shall rule over thee (Genesis 3:16, KJV).

The entrance into flesh and loss of their light vesture resulted in humanity's collective entrance into the Second World Age and 7,000 years of duality in which we, as sons of God, would be given free will to incarnate into the flesh, whereby we would be tested in life to learn through the knowledge of good and evil what existence would be like separate from God. The third creation of Adam, Adam of the Dust, came into being as a result of sixth day Adam and Eve's loss of immortality, or what some scriptures term as their *light vesture.*

The third creation of Adam occurred when both were transformed from immortal, angelic natures into physical flesh bodies on the eighth day, preparing the way for incarnation upon the lower physical Earth, where Lucifer and the rebel angels had already been banished. The Three World Ages reflect the transformation of consciousness from original spiritual innocence and immortality (First World Age) to the fall into flesh (Second World Age) and back to what would be a return to innocence and immortality (Third World Age.) My hope in this chapter is to familiarize the reader with what the Three World Ages are, how they relate to the loss of paradise, and how they explain our current banishment to the world in which we now reside.

Understanding this concept will help one to understand incarnation, why it is we live one flesh life—even though we have memory and consciousness going back to our spiritual beginnings—and why it seems we have memories of events seemingly connected to a conscious existence prior to the one we live out in flesh. This teaching will help one to understand what Yahushuah speaks about in the

Pistis Sophia when He cites how He chose the souls of the apostles for birth in an hour and time specific to fulfill their mission. The election of certain souls for specific roles in their flesh incarnations is also discussed with this Three World Age teaching. This concept also pertains to the later return of Enoch and Elijah as the End of Days witnesses of Revelation.

> Rejoice then and exult and rejoice more and more greatly, for to you it is given that I speak first with you from the beginning of the Truth to its completion. For this cause have I chosen you verily from the beginning through the First Mystery. Rejoice then and exult, for when I set out for the world, I brought from the beginning with me twelve powers, as I have told you from the beginning, which I have taken from the twelve saviours of the Treasury of the Light, according to the command of the First Mystery. These then I cast into the womb of your mothers, when I came into the world, that is those which are in your bodies to-day. For these powers have been given unto you before the whole world, because ye are they who will save the whole world, and that ye may be able to endure the threat of the rulers of the world and the pains of the world and its dangers and all its persecutions, which the rulers of the height will bring upon you.
>
> For many times have I said unto you that I have brought the power in you out of the twelve saviours who are in the Treasury of the Light. For which cause I have said unto you indeed from the beginning that ye are not of the world. I also am not of it. For all men who are in the world have gotten their souls out of [the power of] the rulers of the æons. But the power which is in you is from me; your souls belong to the height. I have brought twelve powers of the twelve saviours of the Treasury of the Light, taking them out of the portion of my power which I did first receive.

And when I had set forth for the world, I came into the midst of the rulers of the sphere and had the form of Gabriel the angel of the æons; and the rulers of the æons did not know me, but they thought that I was the angel Gabriel. It came to pass then, when I had come into the midst of the rulers of the æons, that I looked down on the world of mankind, by command of the First Mystery.

I found Elizabeth, the mother of John the Baptizer, before she had conceived him, and I sowed into her a power which I had received from the little Iao, the Good, who is in the Midst, that he might be able to make proclamation before me and make ready my way, and baptize with the water of the forgiveness of sins. That power then is in the body of John.

Moreover in place of the soul of the ruler which he was appointed to receive, I found the soul of the prophet Elias in the æons of the sphere; and I took him thence, and took his soul and brought it to the Virgin of Light, and she gave it over to her receivers; they brought it to the sphere of the rulers and cast it into the womb of Elizabeth. So the power of the little Iao, who is in the Midst, and the soul of the prophet Elias, they were bound into the body of John the Baptizer.

For this cause then were ye in doubt aforetime, I when I said unto you: John said: I am not the Christ, and ye said unto me: It standeth written in the scripture: When the Christ shall come, Elias cometh before him and maketh ready his way. But when ye said this unto me, I said unto you: Elias verily is come and hath made ready all things, as it standeth written, and they have done unto him as they would. And when I knew that ye had not understood that I had discoursed with you concerning the soul of Elias which is bound into John the Baptizer, I answered you in the discourse in openness face to face: If ye like to accept John the Baptizer: he is Elias, of whom I have said that he will come.

Pistis Sophia, 7

SONS OF GOD

It is important to understand that, with the concept of the Three World Ages, I do not speak about reincarnation in the sense that one is born over and over through time and many lives to evolve to what some refer to as Christ consciousness. When I speak about incarnation I am referring to the prior lives we lived as First World Age spiritual angelic hermaphroditic beings, witness to the temptation, rebellion, war, and subsequent banishment of Lucifer and his rebel angels.

This teaching, however, does leave space for the special election of certain souls tasked for specific assignment, such as Elias as John the Baptist. There are passages that allude to reincarnation but not in the sense that we each are born over and over. For some tasked with special assignment or role, the Lord—if He so chooses—can resend certain spirits here for fulfillment of prophecy but that, as far as judgment and salvation are concerned, we do not incarnate multiple times into the flesh as this would negate the whole reason for our Lord coming on a DNA rescue mission for our flesh. This teaching also helps one to understand what the Lord meant when He said, "Before I formed thee in the belly I knew thee; and before thou camest forth out of the womb I sanctified thee, and I ordained thee a prophet unto the nations" (Jeremiah 1:5, KJV).

> I have loved you, saith the LORD. Yet ye say, Wherein hast thou loved us? Was not Esau Jacob's brother? saith the LORD: yet I loved Jacob, And I hated Esau, and laid his mountains and his heritage waste for the dragons of the wilderness. Whereas Edom saith, We are impoverished, but we will return and build the desolate places; thus saith the LORD of hosts, They shall build, but I will throw down; and they shall call them, The border of wickedness, and, The people against whom the LORD hath indignation forever.
>
> Malachi 1:2, KJV

Unless one knows about and understands the Three World Age teaching, it would be difficult to grasp what the Lord speaks about in the above passage. For how else can one explain why the Lord hated a child that hadn't even been born in the flesh—and in that sense was innocent of sin—unless one understands that we lived prior spiritual lives during the First World Age before incarnation into flesh. There, as spirits, we made choices that would affect our election for life in the Second World Age. The reason Yahweh hated Esau was because he disdained his birthright during the First World Age, which he would repeat in the flesh during the Second World Age. Like flesh beings during the Second World Age, we as spiritual beings during the First World Age were granted free-will dominion to choose whom we would serve in aligning our allegiances to Yahweh/Yahushuah or Lucifer/Yaldaboath and his angels.

During the First World Age, one third of the angels of the Lord willingly abandoned their first estate, one third did nothing, and the other one third fought for Him. Once death came into being with the fall of sixth-day Adam, the Lord would establish the Second World Age as trial for those who either did nothing or rebelled against Him during the First World Age and war in heaven. It would be during the Second World Age that Yahushuah Savior Messiah would be born of woman, die on the cross, defeat death, and offer eternal life and salvation to those who love and honor Yahweh.

The Three World Age teaching verifies judgment and incarnating once into the flesh, and not multiple times through multiple lives, even though as cited Yahushuah can and does utilize certain souls for special assignment, sending them again for certain role as reflected by the parable of Elias, who would return as John the Baptist.

> And his disciples asked him, saying, "Why then say the scribes that Elias must first come?" And Jesus answered and said unto them, "Elias truly shall first come, and restore all things. But I say unto you, That Elias is come already, and they knew him not, but have done unto him

whatsoever they listed. Likewise shall also the Son of man suffer of them." Then the disciples understood that he spake unto them of John the Baptist.

Matthew 17 (KJV)

And they asked him, saying, "Why say the scribes that Elias must first come?" And he answered and told them, "Elias verily cometh first, and restoreth all things; and how it is written of the Son of man, that he must suffer many things, and be set at nought. But I say unto you, That Elias is indeed come, and they have done unto him whatsoever they listed, as it is written of him."

Mark 9 (KJV)

FIRST WORLD AGE

The First World Age had no conceivable beginning that we could understand, but is representative of a space and place before time came into being, when all things were yet still codified in unity and oneness. Prior to the Big Bang and expansion of universal consciousness, only Yahweh existed. As Creator and Creation, He was and is in essence all things in their original state of purity, innocence, and oneness. This unified state of being is Yahweh prior to unfolding creation in all variety and myriad form. The Creator had decided to experience self in expansion and contraction, what would be the breath of life in bringing forth all worlds, visible from the invisible, perishable from the imperishable. It was Yahushuah as the Word and only begotten of the Father who would utilize verbal manifestation to organize everything into existential form. Together they are the breath of life.

In the beginning was the Word, and the Word was with God, and the Word was God. The same was in the beginning with God. All things were made by him; and without him was not any thing made that was made. In him was life; and the life was the light of men. And the light shineth in darkness; and the darkness comprehended it not. And the Word was made flesh, and dwelt among us, (and we beheld his glory, the glory as of the only begotten of the Father,) full of grace and truth.

John 1:1-5:14 (KJV)

This passage from John heralds the connection between Yahushuah, the Son, and Yahweh, the Father, to the primal state of oneness that was prior to what is now. Nothing can exist outside of Them; even darkness is dependent upon light for form. This passage also reveals the connection between Creator and creation to Yahushuah's role as Savior Messiah in that the Son would later adorn the flesh to defeat death and bring salvation to the world. Lucifer and the rebel angels knew that Christ would be born of the line of Adam and did everything they could to deceive and lead astray those He would come to save. They have even attributed the birth, death, and resurrection themes to other personas such as Tammuz, Horus, and even the sun in order to confuse those who would later be born of flesh into believing either Yahushuah Savior Messiah was just a myth, that He was born many times in myriad embodiments, or that many others were equal in regard to His status and power as being the Son of God. This confusion is part of the groundwork that has been laid for the coming great deception wherein the antichrist will unveil himself as Christ to the world.

The angels that participated in the Luciferian rebellion and ensuing war in heaven hate humanity specifically because we are fated to inherit those stations abandoned by them. It is because they have no part in salvation that they are attempting to take with them to the lake of fire as many of the sons and daughters of humanity as they possibly can.

One of the seminal events of the First World Age, besides all of creation being manifest, was Lucifer's refusal to serve as an archangel in heaven under the dominion of Yahushuah. We know from scripture that, prior to the materialization of Adam of Paradise on the sixth day of creation, Lucifer had already been cast out of the upper heavens and that he was able to lure a third of the angels of Yahweh to join him in his rebellion and desire for self rule. The rebellion of these angels leads to a war and their banishment from what are the upper heavens.

This banishment became the cause for why Lucifer would plot revenge against the second creation of Adam and his wife Eve. So what lead to the war in heaven, the rebel angels' banishment, and the destruction of the First World Age—including Tiamat (Earth), Lahmu (Mars) and Kingu (Moon)?

> It is because of this that you are being detained, because you belong to me. When you strip off from yourselves what is corrupted, then you will become illuminators in the midst of mortal men. And this (is the reason) that you will fight against the powers, because they do not have rest like you, since they do not wish that you be saved. Then the apostles worshiped again saying, Lord, tell us: In what way shall we fight against the archons, since the archons are above us?
>
> Then a voice called out to them from the appearance saying, "Now you will fight against them in this way, for the archons are fighting against the inner man. And you are to fight against them in this way: Come together and teach in the world the salvation with a promise. And you, gird yourselves with the power of my Father, and let your prayer be known. And he, the Father, will help you as he has helped you by sending me. Be not afraid, I am with you forever, as I previously said to you when I was in the body." Then there came lightning and thunder from heaven, and what appeared to them in that place was taken up to heaven.
>
> The Letter of Peter to Philip

The Lord would allow the rebel angels a certain period of time and free will to act as gods themselves until they had so corrupted the worlds they inhabited and the places they infiltrated that prayers and cries of justice so reached unto heaven that Yahushua sent His own angels to inspect the actions of the lower order of angels. The Lord would only tolerate a certain manner of injustice before instituting judgments against those whom force His hand. Over and over through time and space He would have to rebuke them in their dedication to evil pursuits.

The rebel angels were joined by the fallen watchers during the time of Jared as another group of the Lord's angels challenged Him on the creation of Adam, claiming that they had been born into flesh bodies that they would never have transgressed any of the commandments of the Law. Taking them up on this challenge, the Lord then transformed them into bodies of flesh and sent them to the earth, where they were tasked with awakening and enlightening humanity to the rule and presence of the Most High. But lusting after the daughters of Cain, they decided instead to mate with the children of humanity, resulting in the birth of the giants or the men of renown of Genesis 6, the children of Anak, or Annunaki.

They would establish kingship through their hybrid demigod giant children and utilize them to oppress, control, and manage the peoples of the earth. That is why the Lord chose Enoch to serve as a witness and assigned him the role of immortalizing the historical account of the fallen angels and their interdiction upon this planet. The judgment brought against them is spoken about in partial account in both *The Book of Enoch* and *The Book of the Giants*. Those hybrid seed lines that they brought into being, specifically the hybrid giant lines, were then wiped out and led by the Lord's angels to war against one another. The rest would be slaughtered in the ultimate judgment of a worldwide deluge with the Lord, sparing Noah (still pure in his generations, meaning uncorrupted by fallen angel DNA) and his family, so that they could then re-populate the planet in pure and replenished innocence. These watchers became evil and joined Lucifer in his rebellion against the Lord, becoming demonic entities themselves.

Four of these angels will be loosed from the river Euphrates during the end of days, or as in the days of Noah. After the flood, the children of Ham resurrect worship of the fallen watchers who then infiltrate their lines birthing hybrid giant lines in Philistia and Bashaan.

The fallen angels and their demigod children are the pantheon of false gods that the various cultures around the world worship. Another phenomenon, which is worldwide in mythology, is the so-called gods raping and stealing spouses from among mortals. The fact that these forgotten stories provide ancient accounts of supposedly superior beings interbreeding with and abducting the daughters of man seems to me the same phenomenon described in Genesis 6— where the Sons of God mated with the daughters of humanity, resulting in the birth of an unnatural creation, a hybrid race of beings termed by the Bible as giants or men of renown.

> For if I were able I would have destroyed you like one of them that were before you. For, indeed, I was formed the first angel: for when God made the heavens, he took a handful of fire and formed me first, Michael second for he had his Son before the heavens and the earth and we were formed, so that we also were created by the will of the Son and the consent of the Father.
>
> Gospel of Bartholomew

Sons of God

To set up the story of the fall of Lucifer and humanity, we must revisit some texts that allude to his station prior to his expulsion from heaven. These quotes provide insight into what he was previous to his refusal to serve and subsequent exile abroad. According to the texts, he had been an anointed cherub, possibly one of those protecting the mercy seat of Yahweh as granted to the Son. He may have even been the first created of the archangels. Once dominion was granted to Yahushuah, Lucifer envisioned seizing the Godhead for himself. For this he was cast down and banished from the upper to the lower heavens.

> When Jesus appeared again, Bartholomew saith unto him: Lord, show us the adversary of men that we may behold him, of what fashion he is, and what is his work, and whence he cometh forth, and what power he hath that he spared not even thee, but caused thee to be hanged upon the tree… Jesus raised him up and said unto him: Bartholomew, wilt thou see the adversary of men? I tell thee that when thou beholdest him, not thou only but the rest of the apostles and Mary will fall on your faces and become as dead corpses. But they all said unto him: Lord, let us behold him. And he led them down from the Mount of Olives and looked wrathfully upon the angels that keep hell (Tartarus), and beckoned unto Michael to sound the trumpet in the height of the heavens. And Michael sounded, and the earth shook, and Beliar came up, being

held by 660 angels and bound with fiery chains. And the length of him was 1,600 cubits and his breadth 40 cubits, and his face was like a lightning of fire and his eyes full of darkness (like sparks, Slav.). And out of his nostrils came a stinking smoke; and his mouth was as the gulf of a precipice, and the one of his wings was four-score cubits. And straightway when the apostles saw him, they fell to the earth on their faces and became as dead.

But Jesus came near and raised the apostles and gave them a spirit of power, and he saith unto Bartholomew: "Come near, Bartholomew, and trample with thy feet on his neck, and he will tell thee his work, what it is, and how he deceiveth men." And Jesus stood afar off with the rest of the apostles. And Barthololmew feared, and raised his voice and said: "Blessed be the name of thine immortal kingdom from henceforth even for ever." And when he had spoken, Jesus permitted him, saying: "Go and tread upon the neck of Beliar," and Bartholomew ran quickly upon him and trode upon his neck: and Beliar trembled.

And Bartholomew was afraid, and fled, and said unto Jesus: "Lord, give me an hem of thy garments that I may have courage to draw near unto him." But Jesus said unto him: "Thou canst not take an hem of my garments, for these are not my garments which I wore before I was crucified." And Bartholomew said: "Lord, I fear Iest, like as he spared not thine angels, he swallow me up also." Jesus saith unto him: "Were not all things made by my word, and by the will of my Father the spirits were made subject unto Solomon? Thou, therefore, being commanded by my word, go in my name and ask him what thou wilt."

The Gospel of Bartholomew

For an extensive introspection into the myriad demonic fallen angels inhabiting our planet with us today, look into the extra-biblical book called the *Testament of Solomon* as it gives a detailed account of how King Solomon was given authority by the Most High to control not only the demons and fallen angels, but also the animal kingdoms. The Lord gave him this ring to not only verify His authority over the demons and fallen angels of this world, but also to prove that it is His choice to whom He grants this kind of power. In this particular passage, the Lord is confirming not only that the Testament of Solomon is true, but that Solomon did utilize the demons and fallen Angels when constructing the grandeur of our Lord's Holy Temple prior to its destruction.

> And Bartholomew made the sign of the cross and prayed unto Jesus and went behind him. And Jesus said to him: "Draw near." And as Bartholomew drew near, fire was kindled on every side, so that his garments appeared fiery. Jesus saith to Bartholomew: "As I said unto thee, tread upon his neck and ask him what is his power." And Bartholomew went and trode upon his neck, and pressed down his face into the earth as far as his ears. And Bartholomew saith unto him: "Tell me who thou art and what is thy name." And he said to him: "Lighten me a little, and I will tell thee who I am and how I came hither, and what my work is and what my power is." And he lightened him and saith to him: "Say all that thou hast done and all that thou doest." And Beliar answered and said: "If thou wilt know my name, at the first I was called Satanael, which is interpreted a messenger of God, but when I rejected the image of God my name was called Satanas, that is, an angel that keepeth hell (Tartarus)." And again Bartholomew saith unto him: "Reveal unto me all things and hide nothing from me." And he said unto him: "I swear unto thee by the power of the glory of God that even if I would hide aught I cannot, for he is near that would convict me. For if I were able I would have destroyed you like one of them that were before you. For, indeed, I was formed (al. called) the first angel: for when God made the heavens, he took a handful of fire and formed me first, Michael second [Vienna MS. for he had his Son before the heavens and the earth and

we were formed (for when he took thought to create all things, his Son spake a word), so that we also were created by the will of the Son and the consent of the Father. He formed, I say, first me, next Michael the chief captain of the hosts that are above], Gabriel third, Uriel fourth, Raphael fifth, Nathanael sixth, and other angels of whom I cannot tell the names. [Jerusalem MS., Michael, Gabriel, Raphael, Uriel, Xathanael, and other 6,000 angels.]

The Gospel of Bartholomew

It's important that one take notice of the fact that Satan says that even though he was formed as the first angel, before even the creation of Michael, the second archangel, that Yahushuah was already in existence and that it was the Son as the embodiment of the Father that created all things into being—a confirmation of John 1, which also verifies this knowledge. And whereas many believe that Lucifer was banished from the heavens for not wanting to bow before sixth-day Adam of Paradise and that he was cast out for not wanting to be a servant to humanity, the truth of the matter is that he was banished for refusing to bow before the dominion of the Son when light was separated from darkness and that all of these things took place prior to even the creation of sixth-day Adam.

For they are the rod-bearers (lictors) of God, and they smite me with their rods and pursue me seven times in the night and seven times in the day, and leave me not at all and break in pieces all my power. These are the angels of vengeance which stand before the throne of God: these are the angels that were first formed. And after them were formed all the angels. In the first heaven are an hundred myriads, and in the second an hundred myriads, and in the third an hundred myriads, and in the fourth an hundred myriads, and in the fifth an hundred myriads, and in the sixth an hundred myriads, and in the seventh is the first firmament (flat surface) wherein are the powers which work upon men.

Bartholomew saith unto him: Flow chastisest thou the souls of men? Beliar saith unto him: Wilt thou that I declare unto thee the punishment of the hypocrites, of the back-biters, of the jesters, of the idolaters, and the covetous, and the adulterers, and the wizards, and the diviners, and of them that believe in us, and of all whom I look upon (deceive)? (38 Lat. 2: When I will show any illusion by them.) But they that do these things, and they that consent unto them or follow them, do perish with me. Dost thou then do these things by thyself alone? And Satan said: "If I were able to go forth by myself, I would have destroyed the whole world in three days: but neither I nor any of the six hundred go forth. For we have other swift ministers whom we command, and we furnish them with an hook of many points and send them forth to hunt, and they catch for us souls of men, enticing them with sweetness of divers baits, that is by drunkenness and laughter, by backbiting, hypocrisy, pleasures, fornication, and the rest of the trifles that come out of their treasures."

The Gospel of Bartholomew

Banished from the upper heavens early in the history of creation for reasons which yet remain an undisclosed mystery, the only thing that makes sense to me in tying the fragments of this story together is that Lucifer was banished from the upper heavens, for refusing to submit to the authority and command of Adam of Light, Yahushuah Savior Messiah called forth as the glory of the world. And while only the Lord knows with certainty as to when Lucifer was banished from the upper heavens, one scripture, the Book of the Secrets of Enoch, ascribes this event as having happened on the second day. Nowhere else have I discovered any mention as to when the expulsion may have occurred.

And for all the heavenly troops I imaged the image and essence of fire, and my eye looked at the very hard, firm rock, and from the gleam of my eye the lightning received its wonderful nature, which is both fire in water and water in fire, and one does not put out the other, nor does the one dry up the other, therefore the lightning is brighter than the sun, softer than water and firmer than hard rock. And from the rock I cut off a great fire, and from the fire I created the orders of the incorporeal ten troops of angels, and their weapons are fiery and their raiment a burning flame, and I commanded that each one should stand in his order. And one from out the order of angels, having turned away with the order that was under him, conceived an impossible thought, to place his throne higher than the clouds above the earth, that he might become equal in rank to my power. And I threw him out from the height with his angels, and he was flying in the air continuously above the bottomless. On the third day I commanded the earth to make grow great and fruitful trees, and hills, and seed to sow, and I planted Paradise, and enclosed it, and placed as armed guardian flaming angels, and thus I created renewal.

The Book of the Secrets of Enoch, 29-30

I affirm, and it is my belief that war in heaven occurred when our Father the Creator called forth Adam of light, His one and only begotten Son Yahushuah Savior Messiah as glory of the universe and gave to Him dominion of all creation. Once dominion was granted to the Son as the word and physical embodiment of the hidden Father, Lucifer—as arch angel and covering cherub of the Lord's mercy seat—rebelled against the Father and Son monarchy, and desiring godhood and universal dominion caused a third of all the angels to fall with him in revolt.

Lucifer sought to be worshipped and praised like the most high among the lower order of angels. The gospels cite Lucifer's rebellion as a conscious decision, but in the Nag Hammadi codices

Yaldaboath, Saklas, or Sammael, the blind god of the lower authorities or demiurge of this planet, did not learn about those existing prior to and above him until he declared himself as the one and only god in all existence. And though we will not know the full detail of exactly what happened during all of those eons of time until our Lord returns to reveal all things, we are given subtle hints and the insight of prophets to shed light on this seemingly undefined story.

> For this they willingly are ignorant of, that by the word of God the heavens were of old, and the earth standing out of the water and in the water: Whereby the world that then was, being overflowed with water, perished: But the heavens and the earth, which are now, by the same word are kept in store, reserved unto fire against the day of judgment and perdition of ungodly men.
>
> 2 Peter 3

DRAGON LORDS

Details of how the Lord separated the visible worlds from the invisible worlds are given by Yahushuah as the Word in second Enoch, or the Book of the Secrets of Enoch. In this account the Lord also mentions why it was that He banished Lucifer and the seraphim angels that rebelled against Him from heaven. What is not talked about in scripture is how the fallen angels came to be imprisoned here in this solar system and upon this Earth. In order to bring clarity to this side of the story, we must revisit ancient Sumerian as well as Babylonian texts written by the fallen ones themselves as to what happened during the account of those early years, or what are referred to as the Prior Times. It's important to realize that the fallen angels as spirit men were here upon this planet long before the creation of modern humanity on the sixth day.

Unless one understands this timeline one may be confused, as most are, into believing that we are at the height of civilization and technological innovation, when in truth we are at the lowest point as far as advancement in human development and spiritual evolution. Sites such as Gobelki Tepe, Tenochtilan, and Baalbek are remains of Annunaki constructed cities built long ago that have survived even to this day. And whereas science will claim that these megalithic structures and cities were built by our so-called primitive ancestors, we modern humans cannot replicate the construction or reproduction of such feats as the Pyramids of Giza, Stonehenge, Puma Punku, or even Petra to this very day. And so we must open ourselves to new possibility in explaining what happened in our solar system's ancient past. Stories such as the Enuma elish, the Babylonian epic tale of creation, and another account of the Prior Times from the Lost Book of Enki must be understood to comprehend our pre-history. These ancient mythologies allude to the forgotten war between the Lord of Hosts and the Dragon, also referenced as the beast, Satan, Tiamat, Rahab, or the adversary. What many do not realize when reading the symbolic account of these ancient creation tales is that what is being described in the text is not the creation of the entire universe by an Annunaki *god* but a depiction of celestial gods or the different planets and members of this solar system as they try to determine orbits and circuits during the early history and development of our solar system. And while many researchers may have never heard of these creation tales being deciphered this way, most ancient cultures celebrate this conflict as the battle that metaphorically depicts how our solar system came into being long ago. These early creation accounts chronicle the primordial capture of Niburu, or what we've come to know as planet X, while immortalizing the cosmic cataclysm that led to the transformation and placement of modern-day Earth along with the capture of one of Tiamat's moons, the one called Kingu. Niburu, known as the planet of the crossing, has, had, and still has an essential role to play as the destroyer in the end of days.

During the early part of the development of our solar system, while the planets were still coalescing into form and establishing their orbital circuits, an interloper planet wandering on the edges of our outer solar system was captured by the gravitational field or *netforce* of Neptune and Uranus and lulled into fusion with this system. With altered trajectory Niburu was steered into conflict with the oncoming paths of the other planets that were inbound, spinning counterclockwise on an ecliptic in opposition to Niburu, which entered moving in a clockwise orbital circuit.

The moons of the Tiamat and Niburu then engage in heavenly combat of unheralded proportion, spawning the stories that later came to be known as the Babylonian creation epic, the Enuma elish. The west wind, moon, or satellite of Niburu gutted Tiamat, smashing her inside out into myriads of comet-like pieces, which linger as testament to Niburu's rising and crossing through the solar ecliptic. The hammered bracelet, or asteroid belt, is evidence that indeed this ancient cataclysm did happen so long ago. The comets and asteroids strewn between the inner and outer planets were all born from this same impact and are nothing more than the leftover debris-field resultant from the heavenly war between Niburu and what was then the large watery planet Tiamat. This story is celebrated by many cultures in one form or another as the slaying of the Dragon Tiamat, destruction of Rahab, and end of the First World Age as described by Jeremiah and Peter. Once one understands what is being discussed, one realizes the story is nothing more than an elaborate description of the creation of our early solar system.

The First World Age ended also in cataclysmic deluge, but not the same one Noah was spared from. The deluge of Noah's day occurred during the Second World Age and after the fall, incarnation into flesh, and incursion of the watchers during the time of Jared that I will cover in a later chapter.

> I beheld the earth, and, lo, it was without form, and void; and the heavens, and they had no light. I beheld the mountains, and, lo, they trembled, and all the hills moved lightly. I beheld, and, lo, there was no man, and all the birds of the heavens were fled. I beheld, and, lo, the fruitful place was a wilderness, and all the cities thereof were broken down at the presence of the LORD, and by his fierce anger. For thus hath the LORD said, "The whole land shall be desolate; yet will I not make a full end."
>
> Jeremiah 4:23-29 (KJV)

> Knowing this first, that there shall come in the last days scoffers, walking after their own lusts, And saying, "Where is the promise of his coming?" For since the fathers fell

SONS OF GOD

asleep, all things continue as they were from the beginning of the creation. For this they willingly are ignorant of, that by the word of God the heavens were of old, and the earth standing out of the water and in the water: Whereby the world that then was, being overflowed with water, perished: But the heavens and the earth, which are now, by the same word are kept in store, reserved unto fire against the day of judgment and perdition of ungodly men. But, beloved, be not ignorant of this one thing, that one day is with the Lord as a thousand years, and a thousand years as one day. The Lord is not slack concerning his promise, as some men count slackness; but is longsuffering to us-ward, not willing that any should perish, but that all should come to repentance. But the day of the Lord will come as a thief in the night; in the which the heavens shall pass away with a great noise, and the elements shall melt with fervent heat, the earth also and the works that are therein shall be burned up. Seeing then that all these things shall be dissolved, what manner of persons ought ye to be in all holy conversation and godliness, looking for and hasting unto the coming of the day of God, wherein the heavens being on fire shall be dissolved, and the elements shall melt with fervent heat? Nevertheless we, according to his promise, look for new heavens and a new earth, wherein dwelleth righteousness.

2 Peter 3:3-13 (KJV)

These two New Testament passages grant insight into not only how the First World Age ended but also testify as to how the Second World Age, the one we are in now, will end ultimately in a judgment of fire. The Revelation of St. John the Theologian grants readers a concise and clearer picture of the great and terrible day of the Lord and how this Earth shall be made flat, high places brought low, low places brought high, until the Earth is renewed white in innocence for preparation of our returning Lord. Because most have never heard of this piece of scripture, I have included it in its entirety at the end of my fourth book.

The Destruction and Re-Creation

It is known, and the story comes down from ancient times, that there was not one creation but two, a creation and a re-creation. It is a fact known to the wise that the Earth was utterly destroyed once then reborn on a second wheel of creation. At the time of the great destruction of Earth, God caused a dragon from out of Heaven to come and encompass her about. The dragon was frightful to behold, it lashed its tail, it breathed out fire and hot coals, and a great catastrophe was inflicted upon mankind. The body of the dragon was wreathed in a cold, bright light and beneath, on the belly, was a ruddy hued glow while behind it trailed a flowing tail of smoke. It spewed out cinders and hot stones, and its breath was foul and stenchful, poisoning the nostrils of men. Its passage caused great thunderings and lightnings to rend the thick, darkened sky, all Heaven and Earth being made hot. The seas were loosened from their cradles and rose up, pouring across the land.

There was an awful, shrilling trumpeting that out-powered even the howling of the unleashed winds. Men, stricken with terror, went mad at the awful sight in the heavens. They were loosed from their senses and dashed about, crazed, not knowing what they did. The breath was sucked from their bodies, and they were burnt with a strange ash.

Then it passed, leaving Earth enwrapped within a dark and glowering mantle, which was ruddily lit up inside. The bowels of the Earth were torn open in great writhing upheavals and a howling whirlwind rent the mountains apart. The wrath of the sky-monster was loosed in the heavens. It lashed about in flaming fury, roaring like a thousand thunders; it poured down fiery destruction amid a welter of thick, black blood. So awesome was the fearfully aspected thing that the memory mercifully departed from man, and his thoughts were smothered under a cloud of forgetfulness. The Earth vomited forth great gusts of foul breath from awful mouths opening up in the midst of the land. The evil breath bit at the throat before it drove men mad and killed them. Those who did not die in this manner were smothered under a cloud of red dust and ashes or were swallowed by the yawning mouths of Earth or crushed beneath crashing rocks.

The first sky-monster was joined by another that swallowed the tail of the one going before, but the two could not be seen at once. The sky monster reigned and raged above Earth, doing battle to possess it, but the many bladed sword of God cut them in pieces, and their falling bodies enlarged the land and the sea. In this manner the first Earth was destroyed by calamity descending from out of the skies. The vaults of heaven had opened to bring forth monsters more fearsome than any that ever haunted the uneasy dreams of men. Men and their dwelling places were gone—only sky boulders and red earth remained where once they were—but amidst all the desolation a few survived, for man is not easily destroyed. They crept out from caves and came down from the mountainsides. Their eyes were wild and their limbs trembled, their bodies shook, and their tongues lacked control. Their faces were twisted, and the skin hung loose on their bones. They were as maddened wild beasts driven into an enclosure before flames; they knew no law, being deprived of all the wisdom they once had and those who had guided them were gone.

The Earth, only true Altar of God, had offered up a sacrifice of life and sorrow to atone for the sins of mankind. Man had not sinned in deed but in the things he had failed to do. Man suffers not only for what he does but for what he fails to do. He is not chastised for making mistakes but for failing to recognize and rectify them. Then the great canopy of dust and cloud that encompassed the Earth, enshrouding it in heavy darkness, was pierced by ruddy light, and the canopy swept down in great cloudbursts and raging storm waters.

Cool moontears were shed for the distress of Earth and the woes of men. When the light of the sun pierced the

Earth's shroud, bathing the land in its revitalizing glory, the Earth again knew night and day, for there were now times of light and times of darkness. The smothering canopy rolled away and the vaults of heaven became visible to man. The foul air was purified and new air clothed the reborn Earth, shielding her from the dark hostile void of heaven.

The rainstorms ceased to beat upon the faces of the land and the waters stilled their turmoil. Earthquakes no longer tore the Earth open, nor was it burned and buried by hot rocks. The land masses were re-established in stability and solidity, standing firm in the midst of the surrounding waters. The oceans fell back to their assigned places and the land stood steady upon its foundations. The sun shone upon land and sea, and life was renewed upon the face of the Earth. Rain fell gently once more and clouds of fleece floated across dayskies. The waters were purified, the sediment sank and life increased in abundance.

Life was renewed, but it was different. Man survived, but he was not the same. The sun was not as it had been and a moon had been taken away. Man stood in the midst of renewal and regeneration. He looked up into the heavens above in fear for the awful powers of destruction lurking there. Henceforth, the placid skies would hold a terrifying secret. Man found the new Earth firm and the Heavens fixed.

He rejoiced but also feared, for he lived in dread that the heavens would again bring forth monsters and crash about him. When men came forth from their hiding places and refuges, the world their fathers had known was gone forever. The face of the land was changed and Earth was littered with rocks and stones which had fallen when the structure of heaven collapsed. One generation groped in the desolation and gloom, and as the thick darkness was dispelled its children believed they were witnessing a new creation. Time passed, memory dimmed and the record of evens was no longer clear. Generation followed generation and as the ages unfolded, new tongues and new tales replaced the old.

Kolbrin Bible

The collapse of the structure of heaven wherein the Earth was gutted, utterly broken, and even lost a moon is the same event that is celebrated in all of the ancient creation epics as the slaying of Tiamat, which became reborn as Ki, the new Earth. On Niburu's second pass through the solar system, the two largest chunks of Tiamat's slain carcass were gravitationally shifted from an orbital position outside of Mars to one inside of Mars. This shift placed the still-coalescing Earth at the perfect distance from Apsu, or the sun, to begin harboring the incredible development of life on this planet. Unless one understands that this account is an early depiction of how our Lord utilized Niburu to create the condition and circumstance necessary to begin a new chapter in the story of life within our solar system, one could not understand how it was this one single cataclysmic event so long ago shifted Tiamat to where the Earth is now, nor would one understand the true nature behind this event and why it was relegated such importance by the Most High, the Annunaki, and the elders of humanity.

Now this is the account of the Earth and its gold;
It is an account of the Beginning
and how the celestial gods created were.
In the Beginning,
When in the Above the gods in the heavens
had not been called into being,
And in the Below Ki, the Firm Ground,
had not yet been named,
Alone in the void there existed Apsu,
their Primordial Begetter.
In the heights of the Above,
the celestial gods had not yet been created;
In the waters of the Below,

the celestial gods had not yet appeared.
Above and Below, the gods had not yet been formed,
destinies were not yet decreed.
No reed had yet been formed, no marshland had
appeared;
Alone did Apsu reign in the void.
Then by his winds the primordial waters were mingled,
A divine and artful spell Apsu upon the waters cast.
On the void's deep he poured a sound sleep;
Tiamat, the Mother of All,
as a spouse for himself he fashioned.
A celestial mother, a watery beauty she was indeed!
Beside him Apsu little Mummu then brought forth,
As his messenger he him appointed, a gift for Tiamat to
present.
A gift resplendent to his spouse Apsu granted:
A shining metal, the everlasting gold, for her alone to
possess!
Then it was that the two their waters mingled,
divine children between them to bring forth.
Male and female were the celestials created;
Lahmu and Lahamu by names they were called.
In the Below did Apsu and Tiamat make them an abode.
Before then had grown in age and in stature,
In the waters of the Above Anshar and Kishar were
formed;
Surpassing their brothers in size they were.
As a celestial couple the two were fashioned;
A son, An, in the distant heavens was their heir.
Then Antu, to be his spouse, as An's equal was brought
forth;
As a boundary of the Upper Waters their abode was
made.
Thus were three heavenly couples,
Below and Above, in the depths created;
By names they were called, the family of Apsu
with Mummu and Tiamat they formed.

At that time, Nibiru had not yet been seen,
The Earth was not yet called into being.
Mingled were the heavenly waters;
by a Hammered Bracelet they were not yet separated.
At that time, circuits were not yet fully fashioned;
The destinies of the gods were not yet firmly decreed;
The celestial kinfolk banded together;
erratic were their ways.
Their ways to Apsu were verily loathsome;
Tiamat, getting no rest, was aggrieved and raged.
A throng to march by her side she formed,
A growling, raging host against the sons of Apsu
she brought forth.

THE MOONS OF TIAMAT

Withal eleven of this kind she brought forth;
She made the firstborn, Kingu, chief among them.
When the celestial gods of this did hear,
for council they rallied.
Kingu she has elevated, to rank as An command to him
she gave! to each other they said.
A Tablet of Destiny to his chest she has attached,
his own circuit to acquire,
To battle against the gods her offspring
Kingu she instructed.
Who shall stand up to Tiamat? the gods asked each other.
None in their circuits stepped forward,
none a weapon for battle would bear.

SEDUCTION OF NIBURU

At that tirne, in the heart of the Deep a god was
engendered,
In a Chamber of Fates, a place of destinies, was he born.
By an artful Creator was he fashioned,
the son of his own Sun he was.
From the Deep where he was engendered,
the god from his family in a rushing departed;

A gift of his Creator, the Seed of Life,
with him away he carried.
To the void he set his course;
a new destiny he was seeking.
The first to glimpse the wandering celestial
was the ever-watchful Antu.
Alluring was his figure, a radiance he was beaming,
Lordly was his gait, exceedingly great was his course.
Of all the gods he was the loftiest,
surpassing theirs his circuit was.
The first to glimpse him was Antu,
her breast by child never sucked.
Come, be my son! she called to him.
Let me your mother become!
She cast her net and made him welcome,
made his course for the purpose suited.
Her words filled the newcomer's heart with pride;
the one who would nurse him made him haughty.
His head to doubled size grew larger,
four members at his sides he sprouted.
He moved his lips in acceptance,
a godly fire from them blazed forth.
Toward Antu his course he turned,
his face to An soon to show.
When An saw him, My son! My son!
with exaltation he shouted.
To leadership you shall be consigned,
a host by your side will be your servants!
Let Nibiru be your name, as Crossing forever known!
He bowed to Nibiru,
turning his face at Nibiru's passage;
He spread his net,
for Nibiru four servants he brought forth,
His host by his side to be: the South Wind, the North
Wind, the Fast Wind, the West Wind.
With joyful heart An to Anshar his forebear
the arrival of Nibiru announced.

Anshar upon this hearing, Gaga, who was by his side,
as an emissary sent forth
Words of wisdom to An deliver,
a task to Nibiru to assign.
He charged Gaga to give voice to what was in his heart,
to An thus say:
Tiamat, she who bore us, now detests us;
She has set up a warring host, she is furious with rage.
Against the gods, her children,
eleven warriors march by her side;
Kingu among them she elevated,
a destiny to his chest she attached without right.
No god among us against her venom can stand up,
her host in us all has fear established.
Let Nibiru become our Avenger!
Let him vanquish Tiamat, let him save our lives!
For him decree a fate, let him go forth
and face our mighty foe!
To An Gaga departed; he bowed before him,
the words of Anshar he repeated.
An to Nibiru his forebear's words repeated,
Gaga's message to him he revealed.
To the words Nibiru with wonder listened;
of the mother who would her children devour
with fascination he heard.
His heart, without saying,
to set out against Tiamat him already prompted.
He opened his mouth, to An and Gaga he thus said:
If indeed I am to vanquish Tiamat your lives to save,
Convene the gods to assembly,
my destiny proclaim supreme!
Let all the gods agree in council to make me the leader,
bow to my command!
When Lahmu and Lahamu heard this,
they cried out with anguish:
Strange was the demand, its meaning cannot be fathomed! Thus they said.

The gods who decree the fates with each other consulted;
To make Nibiru their Avenger they all agreed,
to him an exalted fate decreed.
From this day on, unchallengeable shall be your com-
mandments! to him they said.
No one among us gods shall transgress your bounds!
Go, Nibiru, be our Avenger!
They fashioned for him a princely circuit
toward Tiamat to proceed;
They gave Nibiru blessings,
they gave Nibiru awesome weapons.
Anshar three more winds of Nibiru brought forth:
the Evil Wind, the Whirlwind, the Matchless Wind.
Kishar with a blazing flame filled his body,
a net to enfold Tiamat therewith.
Thus ready for battle,
Nibiru toward Tiamat directly set his course.

WAR IN HEAVEN

Now this is the account of the Celestial Battle,
And how the Earth lead come to be,
and of Nibiru's destiny.
The lord went forth, his fated course he followed,
Toward the raging Tiamat he set his face,
a spell with his lips he uttered.
As a cloak for protection he the Pulser
and the Emitter put on;
With a fearsome radiance his head was crowned.
On his right he posted the Smiter,
on his left the Repeller he placed.
The seven winds, his host of helpers,
like a storm he sent forth;
Toward the raging Tiamat he was rushing,
clamoring for battle.
The gods thronged about him,
then from his path they departed,
To scan Tiamat and her helpers alone he was advancing,

The scheme of Kingu, her host's commander, to conceive.
When he saw valiant Kingu, blurred became his vision;
As he gazed upon the monsters his direction was
distracted,
His course became upset, his doings were confused.
Tiamat's band tightly her encircled,
with terror they trembled.
Tiamat to her roots gave a shudder,
a mighty roar she emitted;
On Nibiru she cast a spell,
engulfed him with her charms.
The issue between them was joined,
the battle was unavoided!
Face to face they came, Tiamat and Nibiru;
against each other they were advancing.
They for battle approached,
they pressed on for single combat.
The Lord spread his net, to encompass her he cast it;
With fury Tiamat cried out,
like one possessed she lost her senses.
The Evil Wind, which had been behind him,
Nibiru drove forward,
in her face he let it loose;
She opened her mouth the Evil Wind to swallow,
but could not close her lips.
The Evil Wind charged her belly,
into her innards it made its way.
Her innards were howling, her body was distended,
her mouth was open wide.
Through the opening Nibiru shot a brilliant arrow
a lightning most divine.
It pierced her innards, her belly it tore apart;
It tore into her womb, it split apart her heart.
Having thus subdued her,
her life-breath he extinguished.
The lifeless body Nibiru surveyed,
like a slaughtered carcass Tiamat now was.

Beside their lifeless mistress,
her eleven helpers trembled with terror;
In Nibiru's net they were captured,
unable they were to flee.
Kingu, who by Tiamat was made the host's chief,
was among them.
The Lord put him in fetters,
to his lifeless mistress he bound him.
He wrested from Kingu the Tablets of Destinies,
unrightly to him given,
Stamped it with his own seal,
fastened the Destine to his own chest.
The others of Tiamat's band as captives he bound,
in his circuit he them ensnared.
He trampled them underfoot, cut them up to pieces.
He bound them all to his circuit;
to turn around he made them, backward to course.
From the Place of the Battle Nibiru then departed,
To the gods who had him
appointed the victory to announce.
He made a circuit about Apsu,
to Kishar and Anshar lie journeyed.
Gaga came out to greet him,
as a herald to the others he then journeyed.

A New Heaven and a New Earth

Beyond An and Antu,
Nibiru to the Abode in the Deep proceeded.
The fate of lifeless Tiamat and of Kingu he then
considered,
To Tiamat, whom he had subdued,
the Lord Nibiru then returned.
He made his way to her,
paused to view her lifeless body;
To artfully divide the monster
in his heart lie was planning.
Then, as a mussel, into two parts he split her,

her chest from her lower parts he separated.
Her inner channels he cut apart,
her golden veins he beheld with wonder.
Trodding upon her hinder part,
the Lord her upper part completely severed.
The North Wind, his helper,
from his side he summoned,
To thrust away the severed head
the Wind he commanded,
in the void to place it.
Nibiru Wind upon Tiamat then hovered,
sweeping upon her gushing waters.
Nibiru shot a lightning, to North Wind he gave a signal;
In a brilliance was Tiamat's upper part
to a region unknown carried.
With her the bound Kingu was also exiled,
of the severed part a companion to be.
The hinder part's fate Nibiru then considered:
As an everlasting trophy of the battle he wished it to be,
A constant reminder in the heavens,
the Place of the Battle to enshrine.
With his mace the hinder part
he smashed to bits and pieces,
Then strung them together
as a band to form a Hammered Bracelet.
Locking them together, as watchmen he stationed them,
A Firmament to divide the waters from the waters.
The Upper Waters above the Firmament
from the Waters Below it he separated;
Artful works Nibiru thus fashioned.
The Lord then crossed the heavens
to survey the regions;
From Apsu's quarter to the abode of Gaga
he measured the dimensions.
The edge of the Deep Nibiru then examined,
toward his birthplace he cast his gaze.
He paused and hesitated; then to the Firmament,

the Place of the Battle, slowly he returned.
Passing again in Apsu's region,
of the Sun's missing spouse he thought with remorse.
He gazed upon Tiamat's wounded half,
to her Upper Part he gave attention;
The waters of life, her bounty,
from the wounds were still pouring.
Her golden veins Apsu's rays were reflecting.
The Seed of Life, his Creator's legacy,
Nibiru then remembered.
When he trod on Tiamat,
when he split her asunder,
to her the seed he surely imparted!
He addressed words to Apsu, to him thus saying:
With your warming rays, to the wounds give healing!
Let the broken part new life be given,
in your family as a daughter to be,
Let the waters to one place be gathered, let firm land
appear!
By Firm Land let her be called,
Ki henceforth her name to be!
Apsu to the words of Nibiru gave heed:
Let the Earth join my family,
Ki, Firm Land of the Below,
let Earth her name henceforth be!
By her turning let there day and night be;
in the days my healing rays to her I shall provide.
Let Kingu be a creature of the night,
to shine at night 1 shall appoint him
Earth's companion, the Moon forever to be!
Nibiru the Words of Apsu with satisfaction heard.
He crossed the heavens and surveyed the regions,
To the gods who had him elevated
he granted permanent stations,
Their circuits he destined that none shall transgress
nor fall short of each other.
He strengthened the heavenly locks,

gates on both sides he established.
An outermost abode he chose for himself,
beyond Gaga were its dimensions.
The great circuit to be his destiny
he beseeched Apsu for him to decree.
All the gods spoke up from their stations:
Let Nibiru's sovereignty be surpassing!
Most radiant of the gods he is,
let him truly the Son of the Sun be!
From his quarter Apsu gave his blessing:
Nibiru shall hold the crossing of Heaven and Earth;
Crossing shall be his name!
The gods shall cross over neither above nor below;
He shall hold the central position,
the shepherd of the gods he shall be.
A Shar shall be his circuit;
that his Destiny will forever be!

Lost Book of Enki 46-54

The battle between the Dragon and the Lord of hosts, once understood, can be found fragmented in all other epic creation tales. The reason I cite this reference about the Prior Times from Zechariah Sitchin's *The Lost Book of Enki* is because the Enuma elish and all of the other creation epics are wrecked with lines missing and passages being undecipherable. I picked this translation because of its completeness, and even though it's not well known, it does detail the account of our solar system's creation better than most available sources. I hope that this info sheds light on what all of the other cultures are speaking about in their accounts of creation and its beginnings.

CREATION OF THE WORLD BY MARDUK

1. The holy house, the house of the gods, in the holy place had not yet been made;

2. 2 . No reed had sprung up, no tree had been created.

3. No brick had been laid, no building had been set up;

4. No house had been erected, no city had been built;

5. No city had been made, no creature had been created.

6. Nippur had not been made, E-kur had not been built;

7. Erech had not been created, E-ana had not been built;

8. The Deep had not been created, Eridu had not been built;

9. Of the holy house, the house of the gods, the habitation had not been made.

10. All lands were sea.

11. At that time there was a movement in the sea;

12. Then was Eridu made, and E-sagil was built,

13. E-sagil, where in the midst of the Deep the god Lugal-dul-azaga 1 dwelleth;

14. The city of Babylon was built, and E-sagil was finished.

15. The gods, the Anunnaki, he 2 created at one time;

16. The holy city, the dwelling, of their hearts' desire, they proclaimed supreme.

17. Marduk laid a reed upon the face of the waters,

18. He formed dust and poured it out beside the reed.

19. That he might cause the gods to dwell in the habitation of their hearts' desire,

20. He formed mankind.

21. The goddess Aruru together with him I created the seed of mankind.

22. The beasts of the field and living creatures in the field he formed.

23. He created the Tigris and the Euphrates, and he set them in their place;

24. Their names he declared in goodly fashion.

25. The grass, the rush of the marsh, the reed, and the forest he created,

26. The green herb of the field he created,

27. The lands, the marshes, and the swamps;

28. The wild cow and her young, the wild calf; the ewe and her young, the lamb of the fold;

29. Plantations and forests;

30. The he-goat and the mountain-goat ... him.

31. The Lord Marduk laid in a dam by the side of the sea;

32. [He ...] a swamp, he made a marsh

33. [...] he brought into existence.

34. [Reeds he form]ed, trees he created;

35. [...] he made in their place.

36. [Bricks he laid], buildings he set up;

37. [Houses he made], cities he built;

38. [Cities he made], creatures he created.

39. [Nippur he made], E-kur he built;

40. [Erech he made, E-an]a he built.

Reverse Relief

1. [...] the decree [...]

2. [...] ... [...]

3f. Thy exalted minister is Papsukal, the wise counsellor of the gods.

5. May Nin-aha-kudû, the daughter of Ea

6. Purify thee with the pure censer,

7. And may she cleanse thee with cleansing fire!

8f. With a cup of pure water from the Deep shalt thou purify thy way!

10. By the incantation of Marduk, the king of the hosts of heaven and earth,

11. May the abundance of the land enter into thee,

12. And may thy decree be accomplished for ever!

13f. O E-zida, thou glorious dwelling, thou art dear unto the hearts of Anu and Ishtar!

15. May (Ezida) shine like the heavens, may it be bright like the earth, may it [be glorious] like the heart of heaven,

16. [And may ...] be firmly established!

Babylonian Creation Tale

Many are now coming to the realization that our solar system reflects deviations and possibilities that are only now becoming topic for discussion. And even though we have ancient creation stories and mythologies that hint at the chaotic nature of the early formation of our own planet and solar system, science is only beginning to confirm what has been prophesied within the Word for thousands of years. Once one understands this timeline and how it correlates with the formation of our universe and this solar system in Genesis 1, one can then understand how it is that the ancient mythologies align with the Revelation of Moses in Genesis. And just to verify that Niburu did in fact come into our solar system as stated by these ancient stories, I present to you this bit of information as it serves as further confirmation.

Rotation of Venus by Fraser Cain on August 4, 2009

Venus is a twin to our own Earth. It has a similar size, mass, density, and chemical composition. Of course, its high temperatures and extreme atmospheric pressure make it different. And there's another aspect of Venus that's different from Earth; the rotation of Venus is longer than its year—oh, and Venus rotates backward.

Remember from science class that a rotation is when an object spins once on its axis, and a revolution is when it travels once around in orbit around another object. So the Earth takes one day to rotate on its axis, and it takes one year to revolve around the Sun in orbit. Venus, on the other hand, takes 243 days to turn once on its axis, and it takes almost 225 days to travel once around the Sun in orbit. As you can see, a day on Venus is longer than its year.

If that's not strange enough, the rotation of Venus is backward. Seen from above, all of the planets in the Solar System rotate counter-clockwise. This means that eastern regions see the sun before western regions. But that rotation on Venus is backward, so it's going clockwise. If you could stand on the surface of Venus you would see the sun rise in the west and then take 116.75 days to travel across the sky and then set in the east.

So why is the rotation of Venus backward? Astronomers think that Venus was impacted by another large planet early in its history billions of years ago. The combined momentum between the two objects averaged out to the current rotational speed and direction.

The deviations of movements within the orbital positions of planets—including the fact that Venus spins opposite to the normal rotation of the other planets of this solar system—is, in my postulation, verification that there is and was a planetary sized interloper that affected the order of the solar system sometime in our ancient past. The ancient accounts cite this interloper as being the 12th member of our solar system, called Niburu or the Destroyer—also called the planet of the crossing. It's my opinion that this planet still has a part to play in the unfolding End of Days scenario of Revelation as laid out by John.

PRIOR TIMES: MISSION EARTH

My assertion that the fallen angels ruled first on this planet—prior to the creation of modern-day humanity—has been criticized by those that believe the entire history of the universe spans only 7,000 years. It seems obvious to me that the history of not only the universe but even that of our own planet are very ancient indeed and that we have much yet much to learn about our past and what we think we know as certain history. I find that once one studies the world's religious traditions and oral histories—and put them together with the collections of mythology fairy tale and folk history available to us from all the cultures of the world—that the same story is repeated over and over everywhere.

Cultures as varied as the peoples of the world, in their ancient past all seem to hold record of god-like beings long ago descending from the stars or heavens to interject themselves into the affairs of this planet. And because they were seemingly superior in knowledge, technology, and ability, ancient peoples accepted them willingly as benevolent emissaries and established cultures and civilizations to cater to their needs even as they began to be mistreated.

> For Primitive Workers, to the Abzu confined,
>> did the Edin heroes clamor.
> For forty Shars was relief only to the Abzu provided!

The heroes in the Edin shouted,
Our toil has increased beyond endurance,
let us have the Workers too!
While Enlil and Enki the matter were debating,
Ninurta the decision into his hands took:
With fifty heroes an expedition to the Abzu he led,
with weapons were they armed.
In the forests and the steppes of the Abzu,
the Earthlings they chased,
With nets they them captured,
male and female to the Edin they them brought.
To do all manner of chores, in the orchards and in the cities,
they trained them.

Lost Book of Enki, 164-165

Once one begins to realize that the fallen ones were responsible for the introduction of evil into the story of our planet and that unless one bases their foundation for reality on this one truth, nothing seemingly will fit into place or makes sense; one will no longer blame the Most High for the perpetuation of evil on this plane of existence and understand why sin was ascribed to the fallen angels.

I heard His voice: Fear not, Enoch, thou righteous man and scribe of righteousness: approach hither and hear my voice. And go, say to the Watchers of heaven, who have sent thee to intercede for them: You should intercede for men, and not men for you: Wherefore have ye left the high, holy, and eternal heaven, and lain with women, and defiled yourselves with the daughters of men and taken to yourselves wives, and done like the children of earth, and begotten giants (as your) sons And though ye were holy, spiritual, living the eternal life, you have defiled yourselves with the blood of women, and have begotten (children) with the blood of flesh, and, as the children of men, have lusted after flesh and blood as those also do who die and perish.

Therefore have I given them wives also that they might impregnate them, and beget children by them, that thus nothing might be wanting to them on earth. But you were formerly spiritual, living the eternal life, and immortal for all generations of the world. And therefore I have not appointed wives for you; for as for the spiritual ones of the heaven, in heaven is their dwelling. And now, the giants, who are produced from the spirits and flesh, shall be called evil spirits upon the earth, and on the earth shall be their dwelling. Evil spirits have proceeded from their bodies; because they are born from men and from the holy Watchers is their beginning and primal origin; they shall be evil spirits on earth, and evil spirits shall they be called. [As for the spirits of heaven, in heaven shall be their dwelling, but as for the spirits of the earth which were born upon the earth, on the earth shall be their dwelling.]

And the spirits of the giants afflict, oppress, destroy, attack, do battle, and work destruction on the earth, and cause trouble: they take no food, but nevertheless hunger and thirst, and cause offences. And these spirits shall rise up against the children of men and against the women, because they have proceeded from them.

From the days of the slaughter and destruction and death of the giants, from the souls of whose flesh the spirits, having gone forth, shall destroy without incurring judgement -thus shall they destroy until the day of the consummation, the great judgement in which the age shall be consummated, over the Watchers and the godless, yea, shall be wholly consummated. And now as to the watchers who have sent thee to intercede for them, who had been aforetime in heaven, (say to them): You have been in heaven, but all the mysteries had not yet been revealed to you, and you knew worthless ones, and these in the hardness of your hearts you have made known to the women, and through these mysteries women and men work much evil on earth. Say to them therefore: You have no peace.

Book of Enoch, 15:1-16:4

A serious truth seeker that dedicates self to studying the Word of Yahweh God will find that the scriptures contain all answers and explain all things. The word details, in my opinion, the true nature of humanity's relationship with these fallen beings and cites how the rebel angels brought evil into the world. The Book of Giants and Enoch speak volumes as to who these groups of celestial beings were, why they decided to act as gods themselves, and how they abandoned their first estate in search of worlds to rule their own. Christians know this story as Lucifer's fall from grace and outright rejection of authority, and yet most do not associate the rebel angels with the Nephilim of Genesis 6 or the Annunaki of Sumerian legend. Most believe these beings to be different groups of mythological entities; however, in my work I have found them to be one and the same. If one does not know that these beings are one and the same, one might possibly be set-up for the strong delusion that these fallen ones are benevolent and that they are—and were—the de facto creators of humanity. This is the strong delusion spoken of in 2 Thessalonians, "And for this cause God shall send them strong delusion, that they should believe a lie."

Having studied much of what is available as far as wisdom texts from all cultures, it's my assertion that the Annunaki, or those from heaven to earth came, are the same Nephilim (fallen angels, not giants) of Genesis 6, powers, principalities, and rulers of darkness of Ephesians 6, archons of the Nag Hammadi codices, and rebel angels described in the Books of Enoch. In order for me to establish who these beings are and that they were here before the creation of humanity on the sixth day, I will cite two pieces of information which together lend credence to the others' accounting—one the Sumerian king list and another similar king list proposed by Berossus—a Hellenized Chaldean philosopher and astrologer commissioned by Antiochus I to account for pre-human history. I mention the king list because, though they seem implausible as far as length of reigns, what people do not realize is that the first rulers on the list were demigods in the sense that they were hybrid beings, children of the Nephilim coupling with the peoples of pre-adamic humanity. And though it seems almost impossible to believe that such beings could have once existed in the ancient past, there are myriad bone fragments, skeletons, skulls, and artifacts discovered from all parts of the world testifying to the existence and presence of these semi-divine beings and the primitive workers they manipulated into existence upon the world stage. For example, in 2011 Peruvian anthropologists unearthed a cone shaped skull of two hybrid, red-haired giants, which other anthropologists classified as "not being human." The reports of red-haired giants were found in a small town and city newspapers countrywide. One such account comes from the San Diego Union Journal of 1947:

> A retired Ohio doctor has discovered relics of an ancient civilization, whose men were 8 to 9 feet tall in the desert near the Nevada-California line, an associate said today. Howard E. Hill of Los Angeles speaking before the Transportation Club, disclosed that several well-preserved mummies were taken yesterday from caverns in an area roughly 180 miles square, extending through much of Nevada and California.

According to the article and Dr. Hill, the remains of this ancient race and their civilization date back some twenty to thirty thousand years ago, prior to the creation of modern day Adam and Eve. One thing of curiosity mentioned in the article is that old cave markings found on site resemble markings "used by the Masonic Order" and that other markings resembled Egyptian hieroglyphs. Dr. Hill speculated that these people were the survivors of Atlantis, concluding that the mummified remains had to be archaic because they were found clothed in a type of leather, which cannot be tied to any known creature in existence today. What is strange about this story is that stories and mythologies of red-haired giants cross the globe, with recent discoveries of Chinese red-haired giants in the Tarim basin area of China. These discoveries prompted National Geographic to produce a 2007 documentary called "Ancient Caucasian Mummies Found In China." This documentary further verifies my conclusion and theories. Truthfully, if one seeks, one will find numerous stories and mythologies worldwide that verify my hypothesis.

And though humanity no longer has access to Beroussus' original writings in complete form, we are blessed to have fragments preserved in the extensively quoted tracts of other ancient historical writers citing from his original five books on the history of Babylonia. It takes years of study to understand the true nature of who these beings really are and what their historical interaction with humans has been. It's only by knowing what happened in the past that we can decide how best to approach such similar modern-day phenomenon as alien abductions.

Berossus' account of angelic interaction, not surprisingly, parallels the Dead Sea Scroll accounts of the Book of Enoch, Book of Giants, as well as Sumerian cuneiform Egyptian hieroglyphic depictions of hybrid monstrosities lurking in the world during our ancient past. Unless one has studied in depth both Hebraic-Christian heritage as well as the Sumerian Egyptian Celtic chronicles, one would not know how to piece these stories together.

Berossus, Mantheo, and even Josephus all confirm that the mutiny of the Annunaki angels took place prior to the creation of modern humanity. It's important to understand this point as it is key for understanding Genesis 1's declaration that the Elohim were involved prior to the creation of sixth day humanity with manipulating the genome of pre-adamic humanity or Bigfoot looking Cro-Magnon Neanderthal man. I will expound upon the Genesis 1 creation story when explaining the circumstances for why Yahushuah created sixth day modern humanity, why Adam was given the breath of life, why he was separated from the fallen angels and placed in a protective enclosure called Paradise, and why it was necessary for

Lucifer to disguise himself in the form of a serpent in order to gain access to the Lord's highest and newest creation.

So much is happening that is not being discussed within Genesis. Unless someone spends a lot of time researching all of the other cultural mythologies, one would have a difficult time piecing together a complete picture of what happened during the previous aeons of Earth history. The Sumerian teachings also provide eye witness account as to what happened during the prior times after the destruction of Tiamat and creation of Ki, the new earth, when Enki, or whom Beroussus calls the demiurge, Cronus, Satan arrived to this planet with a group of fifty other Annunaki somewhere between 450,000 to 432,000 years ago.

> Beroussus, in the first book of his history of Babylonia, informs us that he lived in the age of Alexander the son of Philip. And he mentions that there were written accounts, preserved at Babylon with the greatest care, comprehending a period of above fifteen myriads of years: and that these writings contained histories of the heaven and of the sea; of the birth of mankind; and of the kings, and of the memorable actions which they had achieved. And in the first place he describes Babylonia as a country situated between the Tigris and the Euphrates: that it abounded with wheat, and barley, and ocrus, and sesame; and that in the lakes were produced the roots called gongre, which are fit for food, and in respect to nutriment similar to barley.
>
> That there were also palm trees and apples, and a variety of fruits; fish also and birds, both those which are merely of flight, and those which frequent the lakes. He adds, that those parts of the country which bordered upon Arabia, were without water, and barren; but that the parts which lay on the other side were both hilly and fertile. At Babylon there was (in these times) a great resort of people of various nations, who inhabited Chaldæa, and lived in a lawless manner like the beasts of the field. In the first year there appeared, from that part of the Erythræan sea

which borders upon Babylonia, an animal destitute of reason, by name Oannes, whose whole body (according to the account of Apollodorus) was that of a fish; that under the fish's head he had another head, with feet also below, similar to those of a man, subjoined to the fish's tail. His voice too, and language, was articulate and human; and a representation of him is preserved even to this day.

Impatient, Ea donned his Fish's suit;
   within his chest his heart was like a drum beating.
Into the marsh he jumped,
   toward its edge hurried steps he directed.

Lost Book of Enki

This Being was accustomed to pass the day among men; but took no food at that season; and he gave them an insight into letters and sciences, and arts of every kind. He taught them to construct cities, to found temples, to compile laws, and explained to them the principles of geometrical knowledge. He made them distinguish the seeds of the earth, and shewed them how to collect the fruits; in short, he instructed them in every thing which could tend to soften manners and humanize their lives. From that time, nothing material has been added by way of improvement to his instructions. And when the sun had set, this Being Oannes, retired again into the sea, and passed the night in the deep; for he was amphibious. After this there appeared other animals like Oannes, of which Berossus proposes to give an account when he comes to the history of the kings.

Moreover Oannes wrote concerning the generation of mankind; and of their civil polity; and the following is the purport of what he said: There was a time in which there existed nothing but darkness and an abyss of waters, wherein resided most hideous beings, which were produced of a two-fold principle. There appeared men, some of whom were furnished with two wings, others with four, and with two faces. They had one body but two heads:

the one that of a man, the other of a woman: and likewise in their several organs both male and female. Other human figures were to be seen with the legs and horns of goats: some had horses' feet: while others united the hind quarters of a horse with the body of a man, resembling in shape the hippocentaurs. Bulls likewise were bred there with the heads of men; and dogs with fourfold bodies, terminated in their extremities with the tails of fishes: horses also with the heads of dogs: men too and other animals, with the heads and bodies of horses and the tails of fishes. In short, there were creatures in which were combined the limbs of every species of animals. In addition to these, fishes, reptiles, serpents, with other monstrous animals, which assumed each other's shape and countenance. Of all which were preserved delineations in the temple of Belus at Babylon.

The person, who presided over them, was a woman named Omoroca; which in the Chaldæan language is Thalatth; in Greek Thalassa, the sea (Tiamat); but which might equally be interpreted the Moon. All things being in this situation, Belus came, and cut the woman asunder: and of one half of her he formed the earth, and of the other half the heavens; and at the same time destroyed the animals within her. All this (he says) was an allegorical description of nature. For, the whole universe consisting of moisture, and animals being continually generated therein, the deity above-mentioned took off his own head: upon which the other gods mixed the blood, as it gushed out, with the earth; and from thence were formed men.

On this account it is that they are rational, and partake of divine knowledge. This Belus, by whom they signify Jupiter (Niburu), divided the darkness, and separated the Heavens from the Earth, and reduced universe to order. But the animals, not being able to bear the prevalence of light, died. Belus upon this, seeing a vast space unoccupied, though by nature fruitful, commanded one of the gods to take off his head, and to mix the blood with the earth; and from thence to form other men and animals, which should be capable of bearing the air. Belus formed also the stars, and the sun, and the moon, and the five planets. (Such, according to Polyhistor Alexander, is the account which Berossus gives in his first book.) (In the second book was contained the history of the ten kings of the Chaldæans, and the periods of the continuance of each reign, which consisted collectively of an hundred and twenty sari (shar), or four hundred and thirty-two thousand years (120 by 3,600); reaching to the time of the Deluge.

Fragments of Chaldean History,
Berossus: Alexander Polyhistor

Berossus's early account is important as it verifies the fallen angel corruption of pre-adamic humanity as well as their rule upon the earth previous to even the creation of modern-day humanity. Another mention of extreme importance is Oannes as the bringer of knowledge and civilization to the ancient pre-adamic peoples. Oannes, for anybody that researches the story, was called the Lord of the Waves by the Babylonians and is depicted as a partially amphibious being with the torso and head of a man and lower portion representing that of a fish with scales. This myth was the forerunner for the mermaid, siren, and merfolk legends.

Oannes is also Greek for the Akkadian Lord Ea, Gnostic Demiurge Yaldaboath Saklas Samael, Christian Lucifer or Satan, Targum Sammael, and Islamic Iblis, as all are just different names for the same god of the first Annunaki civilization called Eridu, the Sumerian Prince Ea, later Enki. Many cultures attribute the bringing of higher civilization to a form of Enki or Oannes, the lightbringer whom, according to legend, came in the guise of a fish, eagle, serpent, or hybrid mix of these such as Quetzlcoatl, the plumed serpent.

The Sumerian texts speak of a fish/eagle suit the Annunaki wear when exploring other worlds. Perhaps it was just such a suit that gave them the ability to present themselves in one form or another to various cultures and civilizations, or perhaps as the Bible and other extra-biblical books suggest, Lucifer and his fallen angels possess the ability to shape shift into any form, even that of an angel of light and can assume appearance in any guise. It is my belief that all of these various, seemingly unconnected embodiments are in fact the same phenomena, and that Oannes, Quetzlcoatl, and Kulkulcan, among others, all represent the same historical verification that Satan and the fallen ones did long ago interdict themselves into the affairs of humanity as the hybrid demigods worshiped of old.

There is a tribe from Mali, Africa, called the Dogon that still worships Oannes in idol form. Called the Nommos, they claim the olden gods descended to Earth in an ark thousands of years ago from a planet that orbited another star in a then unknown binary star system. The Nommos, according to legend, gave the Dogon knowledge about Sirius B and even left them in possession of a 400-year-old artifact that apparently depicts the Sirius configuration as a binary star system, a fact discovered only a few years before anthropologists recorded the Dogon stories. Would it surprise you to know that after six months of spiritual initiation the Dogon spiritual leader, called Hogon, appears publically, wearing a red fez much like the Shriner's of America and that the Fez is tied to the worship of these ancient star gods? Would it surprise you to know that the pope's hat, called a mitre, is also representation of the fish cap worn by Oannes? The pope's hat is connected directly to the worship of Oannes, or whom the Philistines and the Bible reference as Dagon. So why is the Roman Catholic Church seemingly tied to the worship of ancient pagan deities?

> Then the lords of the Philistines gathered them together for to offer a great sacrifice unto Dagon their god, and to rejoice: for they said, Our god hath delivered Samson our enemy into our hand. And when the people saw him, they praised their god: for they said, Our god hath delivered

into our hands our enemy, and the destroyer of our country, which slew many of us.

And it came to pass, when their hearts were merry, that they said, Call for Samson, that he may make us sport. And they called for Samson out of the prison house; and he made them sport: and they set him between the pillars. And Samson said unto the lad that held him by the hand, Suffer me that I may feel the pillars whereupon the house standeth, that I may lean upon them.

Now the house was full of men and women; and all the lords of the Philistines were there; and there were upon the roof about three thousand men and women, that beheld while Samson made sport. And Samson called unto the Lord, and said, O Lord GOD, remember me, I pray thee, and strengthen me, I pray thee, only this once, O God, that I may be at once avenged of the Philistines for my two eyes. And Samson took hold of the two middle pillars upon which the house stood, and on which it was borne up, of the one with his right hand, and of the other with his left. And Samson said, Let me die with the Philistines. And he bowed himself with all his might; and the house fell upon the lords, and upon all the people that were therein. So the dead which he slew at his death were more than they which he slew in his life.

Judges 16:23-30

When the Philistines took the ark of God, they brought it into the house of Dagon, and set it by Dagon. And when they of Ashdod arose early on the morrow, behold, Dagon was fallen upon his face to the earth before the ark of the Lord. And they took Dagon, and set him in his place again. And when they arose early on the morrow morning, behold, Dagon was fallen upon his face to the ground before the ark of the Lord; and the head of Dagon and both the palms of his hands were cut off upon the threshold; only the stump of Dagon was left to him.

Therefore neither the priests of Dagon, nor any that come into Dagon's house, tread on the threshold of Dagon in Ashdod unto this day. But the hand of the LORD was heavy upon them of Ashdod, and he destroyed them, and smote them with emerods, even Ashdod and the coasts thereof. And when the men of Ashdod saw that it was so, they said, The ark of the God of Israel shall not abide with us: for his hand is sore upon us, and upon Dagon our god. They sent therefore and gathered all the lords of the Philistines unto them, and said, What shall we do with the ark of the God of Israel? And they answered, Let the ark of the God of Israel be carried about unto Gath. And they carried the ark of the God of Israel about thither.

Samuel 5:2-7 (KJV)

And when they had stripped him, they took his head, and his armour, and sent into the land of the Philistines round about, to carry tidings unto their idols, and to the people. And they put his armour in the house of their gods, and fastened his head in the temple of Dagon.

Chronicles 10:10 (KJV)

Oannes is none other than Prometheus of Greek legend, or the Lucifer of Masonic tradition that was the light bearer or bringer of wisdom who, according to occultist lore, abandoned his first estate in order to bring knowledge in the form of light to humanity locked away in darkness by a supposed "cruel, uncaring tyrant god." According to Masons, Lucifer only wanted to help humanity by extending to us our own right to godhood and experience of the lavish pleasures of life in the flesh. The Masons believe that Lucifer sacrificed himself to bring humanity the possibilities of free will in this temporal world. Those that embrace the Luciferian creed of "do as thou wilt," are they who would rather indulge in all grandiose self pleasure than exist in an eternal world where they must adhere to the commandment and law of a Creator of us all. They, like Lucifer, deny Christ as the Son of God and arbiter of future judgment, for how can one truly be evil if one possesses any shred of faith or belief in the eternal condemnation or the salvation of soul? And though the Masons worship Lucifer as the liberator of free will, what they won't tell you is that Lucifer as Satan was responsible for our collective fall as humanity and our current imprisonment within the flesh.

With the insight of Berossus, Mantheo, and other ancient historians we can detail the fallen angels' connection to the worship of the ancient star gods in their various embodiments and to those entities that were said to have delivered advanced knowledge to various cultures early in their history of this planet. Many may still doubt my assertion that the fallen ones inhabited this planet prior to our creation, and yet ancient sites are being discovered in places where no city, people, or civilization should have been in existence, especially not one advanced beyond even modern day standards. And even though modern-day science currently considers Sumer as the oldest historical culture and civilization to have ever existed upon the planet, they do not take into account pre-deluge history or those cultures and civilizations that have become largely buried by earth and sea. New evidence has come to light recently with the discovery of a forgotten lost Atlantis-type city submerged off the coast of Japan near Yonaguni, Jima.

Investigators cite the ancient city as being 5,000 years old and date its destruction to an earthquake over 2,000 years ago. I believe the site to be much older and part of those cultures, which existed prior to the flood of Noah's day. I believe that this city, like the myth of Atlantis, was part of previous judgments that took place on cities inhabited by the fallen ones and the creatures they brought into existence prior to even the creation of modern humanity.

We know that the Lord has had to destroy the fallen angels in their celestial and earthly habitations many times because of their insistence upon acting as gods themselves and for specifically destroying planets peoples and creatures. The planets in this solar system are riddled with evidence of the Lord's judgments against them.

> Such was his glory that he governed the virtues of heaven... Satan was the master of all those who imitated the Father, and his power descended from the sky to the inferno and rose again from the inferno to the throne of the invisible Father. And he observed the glory of Him who transformed the skies. And he dreamed of placing his seat on the clouds of heaven because he wanted to be like the very high.
>
> The Gospel of the Secret Supper

THE CELESTIAL BATTLE
AND END OF THE
FIRST WORLD AGE

Scripture refers to a time when Lucifer refused to humble himself before the dominion of Yahushuah and was cast from heaven, and also about a time when—after the creation of sixth-day—Adam Lucifer refused to bow to humanity and the dominion of Adam in Paradise. The Lord allows cycles to repeat even in our lives so that those that watch vigilantly will know what's coming and not be fated to repeat mistakes, recognizing patterns such as the warning of in the days of Noah. The first instance of Lucifer's rebellion occurred when Yahushuah, or Adam of Light, was unveiled to the world. His revealing caused the separation of light and darkness, and His dominion became the reason for Lucifer's rage and envy. Most have never heard of Adam of Light nor His association with Yahushuah as being the original Adam; however, if the *Book of the Secrets of Enoch* is correct and Lucifer was banished from the upper heavens on the second day, the only thing that can tie all of these stories together is that Lucifer refused to submit to the dominion of our Lord, Adam of Light, and for this he was cast out of the upper heavens. This separation of light and darkness is also the point where he would challenge the Lord to the same death and incarnation in the flesh to which the Lord sentenced Satan and his angels. While there are not many passages detailing who Adam of Light is and what role He is to play within the creation, one passage from *On the Origin of the World* also correlates Yahushuah with being the first created Adam, Adam of Light.

> Now when Adam of Light conceived the wish to enter his light—i.e., the eight heaven—he was unable to do so because of the poverty that had mingled with his light. Then he created for himself a vast eternal realm. And within that eternal realm he created six eternal realms and their adornments, six in number, that were seven times better than the heavens of chaos and their adornments. Now all these eternal realms and their adornments exist within the infinity that is between the eighth heaven and the chaos below it, being counted with the universe that belongs to poverty. If you want to know the arrangement of these, you will find it written in the Seventh Universe of the Prophet Hieralias.
>
> And before Adam of Light had withdrawn in the chaos, the authorities saw him and laughed at the prime parent because he had lied when he said, It is I who am God. No one exists before me. When they came to him, they said, Is this not the god who ruined our work? He answered and said, Yes. If you do not want him to be able to ruin our work, come let us create a man out of earth, according to the image of our body and according to the likeness of this being, to serve us; so that when he sees his likeness, he might become enamored of it. No longer will he ruin our work; rather, we shall make those who are born out of the light our servants for all the duration of this eternal realm... Now these through the will <...> The souls that were going to enter the modeled forms of the authorities were manifested to Sabaoth and his Christ. And regarding these, the holy voice said, Multiply and improve! Be lord over all creatures. And it is they who were taken captive,

according to their destinies, by the prime parent. And thus they were shut into the prisons of the modelled forms until the consummation of the age.

On the Origin of the World

In the passage "come let us create a man out of the Earth," Yaldaboath is speaking to the lower order of angels about the third creation of Adam, Adam of dust, which came into being on the eighth day as an agreement between the angels of both the lower and higher order. The third creation of Adam is a very difficult topic to understand and that's partially one of the reasons for my efforts in producing this book. My hope is to detail the many creations of Adam and the various world ages so that you can understand how and why each came into being and how and why it led us to our current condition as a spiritual being caught in a fallen state of physical flesh. I will discuss in a later chapter the third creation of Adam, but suffice it to say there are many texts that I will use to not only describe the fall of humanity, but also the elevation of humanity once dust Adam and Eve are recreated on the eighth day into flesh form. The Nag Hammadi collection, the Kolbrin Bible, as well as many other texts also gives insight into how humanity was lifted from their fallen state to recognize that they were living among the fallen ones.

Remember in the book of Luke? The Lord says that He was witness to Satan falling as lightning from heaven. How could this be if He was not Himself already with the Father? If one reads closely the passage from John 1, one will see that the Father and the Son are one, that He was with Him since before the beginning, that all things were created through Him and by Him, and that nothing came into existence that was not done through Him/Them. We have to understand that Yahushuah, or who many know as Jesus Christ, has always been with God the Father, and as Son He and the Father are one. Our Lord has been with the Father since before the beginning and it was in fact He, as the word and verbal expression of the Father, that brought all these things into being; not only that, but He as the light was what brought the entirety of creation to visibility.

I know that it's difficult for people to grasp this concept, yet I think it's important for people to at least ponder the incredible nature of this thought. Because if one can grasp this simple concept as laid out by John, one would know that never could they—or we as creatures—ever aspire to be Christ in the fullness of His glory. Even as sons of God and children made in the image of the word as physical embodiment of the Father, we are still not the Christ and never could aspire to that role. Christ is the only begotten of Yahweh God, and it was only to Him that role as God in flesh was given, to die as a sacrificial lamb for the sins of those whom had rebelled and fallen prior to His taking on form to defeat death. Only Yahushuah would fulfill this role, and at a date and time specific to fulfill the feasts and prophecies of the Father.

Our Lord is the light of the universe, and we, like the angels, should know to whom all praise worship, gratitude, and blessings should be directed in servicing the grand monarchy of the Morningstar administration. Please understand we can never aspire to be the Christ in such a way that we equal His glory. Even when we allow self to become a vessel of His will, it is He that works through us that is the power, and yet even when He works through us it is not us but he that is the Christ within us that accomplishes miracles. This is what it means to be born again and filled with the Holy Spirit, for we are to implement the laws and commandments of the Lord in exampling to others.

Yahushuah, as the embodiment of Yahweh and the light that was called forth that separated darkness from the upper heavens, was the Adam to whom Lucifer refused servitude on the second day. It was on that day also that he entertained the thought of exalting himself above the throne and dominion of the Holy Trinity. For these two incidences, he and those that sided with him were cast out of the upper heavens. Later He would exact his revenge on the second creation of Adam, Adam of Paradise, since he had no power or authority to rebuke the glory or might of our Lord, Adam of Light.

> And I said, Lord, before Satan fell, what was his glory beside your Father's? And he told me, Such was his glory that he governed the virtues of heaven. As for me, I sat next to my Father. Satan was the master of all those who imitated the Father, and his power descended from the sky to the inferno and rose again from the inferno to the throne of the invisible Father. And he observed the glory of Him who transformed the skies. And he dreamed of placing his seat on the clouds of heaven because he wanted to be like the very high...
>
> When he descended farther down, he found himself in the presence of clouds weighing on the tidal waves of the sea. He went on until he got to his ossop, which is the principle of fire. After that he could not descend farther because of the intense flame of the fire. Then Satan came in from behind and filled his own heart with malice, and reaching the angel of the air and the one who was above the waters, he said to them, Everything belongs to me. If you listen to me, I will place my seat on the clouds and I shall be similar to the very high. I will withdraw the waters of the upper firmament and assemble all the areas occupied by the sea into one entity of vast seas. That done, there will be no water on the face of the entire earth, and I shall reign with you through the centuries of the centuries.
>
> The Gospel of the Secret Supper

Yahushuah as Adam of Light was the image that the second Adam, Adam of Paradise, was formed as on the sixth day. This creation of humanity would be unique in that we would be endowed with the Holy Spirit and infused with the breath of life that is Christ within us. The Lord would utilize this spirit-filled being to not only bring righteousness to the world but also judgment to those that were

SONS OF GOD

then ruling in deceit upon the lower earth. Sixth-day humanity was made in the image of the Holy Trinity before falling from grace:

> He answered and said unto them, He that soweth the good seed is the Son of man; The field is the world; the good seed are the children of the kingdom; but the tares are the children of the wicked one; The enemy that sowed them is the devil; the harvest is the end of the world; and the reapers are the angels. As therefore the tares are gathered and burned in the fire; so shall it be in the end of this world.
>
> Matthew 13:36-40 (KJV)

Before Lucifer was to be cast from the upper heavens, the Lord allowed him to tempt the resolve of all the angels; He wanted to see which would be incited for rebellion and which would remain loyal to His dominion and monarchy. While Lucifer was going to and fro among the angels of the Lord, testing their allegiance, many were in quandary as to whom they should serve. With war impending, sides would have to be chosen carefully as the winner would rule supreme over heavenly affairs.

Contrary to belief, Satan never had a chance to usurp the throne of Yahweh or the dominion of Yahushuah, for how can a creature ever rule supreme over its Creators? Such a thought is beyond comprehension, and yet Lucifer's appeal was so great that he convinced one third of the angels of every order to side with his rebellion. One third was loyal to Yahweh and Yahushuah, yet one third wavered in commitment as to whom to serve—Lucifer and the New World Order or Yahweh and the Natural Order. This rebellion caused Yahushuah to reconstitute a plan by which to redeem the angels of the First World Age by giving them/us free will to incarnate into flesh during the Second World Age. As sons of God and spirits of the First World Age, we would be tried and tested through life in mortal flesh where, as humans, we would learn about creation through the experience of both good and evil. Lucifer's persuasive abilities incited those that followed him to attempt an overthrow of Yahushuah's dominion. As war in heaven ensued, he and his hosts fought against Michael and one third of the Cherubim angels, of which Lucifer had once been. For his insurrection, he became head of the Seraphim angels, which together were banished from the realms above the six heavens.

Yahweh allowed the Lucifer rebellion to test the loyalty of all of His angels as the one third (Ophanim) that wavered in choosing sides would now be given chance again to prove allegiance and loyalty by incarnating into flesh. The one third (Seraphim) that affixed themselves to Lucifer, believing the same lie that caused his own downfall, that being the promise, desire of godhood, and selfish rule, would have no part in salvation and at the end of days be eradicated as if they had never been. The one third (Cherubim) that remained loyal would be given special election and chance to volunteer service in the flesh, incarnating for special purpose much like the Apostles and John the Baptist. While not much has been written to clarify this accounting, there is a quote from the First Book of Adam and Eve that gives readers insight into this little known War in Heaven.

> But now, O Adam, we will make known to you, what came over us through him, before his fall from heaven. He gathered together his hosts, and deceived them, promising to give them a great kingdom, a divine nature; and other promises he made them. His hosts believed that his word was true, so they yielded to him, and renounced the glory of God. He then sent for us—according to the orders in which we were—to come under his command, and to accept his vain promise. But we would not, and we did not take his advice. Then after he had fought with God, and had dealt forwardly with Him, he gathered together his hosts, and made war with us. And if it had not been for God's strength that was with us, we could not have prevailed against him to hurl him from heaven. But when he fell from among us, there was great joy in heaven, because

of his going down from us. For if he had remained in heaven, nothing, not even one angel would have remained in it. But God in His mercy, drove him from among us to this dark earth; for he had become darkness itself and a worker of unrighteousness. And he has continued, O Adam, to make war against you, until he tricked you and made you come out of the garden, to this strange land, where all these trials have come to you. And death, which God brought to him, he has also brought to you, O Adam, because you obeyed him, and trespassed against God. Then all the angels rejoiced and praised God, and asked Him not to destroy Adam this time, for his having sought to enter the garden; but to bear with him until the fulfillment of the promise; and to help him in this world until he was free from Satan's hand.

The First Book of Adam and Eve, 55

Cast out of the upper heavens, Lucifer as Satan (the adversary) was banished with his hosts to wander the lower heavens in search of worlds to destroy and kingdom to rule. From the second until the sixth day, he and his rebel angels had free reign of the lower heavens, and as the Sumerian tales of the Annunaki relate, could and possibly did explore the myriad planets and moons of this solar system, establishing what are termed as *waystations* throughout. How far and wide his exploration encompassed we may never know, and yet daily it seems someone from NASA personnel, astronauts, or members from other national alphabet agencies are leaking stories, photos, and even videos detailing the connection of the ancient *star gods* to possible megalithic type structures and cities having been in existence upon not only our own moon and Mars but perhaps also other planets and moons within this solar system. Having free roam of the planets from the second until the sixth day, Satan and his hosts had plenty of time to build such structures and to establish such cities.

Thou shalt not be joined with them in burial, because thou hast destroyed thy land, and slain thy people: the seed of evildoers shall never be renowned. Prepare slaughter for his children for the iniquity of their fathers; that they do not rise, nor possess the land, nor fill the face of the world with cities. For I will rise up against them, saith the LORD of hosts.

Isaiah 14:20-22 (KJV)

Pre-Adamic Earth

In order for me to clarify whom the sixth-day, spirit-filled, breath of life, hermaphroditic Adam was from the eighth-day, dual-natured, fallen-dust Adam, I must explain the Genesis 2 pre-adamic creation—as molded by the Elohim—to establish how this story fits in with the Three World Ages and three creations of Adam. Most do not realize that the early chapters of Genesis 2 actually describe the molding of a creature prior to the creation of modern humanity and that one was molded by the Annunaki Elohim and the other formed by the Holy Trinity.

> And God said, Let us make man in our image, after our likeness: and let them have dominion over the fish of the sea, and over the fowl of the air, and over the cattle, and over all the earth, and over every creeping thing that creepeth upon the earth. So God created man in his own image, in the image of God created he him; male and female created he them. And God blessed them, and God said unto them, Be fruitful, and multiply, and replenish the earth, and subdue it: and have dominion over the fish of the sea, and over the fowl of the air, and over every living thing that moveth upon the earth. And God said, Behold, I have given you every herb bearing seed, which is upon the face of all the earth, and every tree, in the which is the fruit of a tree yielding seed; to you it shall be for meat. And to every beast of the earth, and to every fowl of the air, and to every thing that creepeth upon the earth, wherein there

is life, I have given every green herb for meat: and it was so. And God saw every thing that he had made, and, behold, it was very good. And the evening and the morning were the sixth day.

Gemesis 2:26-31 (KJV)

If you look up the translation for God in the prior Genesis passages one will find that the word *God* translates as plural Elohim, which like *sons of God* stands for the sum total of angels in both the higher and lower orders. God in these early passages actually represents the angels of God—in this case the rebel angels that were cast out of their first estate.

If one looks very closely at these particular passages, one will notice a very delicate shift from Elohim (God) to Yahweh Elohim (Lord God). This shift is very important in that it very subtly veils fallen-angel involvement with the pre-adamic creature of Genesis 2. The Annunaki, as indicative of this passage, were involved in the prior genetic manipulation of an ancestor of Cro-magnon Neanderthal pre-adamic apeman already in existence here on the planet. The Sumerian teachings also confirm that the Annunaki had created what they term a primitive worker from this big-foot type of creature.

This Genesis 2 account also verifies a division of capability in that the Annunaki-molded creature was very different than the sixth-day Adam created by Yahweh Elohim as what the Sumerian teachings call the Civilized Man. The first molded creature did not possess intelligence enough to farm the land or to shepherd domesticated animals. This being was neither endowed with the ability to speak nor to understand language. It was also vegetarian, as it was the Annunaki giants that were the first to consume flesh as carnivores on the planet. The destruction and recreation of Tiamat, as referenced in the Kolbrin, is also implied within the early Genesis account, and both shroud within them the destruction of those cities that were inhabited by the fallen ones and the slave race they had molded prior to the Holy Trinity creating modern humanity in Genesis 2.

During the early part of earth history, both the fallen ones, as well as their slave race, numbered few. Both groups were sustained directly from the land and were easily nourished by the abundance that nature provided. Once both groups began to multiply, life became increasingly difficult for both groups. It is my contention that the Annunaki, though they have very long and seemingly immortal life spans, are not eternal, immortal beings, especially in their current state as Annunaki spirit men. I believe they are similar in likeness to ourselves in that they also must eat, drink, sleep and defecate just like the rest of us mere mortals. As such, they can be killed, and do in fact die. This does not deter from their ability to, like Legion, sustain self in seeming immortality, possessing body after body through lifetime age and space of time to shrug off the limitations of flesh and death.

We are told in the book of Enoch that after their deaths in the flood, the children of Anak, the hybrid giant seedlines—because they were not a natural creation and had no part in salvation—would be condemned by the Lord to wander the post-deluge Earth as demonic entities, seeking bodies to possess for indwelling. It would be through the bodies of others that the condemned would again feed on the flesh and blood of humanity, as they had prior as the embodiment of the mythological titans of old.

The fallen ones are inter-dimensional beings that can live in and out of flesh. Even these seemingly immortal rebel angels will be judged to die mortal deaths during the harvest, at the end of days, with the coming separation of the wheat and the tares. They, like evil, have been given only a short time to exist, and once that time is up, all those that are associated with evil shall be wiped from existence as if they had never been. My contention that the fallen angels inhabit flesh and human form is also backed up by Ezekiel 28 and Isaiah 14, which are both very familiar passages written in reference to Lucifer and his station prior to his fall. These quotes also verify that Satan is now a man, holding the form of a man, possessing the shape of a man, and that the Lord will judge him to die the death of a man by burning him inside out in the presence of kings and rulers.

How art thou fallen from heaven, O Lucifer, son of the morning! how art thou cut down to the ground, which didst weaken the nations! For thou hast said in thine heart, I will ascend into heaven, I will exalt my throne above the stars of God: I will sit also upon the mount of the congregation, in the sides of the north: I will ascend above the heights of the clouds; I will be like the most High. Yet thou shalt be brought down to hell, to the sides of the pit. They that see thee shall narrowly look upon thee, and consider thee, saying, Is this the man that made the earth to tremble, that did shake kingdoms; That made the world as a wilderness, and destroyed the cities thereof; that opened not the house of his prisoners? All the kings of the nations, even all of them, lie in glory, every one in his own house. But thou art cast out of thy grave like an abominable branch, and as the raiment of those that are slain, thrust through with a sword, that go down to the stones of the pit; as a carcase trodden under feet. Thou shalt not be joined with them in burial, because thou hast destroyed thy land, and slain thy people: the seed of evildoers shall never be renowned. Prepare slaughter for his children for the iniquity of their fathers; that they do not rise, nor possess the land, nor fill the face of the world with cities. For I will rise up against them, saith the LORD of hosts...

Isaiah 14:12-22 (KJV)

Son of man, say unto the prince of Tyrus, Thus saith the Lord GOD; Because thine heart is lifted up, and thou hast said, I am a God, I sit in the seat of God, in the midst of the seas; yet thou art a man, and not God, though thou set thine heart as the heart of God: Behold, thou art wiser than Daniel; there is no secret that they can hide from thee: With thy wisdom and with thine understanding thou hast gotten thee riches, and hast gotten gold and silver into thy treasures: By thy great wisdom and by thy traffick hast thou increased thy riches, and thine heart is lifted up because of thy riches: Therefore thus saith the Lord GOD; Because thou hast set thine heart as the heart of God; Behold, therefore I will bring strangers upon thee, the terrible of the nations: and they shall draw their swords against the beauty of thy wisdom, and they shall defile thy brightness. They shall bring thee down to the pit, and thou shalt die the deaths of them that are slain in the midst of the seas. Wilt thou yet say before him that slayeth thee, I am God? but thou shalt be a man, and no God, in the hand of him that slayeth thee. Thou shalt die the deaths of the uncircumcised by the hand of strangers: for I have spoken it, saith the Lord GOD.

Ezekiel 28:2-10 (KJV)

It wasn't until the Lord breathed the spirit of life into sixth-day Adam that humanity was endowed with the ability to speak and recognize language. It's important to understand that the counterfeit creation, the primitive worker molded by the fallen angels, had no capacity to speak or understand language and was very limited in ability to provide service to the Annunaki as a slave race. Both the Sumerian as well as biblical accounts verify this little known and seldom understood truth.

Pre-adamic man was already present on the planet with dinosaurs and the dragons that were the Nachash of Genesis 3; this is the era when the Annunaki giants ruled upon the earth. The reason the Annunaki worked to mold this early prototype apelike human into being was to alter a slave needed to mine the gold necessary for them to protect their own planet's atmosphere. It is said in the Sumerian texts that Niburu was undergoing ecological disaster and that wars and planetary cataclysms had over time weakened and punctured holes through the protective layers of their atmosphere. The inability to deflect harmful rays affected Niburu each time it encroaches upon the sun or what they call Apsu in orbital rotation. Niburu would undergo massive upheaval in the form of volcanic, seismic, and tectonic activity, which would threaten the inhabitants of that world. Depletion of their ozone allowed too much sunlight to bombard the surface, making life there a dangerously precarious affair.

A solution was found in the form of gold as the Annunaki scientists determined a plan of action to attempt repair of the breach. They would crush massive amounts of gold into powder form and then suspend it into the atmosphere to see if it would help refract the sun's rays. Gold would be the reason why Earth was targeted for exploration and occupation. It was known since the war in heaven between Niburu and Tiamat, that this planet was riddled with an abundance of gold. Gold is limited in quantity on Niburu. Alalu, the Niburian king that first decided on coming to the Earth, did so because he knew from their ancient accounts that this planet contained veins that lie exposed where the Annunki would be able to gain easy access to an abundance of it. After Alalu's pioneering voyage, other Annunaki explorers were sent here en mass to begin operations to locate and secure the large quantities of gold needed to repair their own atmosphere.

Finding the work difficult and tedious, a council of Annunaki elders approved a plan to alter the DNA of the pre-adamic being already in existence upon the Earth. Once successfully fashioned, it would be utilized as the labor force needed to eradicate the gold required for transport to Niburu. The council determined it better to jump the gun on evolution even though universally forbidden, rather than risk mutiny from their fellow Annunaki.

The being whose material they used initially in modification was described as a seven to eight-foot-tall, large, humanoid type fully covered in red hair that wore no clothing, had no language, drank, ate, and dwelt among the other creatures of the Earth. They knew that they would break a universal rule on mixing seed and jumping the gun on the evolution of creatures on other planets, and yet they did so anyway, citing the need to secure gold and heal the ozone of Niburu.

THE PRIMITIVE WORKER

A solution is possible! Enki was saying:
Let us create a Lulu, a Primitive Worker,
the hardship work to take over,
Let the Being the toil of the Anunnaki carry on his back!
Astounded were the besieged leaders,
speechless indeed they were.

Whoever heard of a Being afresh created,
a worker who the Anunnaki's work can do?
They summoned Ninmah,
one who of healing and succor was much knowing.
Enki's words to her they repeated:
Whoever of such a thing heard? they her asked,
The task is unheard of! she to Enki said.
All beings from a seed have descended,
One being from another over aeons did develop,
none from nothing ever came!
How right you are my sister! Enki said, smiling.
A secret of the Abzu let me to you all reveal:
The Being that we need, it already exists!

All that we have to do is
put on it the mark of our essence,
Thereby a Lulu, a Primitive Worker, shall be created!
So did Enki to them say.
Let us hereby a decision make,
a blessing to my plan give:
To create a Primitive Worker,
by the mark of our essence to fashion him!

To create a Primitive Worker,
by the mark of our essence to fashion him!

So was Enki to the leaders saying.
The Being that we need, it already exists!
Thus did Enki to them a secret of the Abzu reveal.
With astonishment did the other leaders Enki's words hear;
by the words they were fascinated.
Creatures in the Abzu there are, Enki was saying,
that walk erect on two legs,
Their forelegs they use as arms,
with hands they are provided.
Among the animals of the steppe they live.
They know not dressing in garments,
They eat plants with their mouths,
they drink water from lake and ditch.

Shaggy with hair is their whole body,
their head hair is like a lion's;
With gazelles they jostle,
with teeming creatures in the waters they delight!
The leaders to Enki's words with amazement listened.
No creature like that has ever in the Edin been seen!
Enlil, disbelieving, said.
Aeons ago, on Nibiru, our predecessors like that might
have been! Ninmah was saying.
It is a Being, not a creature!
Ninmah was saying. To behold it must be a thrill!
To the House of Life Enki led them;
in strong cages there were some of the beings.
At the sight of Enki and the others they jumped up,
with fists on the cage bars they were beating.
They were grunting and snorting;
no words were they speaking.
Male and female they are!
Enki was saying; malehoods and femalehoods they have,
Like us, from Nibiru coming, they are procreating.
Ningishzidda, my son,
their Fashioning Essence has tested;
Akin to ours it is, like two serpents it is entwined;

When their with our life essence shall be combined,
our mark upon them shall be,
A Primitive Worker shall be created!
Our commands will he understand,
Our tools he will handle,
the toil in the excavations he shall perform;
To the Anunnaki in the Abzu relief shall come!
So was Enki with enthusiasm saying,
with excitement his words came forth.
Enlil at the words was hesitating:
The matter is one of great importance!
On our planet, slavery has long ago been abolished,
tools are the slaves, not other beings!

A new creature, beforehand nonexisting,
you wish to bring into being;
Creation in the hands of the
Father of All Beginning alone is held!
So was Enlil in opposing saying; stern were his words.
Enki to his brother responded: Not slaves,
but helpers is my plan!
The Being already exists! Ninmah was saying.
To give more ability is the plan!
Not a new creature, but one existing more in our image
made! Enki with persuasion said,
With little change it can be achieved,
only a drop of our essence is needed!

A grave matter it is, it is not to my liking! Enlil was saying.
Against the rules of from planet to planet journeying it is,
By the rules of to Earth coming it was forbidden.
To obtain gold was our purpose, to replace the Father of
All Beginning it was not!

After Enlil thus had spoken,
Ninmah was the one to respond:
My brother! Ninmah to Enlil was saying,

With wisdom and understanding
has the Father of All Beginning us endowed,
To what purpose have we so been perfected,
else of it utmost use to make?
With wisdom and understanding
has the Creator of All our life essence filled,
To whatever using of it we capable are,
is it not that for which we have been destined?
So was Ninmah words to her brother Enlil directing.
With that which in our essence was granted,
tools and chariots we have perfected,
Mountains with terror weapons we shattered,
skies with gold we are healing!
So was Ninurta to his birth-giving mother saying.
Let us with wisdom new tools fashion,
not new beings create,
Let by new equipments, not by slave beings,
the toil be relieved!
Where to our understanding does us lead,
to that we have been destined!
So was Ningishzidda saying,
with Enki and Ninmah he in agreement was.
What knowledge we possess, its use cannot be prevented!
Ningishzidda was saying.
Destiny indeed cannot be altered,
from the Beginning to the End it has been determined!
To them Enlil was thus saying. Destiny it is, or Fate it is,
That to this planet us has brought,
to gold from the waters foil,
To put Anunnaki heroes to excavating toil,
to a Primitive Worker create to be planning?
That, my kinfolk, is the question!
Thus, with graveness, Enlil was saying.
Is it Destiny, is it Fate; That is what deciding requires,
Is it from the Beginning ordained,
or by us for choosing?
To put the matter before Anu they decided;

Anu before the council the matter presented.
The elders, the savants, the commanders were consulted.
Long and bitter the discussions were,
of Life and Death, Fate and Destiny words were spoken.
Can there be another way the gold to obtain?
Survival is in danger!

If gold must be obtained,
let the Being be fashioned!
the council decided.
Let Anu forsake the rules of planetary journeys,
let Nibiru be saved!
From Anu's palace the decision to Earth was beamed;
it Enki delighted.
Let Ninmah my helper be,
of such matters understanding she has!
Thus was Enki saying.
At Ninmah with a longing he was gazing.
Let it so be! Ninmah was saving. Let it so be! Enlil did say.
By Ennugi was the decision
to the Anunnaki in the Abzu announced:
Until the Being is achieved,
to the toil willingly you must return! he said.
There was disappointment; rebellion there was not;
to the toil the Anunnaki returned.
In the House of Life, in the Abzu,
how to fashion the Being
Enki to Ninmah was explaining.
To a place among the trees Ninmah he directed,
a place of cages it was.
In the cages there were odd creatures,
their likes in the wild no one had seen:
Foreparts of one kind they had,
hindparts of another creature they possessed;
Creatures of two kinds by their essences combined
to Ninmah Enki was showing!

To the House of Life they returned, to a clean place with
brightness shining they led her.
In the clean place Ningishzidda to Ninmah
the life-essence secrets was explaining,
How the essence from two kinds combined can be,
he to her was showing.
The creatures in the tree cages are too odd,
monstrous they are! Ninmah was saying.
Indeed so! Enki responded. To attain perfection,
for that you are needed!
How the essences to combine, how much of this,
how much of that to put together,
In which womb conception to begin,
in which womb should the birth be given?

For that your succor and healing understanding are needed;
The understanding of one who gave birth,
who a mother is, is required!
A smile on the face of Ninmah was;
the two daughters that by Enki she mothered
she well remembered.
With Ningishzidda she surveyed the sacred formulas that
on ME's were secreted,
How this and that were done of him she inquired.
The creatures in the tree cages she examined,
the two-legged creatures she contemplated.
By a male inseminating
a female are the essences transmitted,
The two entwined strands separate
and combine an offspring to fashion.
Let a male Anunnaki a two-legged female impregnate,
let a combination offspring be born!
Thus did Ninmah say.
That we have tried, with failures it resulted!
to her Enki responded.
There was no conceiving, there was no birth!

Lost Book of Enki

I know this is a difficult teaching to understand, yet it is vital for understanding what exactly is being discussed in the early chapters of Genesis. This story is important when laying the foundations for the rest of the creations of Adam, for otherwise one would be hard-pressed to make sense of all that is going on within the Genesis account. The Annunaki corruption of the earth is alluded to in all cultures of the world. What is described in Genesis 6 is verified by literally hundreds, if not thousands, of texts and oral traditions. The Sumerian account of genetic experimentation is reminiscent of the rumors of nightmarish Dr. Moreau type creatures being molded currently in deep underground bases. This information, though lunatic fringe, matches a Dead Sea Scroll text called the *Book of Giants*.

> 1Q23 Frag. 9 + 14 + 15 2 […] they knew the secrets of […] 3 [… si]n was great in the earth […] 4 […] and they killed many [. .] 5 [… they begat] giants […]
>
> 4Q531 Frag. 3 2 [… everything that the] earth produced […] […] the great fish […] 14 […] the sky with all that grew […] 15 [… fruit of] the earth and all kinds of grain and all the trees […] 16 […] beasts and reptiles … [al]l creeping things of the earth and they observed all […] |8 [… eve]ry harsh deed and […] utterance […] 19 […] male and female, and among humans […]
>
> 1Q23 Frag. 1 + 6 [… two hundred] 2 donkeys, two hundred asses, two hundred … rams of the] 3 flock, two hundred goats, two hundred [… beast of the] 4 field from every animal, from every [bird …] 5 […] for miscegenation […]
>
> 4Q531 Frag. 2 […] they defiled […] 2 [… they begot] giants and monsters […] 3 […] they begot, and, behold, all [the earth was corrupted …] 4 […] with its blood and by the hand of […] 5 [giant's] which did not suffice for them and […] 6 […] and they were seeking to devour many […] 7 […] 8 […] the monsters attacked it.
>
> 4Q532 Col. 2 Frags. 1—6 2 […] flesh […] 3al [1 …] monsters […] will be […] 4 […] they would arise […]

lacking in true knowledge [...] because [...] 5 [...] the earth [grew corrupt...] mighty [...] 6 [...] they were considering [...] 7 [...] from the angels upon [...] 8 [...] in the end it will perish and die [...] 9 [...] they caused great corruption in the [earth ...] [... this did not] suffice to [...] they will be [...]

The Book of Giants

The creation of myriads of hybrid monstrosities by the fallen ones prompted our Lord to bring judgment to their works and efforts. This would also be a determining factor for the Lord to create His own creature made in His own image to inherit the bounty of the Earth. Righteousness would descend to this fallen world through those who would incarnate into flesh as the children of modern sixth day Adam and Eve. Lucifer would plot his revenge against Adam of Light by deceiving them. His seduction of Eve would cause all three to transgress the law concerning the tree of death and consequentially Adam and Eve were cast to the lowest region of physical creation, the lower visible Earth, to whence Satan and his angels had already been banished. Here the Second World Age, the age of flesh, would begin with the serpent's line and birth of Cain.

After the clothing of fig-leaves they put on clothing of skins, and that is the skin of which our bodies are made, being of the family of man, and it is a clothing of pain. The entrance of Adam into Paradise was at the third hour. He and Eve passed through great power in three hours, they were naked for three hours, and in the ninth hour they went out from Paradise, unwillingly, with much grief, great weeping, mourning and sighing.

KITAB AL-MAGALL

ADAM OF PARADISE AND THE SECOND WORLD AGE

[Friday]. On the sixth day I commanded my wisdom to create man from seven consistencies: one, his flesh from the earth; two, his blood from the dew; three, his eyes from the sun; four, his bones from stone; five, his intelligence from the swiftness of the angels and from cloud; six, his veins and his hair from the grass of the earth; seven, his soul from my breath and from the wind. And I gave him seven natures: to the flesh hearing, the eyes for sight, to the soul smell, the veins for touch, the blood for taste, the bones for endurance, to the intelligence sweetness (sc. enjoyment). I conceived a cunning saying to say, I created man from invisible and from visible nature, of both are his death and life and image, he knows speech like some created thing, small in greatness and again great in smallness, and I placed him on earth, a second angel, honourable, great and glorious, and I appointed him as ruler to rule on earth and to have my wisdom, and there was none like him of earth of all my existing creatures.

And I appointed him a name, from the four component parts, from east, from west, from south, from north, and I appointed for him four special stars, and I called his name Adam, and showed him the two ways, the light and the darkness, and I told him: 'This is good, and that bad,' that I should learn whether he has love towards me, or hatred, that it be clear which in his race love me. For I have seen his nature, but he has not seen his own nature, therefore through not seeing he will sin worse, and I said 'After sin what is there but death?' And I put sleep into him and he fell asleep. And I took from him a rib, and created him a wife, that death should come to him by his wife, and I took his last word and called her name mother, that is to say, Eva.

The Book of the Secrets of Enoch, 30

THE SIXTH-DAY, SECOND-CREATION ADAM OF PARADISE

After thousands of years where the fallen angels ruled upon this planet, the Lord would institute a plan to not only condemn the Elohim angels that rebelled against Him but also grant a chance for redemption to the angels that sat on the fence during the First World Age. With the creation of this new being, the Lord would allow light to descend into darkness for the elevation of this world. The lower Earth would become a middle road battleground for the incarnation of spirit and soul. That's when Yahushuah as the Word and embodiment of the Father took dust from the earth and breathed the spirit of life into it so that humanity was no longer just a carnal soul, but was now imbued with the spirit which could inherit eternal life.

This creation was the sixth-day, modern, hermaphroditic Adam and Eve before she was split off from him creating separate male and female genders. Adam, in his bright natured form, was much like the angels that serve our Lord. Most do not realize that He was blessed with an even greater capacity for understanding and comprehension of the mysteries than the fallen angels themselves. Another thing that most do not realize is that Adam was created in the presence of both the higher angels of heaven and the lower angels of Earth before he was separated and taken to paradise under the protection of the Lord.

When the lower angels witnessed this image, it was then that they instituted a plan to lure that heavenly being to the Earth. What they did not realize, however, was that they were following preparations as laid out by the intent of the Most High, and once they created this modeled form, the Lord would vitalize it with His own breath, thereby elevating above them the creature they were attempting to mold as prisoners for the angels of light. When initially created, sixth-day Adam was an immortal being that did not eat drink, sleep, or defecate. He also was endowed with twin sight in that he was able to perceive both the spiritual and physical worlds. After Adam was taken to the protection of paradise, the Lord separated Eve from him. Even after the separation, both were spiritual, angelic beings not yet impoverished by the physical limitations of bodily senses.

Once Eve is split off from Adam, she becomes the vehicle by which Satan, as the serpent, tempts her to eat from the tree of the knowledge of good and evil. This treachery would lead to the condition of death, loss of their bright natures, and fall into flesh form where they would then fulfill all the prophecies of Genesis 3 as foretold by the Lord when He banished them from Paradise and placed them upon the wilderness of the earth with all of the other fallen angels. This transformation would take place on the eighth day and come about as an agreement between the higher and lower angels.

> On the sixth day God created from the earth all the beasts, and animals and insects and creeping reptiles. This day is Friday, and on it God created Adam of dust, and formed Eve from his rib. On the seventh day God had completed all creation, and He called it Sabbath. God had created Adam in the third hour of Friday the sixth day. Iblis had laid claim to Godhead which had entered him in the second hour of that day, and God had hurled him down from heaven to earth. Before God the Lord created Adam, rest fell upon all the powers; and God said, 'Come, let us create a Man in our likeness and form and image.' When

the Angels heard this saying from the Lord they became frightened and much terrified, and they said to one another, 'What is this great wonder which we hear, and how is it possible that the form of our God and Creator can appear to us?' Then all the Angels looked towards the right hand of the Lord, which was stretched out above all creation, and all of it was in His right hand. Then they looked towards the right hand of the Lord, and it took from all the earth a little handful of dust, and from all the waters a drop of water, and from the air a soul and a spirit, and from fire the force of heat, and it became in the grasp of the Lord portions of the four elements, heat and cold, moisture and drought. Verily God, the glorious and strong, created Adam from these four weak elements, which have no power, that all creatures created from them might hear and obey him: dust, that man might obey him; water, that all that is born of it and in it might obey him; air, that it might be possible for him to breathe it and to feel its breezes, and that its birds might obey him; and fire, that the heat of forces created from it should be a powerful helper to his sense.

The reason why God, may His holy names be sanctified! created Adam with His holy hand in His form and image was that he should receive wisdom and speech and animal motion, and for the knowledge concerning things. When the glorious and illustrious Angels saw one like Him in Adam, they were affrighted. The wondrous glory upon his face terrified them, his form appeared shining with divine light greater than the light of the sun, and his body was bright and brilliant like the well-known stars in the crystal. When the figure of Adam drew itself up, he leapt standing; he was in the centre of the earth, he stretched out his right hand and his left hand and put his feet in order upon Golgotha, which is the place where was put the wood (cross) of our Saviour Jesus the Christ. The Angels and the Powers heard the voice of God, may He be glorified and exalted! saying to Adam, 'O Adam, I have made thee king and priest and prophet and ruler and chief and governor over all creatures that are made. All creation shall obey thee and follow thy voice. Under thy grasp they shall be.

To thee alone I have given this power; I have placed thee in possession of all that I have created.' When the Angels heard this saying from the Lord they redoubled honour and respect to Adam. When the Devil saw the gift that was given to Adam from the Lord, he envied him from that day and the schismatic from God set his mind in cunning towards him to seduce him by his boldness and his curse; and when he denied the grace of the Lord towards him, he became shameless and warlike. God, may His names be sanctified! deprived the Devil of the robe of praise and dignity and called his name Devil, he is a rebel against God, and Satan, because he opposes himself to the ways of the Lord, and Iblis, because He took his dignity from him.

While Adam was listening to the speech of his Lord to him, and standing upon the place of Golgotha, all the creatures being gathered together that they might hear the conversation of God with him, lo! a cloud of light carried him and went with him to Paradise and the choirs of Angels sang before him, the cherubim among them blessing and the seraphim crying 'Holy!' until Adam came into Paradise. He entered it at the third hour on Friday, and the Lord, to Him be praise! gave him the commandment, and warned him against disobedience to it. Then the Lord, to Him be praise! threw upon Adam a form of sleep, and he slept a sweet sleep in Paradise. And God took a rib from his left side, and from it He created Eve. When he awoke and saw Eve he rejoiced over her and lived with her, and she was in the pleasant garden of Paradise. God clothed them with glory and splendour. They outvied one another in the glory with which they were clothed, and the Lord crowned them for marriage, the Angels congratulated them, and there was joy there such as never has been the like and never will be till the day in which the people at the right hand shall hear the glorious voice from the Lord. Adam and Eve remained in Paradise for three hours.

The site of Paradise was high up in the air, its ground was heavenly, raised above all mountains and hills, that were thirty spans high, that is fifteen cubits, according to the cubit of the Holy Ghost. This Paradise stretches round from the east by a wall from the hollow to the southern place of darkness where the cursed Prince was thrown, it is the place of sorrows. Eden is a fountain of God lying eastwards, to a height of eight degrees of the rising of the sun, and this is the mercy of God on which the children of men put their trust, that they shall have a Saviour from thence, because God, may He be exalted and glorified! knew in His foreknowledge what the Devil would do to Adam. Eden is the Church of God, and the Paradise in which is the altar of rest, and the length of life which God has prepared for all the saints.

Then God planted the tree of life in the middle of Paradise and it was the form of the cross which was stretched upon it, and it was the tree of life and salvation. Satan remained in his envy to Adam and Eve for the favour which the Lord shewed them, and he contrived to enter into the serpent, which was the most beautiful of the animals, and its nature was above the nature of the camel. He carried it till he went with it in the air to the lower parts of Paradise. The reason for Iblis the cursed hiding himself in the serpent was his ugliness, for when he was deprived of his honour he got into the acme of ugliness, till none of the creatures could have borne the sight of him uncovered, and if Eve had seen him unveiled in the serpent, when she spoke to him, she would have run away from him, and neither cunning nor deceit would have availed him with her; but he contrived to hide himself in the serpent, the cunning creature, to teach the birds with round tongues the speech of men in Greek and such like... But the cursed Devil, when he entered the serpent, came towards Eve, when she was alone in Paradise away from Adam, and called her by her name.

She turned to him, and looked at her likeness behind a veil, and he talked to her, and she talked to him, and he led her astray by his speech, for woman's nature is weak, and she trusts in every word, and he lectured her about the forbidden tree in obedience to her desire, and described to her the goodness of its taste, and that when she should eat of it she should become a god; and she longed for what the cursed one made her long for, and she would not hear from the Lord, may His names be sanctified! what He had commanded Adam about the tree.

She hastened eagerly towards it, and seized some of its fruit in her mouth. Then she called Adam, and he hastened to her, and she gave him of the fruit, telling him that if he ate of it he would become a god. He listened to her advice because he should become a god as she said. When he and she ate the deadly fruit they were bereft of their glory, and their splendour was taken from them, and they were stripped of the light with which they had been clothed. When they looked at themselves, they were naked of the grace which they had worn, and their shame was manifest to them; they made to themselves aprons of fig-leaves, and covered themselves therewith, and they were in great sadness for three hours. They did not manage to continue in the grace and the power with which the Lord had endued them before their rebellion for three hours, till it was taken from them and they were made to slip and fall down at the time of sunset on that day, and they received the sentence of God in punishment. After the clothing of fig-leaves they put on clothing of skins, and that is the skin of which our bodies are made, being of the family of man, and it is a clothing of pain. The entrance of Adam into Paradise was at the third hour. He and Eve passed through great power in three hours, they were naked for three hours, and in the ninth hour they went out from Paradise, unwillingly, with much grief, great weeping, mourning and sighing.

They slept towards the East of it near the altar. When they awoke from their sleep, God spoke to Adam and comforted him, saying to him, blessed be His names! 'O Adam! do not grieve, for I will restore thee to thine inheritance, out of which thy rebellion has brought thee. Know that because of my love to thee I have cursed the earth, and I will not have pity upon it, on account of thy sin. I have cursed also the serpent by whom thou hast been led astray, and I have made its feet go within its belly. I have made dust its food. I have not cursed thee. I have decreed against Eve that she shall be at thy service. Know certainly that when thou hast accomplished the time that I have decreed for thee to dwell outside, in the accursed land, for thy transgression of my commandment, I will send my dear Son; He will come down to the earth, He will be clothed with a body from a Virgin of thy race, named Mary. I will purify her and choose her, and bring her into power generation after generation until the time that the Son comes down from Heaven. In that time shall be the beginning of thy salvation and restoration to thine inheritance.

KITAB AL-MAGALL

Please notice that in this very important quote that Adam is crowned King in sight of the fallen ones before he is taken to paradise to be under the protection of the Lord and his angels. Unbeknownst to Satan, Adam, or Eve, the Lord was establishing plans to not only rectify the Nephilim corruption of the earth, but also redeem fallen humanity, as He knew that Adam would fall and the devil would tempt them. It was in paradise and not on the Earth that male and female genders came into being. After Adam names the creatures, the Lord fashioned—from and out of Adam—his twin soul Eve. It was in this garden of the Lord that Satan would have to enter in the guise of a serpent in order to tempt the Lord's newly created and highest creatures. His beguiling caused Eve to desire the same promise that caused Lucifer's initial fall from grace and banishment from the upper heavens—the desire to be as gods themselves. This desire caused Adam and Eve to lose their bright natures or light vestures since their bodies had initially been clothed in light and immortality.

This eating of the fruit of the tree of the knowledge of good and evil would result in their incarnation into flesh upon the lower Earth where they would be living among the devils and demons already banished there. This text even mentions that the result of eating of that forbidden fruit was in fact incarnation into the flesh.

> [Friday]. On the sixth day I commanded my wisdom to create man from seven consistencies: one, his flesh from the earth; two, his blood from the dew; three, his eyes from the sun; four, his bones from stone; five, his intelligence from the swiftness of the angels and from cloud; six, his veins and his hair from the grass of the earth; seven, his soul from my breath and from the wind. And I gave him seven natures: to the flesh hearing, the eyes for sight, to the soul smell, the veins for touch, the blood for taste, the bones for endurance, to the intelligence sweetness (sc. enjoyment). I conceived a cunning saying to say, I created man from invisible and from visible nature, of both are his death and life and image, he knows speech like some created thing, small in greatness and again great in smallness, and I placed him on earth, a second angel, honourable, great and glorious, and I appointed him as ruler to rule on earth and to have my wisdom, and there was none like him of earth of all my existing creatures. And I appointed him a name, from the four component parts, from east, from west, from south, from north, and I appointed for him four special stars, and I called his name Adam, and showed him the two ways, the light and the darkness, and I told him: 'This is good, and that bad,' that I should learn whether he has love towards me, or hatred, that it be clear which in his race love me. For I have seen his nature, but he has not seen his own nature, therefore through not see-

ing he will sin worse, and I said 'After sin what is there but death?' 16 And I put sleep into him and he fell asleep. And I took from him a rib, and created him a wife, that death should come to him by his wife, and I took his last word and called her name mother, that is to say, Eva.

The Book of the Secrets of Enoch, 30

ADAM has life on earth, and I created a garden in Eden in the east, that he should observe the testament and keep the command. I made the heavens open to him, that he should see the angels singing the song of victory, and the gloomless light. And he was continuously in paradise, and the devil understood that I wanted to create another world, because Adam was lord on earth, to rule and control it. The devil is the evil spirit of the lower places, as a fugitive he made Sotona from the heavens as his name was Satanail, thus he became different from the angels, but his nature did not change his intelligence as far as his understanding of righteous and sinful things. And he understood his condemnation and the sin which he had sinned before, therefore he conceived thought against Adam, in such form he entered and seduced Eva, but did not touch Adam. But I cursed ignorance, but what I had blessed previously, those I did not curse, I cursed not man, nor the earth, nor other creatures, but man's evil fruit, and his works.

The Book of the Secrets of Enoch, 31:1-6

In this chapter I endeavor to remind you of our intended providence, for Yahweh desired to establish us as part of the heavenly hosts that serve Him all moments of being. It is my hope to piece together for you a forgotten story, a hidden tale recapturing the reasons behind the fall of Lucifer and its consequence for Adam of Paradise, Eve, and eventual humanity. It is my assertion that the real reason for humanity's fall into flesh was to set the stage for the final and ultimate battle between Yahweh/Yahushuah and Lucifer. Unless one understands this singular aspect of the story, one will not comprehend where we are in the ancient war between the two bloodlines (Genesis 3:15). When Yahushuah created the sixth-day, second-creation of Adam, the soul-endowed Adam, *that* Adam was given dominion over the third heaven, or Paradise. This creation of Adam had no idea as to why Lucifer hated him or that war once ensued in heaven. He only knew that Satan, for whatever reason, was adamant in persecuting him and Eve. Both were in an innocent state, having never experienced evil, so the idea that an angel of the Lord could actually hate them just never crossed their minds.

The Latin version of the *Life of Adam and Eve* retells this story, describing in detail the innocent ignorance of both as they directly question Satan as to why he was so egregiously persecuting them. Neither knew why Satan deplored them, and neither ever conceived the thought that an angel would or could ever plot evil against them.

> And she cried out and said: 'Woe unto thee, thou devil. Why dost thou attack us for no cause? What hast thou to do with us? What have we done to thee? for thou pursuest us with craft? Or why doth thy malice assail us? Have we taken away thy glory and caused thee to be without honour? Why dost thou harry us, thou enemy (and persecute us) to the death in wickedness and envy?' And with a heavy sigh, the devil spake: 'O Adam! all my hostility, envy, and sorrow is for thee, since it is for thee that I have been expelled from my glory, which I possessed in the heavens in the midst of the angels and for thee was I cast out in the earth.' Adam answered, 'What dost thou tell me? What have I done to thee or what is my fault against thee? Seeing that thou hast received no harm or injury from us, why dost thou pursue us?'
>
> The devil replied, 'Adam, what dost thou tell me? It is for thy sake that I have been hurled from that place. When thou wast formed. I was hurled out of the presence of God and banished from the company of the angels. When God blew into thee the breath of life and thy face and likeness

was made in the image of God, Michael also brought thee and made (us) worship thee in the sight of God; and God the Lord spake: Here is Adam. I have made thee in our image and likeness.'

And Michael went out and called all the angels saying: 'Worship the image of God as the Lord God hath commanded.' And Michael himself worshipped first; then he called me and said: 'Worship the image of God the Lord.' And I answered, 'I have no (need) to worship Adam.' And since Michael kept urging me to worship, I said to him, 'Why dost thou urge me?

I will not worship an inferior and younger being (than I). I am his senior in the Creation, before he was made was I already made. It is his duty to worship me.' When the angels, who were under me, heard this, they refused to worship him. And Michael saith, 'Worship the image of God, but if thou wilt not worship him, the Lord God will be wrath with thee.' And I said, 'If He be wrath with me, I will set my seat above the stars of heaven and will be like the Highest.'

And God the Lord was wrath with me and banished me and my angels from our glory; and on thy account were we expelled from our abodes into this world and hurled on the earth. And straightway we were overcome with grief, since we had been spoiled of so great glory. And we were grieved when we saw thee in such joy and luxury. And with guile I cheated thy wife and caused thee to be expelled through her (doing) from thy joy and luxury, as I have been driven out of my glory.

The Vitae of Adam and Eve, 11:2-16:4

The sixth-day second creation of Adam, wrought in immortal innocence, knew not the experience of hate or evil and never fathomed the idea that Satan could or would loathe him. He was created pure—without fail—and did not understand the loneliness of his situation until, naming all of the other creatures, he recognized none like him. This recognition became cause for the Lord to separate from him a female helpmate. The separation of the feminine from the masculine was relegated a separate embodiment, that of Eve, and once the androgynous nature was divided Eve became the focus of Lucifer's plot to cause the fall of humanity. It wasn't until the feminine aspect had been separated from Adam's initial androgynous nature that separate female and male forms came into being.

Yahweh forewarned Adam to not eat of or touch of the tree of the knowledge of good and evil lest he die. He did so because He knew Satan would tempt both Adam and Eve to fall. Adam, not understanding the importance of this message, did not admonish Eve with the same warning once split off from him.

> And of Your goodwill, O Lord, You made us both with bodies of a bright nature, and You made us two, one; and You gave us Your grace, and filled us with praises of the Holy Spirit; that we should be neither hungry nor thirsty, nor know what sorrow is, nor yet faintness of heart; neither suffering, fasting nor weariness.
>
> The First Book of Adam and Eve, 34

> If the woman had not separated from the man, she should not die with the man. His separation became the beginning of death. Because of this, Christ came to repair the separation, which was from the beginning, and again unite the two, and to give life to those who died as a result of the separation, and unite them.
>
> The Gospel of Phillip

> When Eve was still with Adam, death did not exist. When she was separated from him, death came into being. If he enters again and attains his former self, death will be no more.
>
> The Gospel of Phillip

Satan believed that if he could cause the fall of Adam and Eve that their children would be born under his authority and within the dominion of the lower Earth. What Satan did not realize is that the Lord would only allow him a certain allotment of time in which to attempt to fulfill this plan. He would be granted dominion of the lower Earth for only a short time—7,000 years, seventy weeks, or seventy generations. Once humanity began incarnating into flesh, Lucifer would seek to thwart the birth of the Messiah, who— born of woman and through the line of Adam—would bring salvation and forgiveness to the children of Earth, extending grace even unto the Gentile nations who serve Satan as the children of Cain. Satan sought to prevent the birth of Yahushuah and incited Herod to decimate all male children up to the age of two born into the Hebrew nation. He thought that if he could kill the Savior, salvation would never be established, and judgment would never arrive. Satan understood that once the Second World Age began, Yahushuah, the Son, would be born of the flesh and be crucified, defeat death, restore hope, and deliver to paradise all of the souls of the righteous who, until then, had been collected in Sheol. His incarnation would occur 5,500 years after Adam and Eve were banished from Paradise.

Yahushuah would then establish the church to instill the world with the laws, commandments, and ordinances of the Father as written in the Torah. Once Yahushuah incarnated in the flesh, there would be but a short time until His second coming and end of the Second World Age. He would bring eternal rest and everlasting life to the righteous and death, destruction, and permanent disgrace to Satan and his fallen angels.

Many people ask why Yahweh would even allow evil to exist for any length of time. The reason that the Father did not slay Lucifer immediately and bring the entire creation back into unity and order is precisely because the Lord also loved Lucifer and hoped that he, too, would repent of his wickedness. The rebel angels and fallen watchers are sons of God, too, though they cannot desist from evil.

It wasn't until the fallen watchers joined the rebel angels and interdicted themselves into the affairs of humanity, took earthly wives, and sired an unnatural race of cannibalistic giants into the world that the Lord decided on forgiving their trespass no more. Both of these groups are now only tolerated until judgment rewards them according to their deeds.

> And yet he could not curse Satan, nor injure him by word, because he had no authority over him, neither did he take to doing so with words from his mouth. Therefore the angel tolerated him, without saying one bad word, until the Word of God came who said to Satan, Go away from here; once before you deceived My servants, and this time you seek to destroy them. Were it not for My mercy I would have destroyed you and your hosts from off the earth. But I have had patience with you, until the end of the world.
>
> First Book of Adam and Eve, 43

As the Father loved Adam, so does Yahweh love Lucifer and hoped he would repent of his evil intention. Lucifer had once been honored by the Lord as his first created Cherubim archangel; he was given high authority previous to his fall. Vanity and power clouded his sense, corrupted his heart, and lead him to be cast out of heaven. His reign upon the Earth would only be for a short time as he, Death, and the false prophet themselves would suffer ultimate demise for engendering the downfall of humanity.

> Sedrach said to him, It was by your will that Adam was deceived, my Master. You commanded your angels to worship Adam, but he who was first among the angels disobeyed your order and did not worship him; and so you banished him, because he transgressed your commandment and did not come forth (to worship) the creations of your hands. If you loved man, why did you not kill the devil, the artificer of all iniquity?

God saith to him: Be it known unto thee that I ordered all things to be placable to him: I gave him understanding and made him the heir of heaven and earth, and I subjected all things to him, and every living thing flees from him and from before his face: but he, having received of mine, became alien, adulterous, and sinful: tell me, what father, having given his son his portion, when he takes his substance and leaves his father and goes away and becomes an alien and serves an alien, when the father sees that the son has deserted him, does not darken his heart, and does not the father go and take his substance and banish him from his glory because he deserted his father? And how have I, the wonderful and jealous God, given him everything, and he having received these things has become an adulterer and a sinner?

Apocalypse of Sedrach 5-6

Yahweh would use the fall of humanity as the scenario necessary to test the allegiance and loyalties of all of His angels, as most would be forced to incarnate into flesh bodies for what would be the Second World Age.

ADAM has life on earth, and I created a garden in Eden in the east, that he should observe the testament and keep the command. I made the heavens open to him, that he should see the angels singing the song of victory, and the gloomless light. And he was continuously in paradise, and the devil understood that I wanted to create another world, because Adam was lord on earth, to rule and control it.

The devil is the evil spirit of the lower places, as a fugitive he made Sotona from the heavens as his name was Satanail, thus he became different from the angels, but his nature did not change his intelligence as far as his understanding of righteous and sinful things. And he understood his condemnation and the sin which he had sinned before, therefore he conceived thought against Adam, in such form he entered and seduced Eva, but did not touch Adam. But I cursed ignorance, but what I had blessed previously, those I did not curse, I cursed not man, nor the earth, nor other creatures, but man's evil fruit, and his works.

The Book of the Secrets of Enoch, 31:1-6

It was part of the Lord's plan to allow for the seduction of Eve and the consequential fall of humanity, as all would now be forced to incarnate into flesh and through free will determine their lot in judgment. The benefactors of salvation will have to prove through life and being that they/we are worthy of salvation and to be the inheritors of those positions abandoned by the rebel and watcher angels that held not their first estate.

For I knew you would sin and transgress, and come out into this land. Yet I wouldn't force you, nor be heard over you, nor shut up; nor doom you through your fall; nor through your coming out from light into darkness; nor yet through your coming from the garden into this land.

For I made you of the light; and I willed to bring out children of light from you and like to you. But you did not keep My commandment one day; until I had finished the creation and blessed everything in it. Then, concerning the tree, I commanded you not to eat of it. Yet I knew that Satan, who deceived himself, would also deceive you. So I made known to you by means of the tree, not to come near him. And I told you not to eat of the fruit thereof, nor to taste of it, nor yet to sit under it, nor to yield to it.

Had I not been and spoken to you, O Adam, concerning the tree, and had I left you without a commandment, and you had sinned—it would have been an offence on My part, for not having given you any order; you would turn around and blame Me for it. But I commanded you, and warned you, and you fell. So that My creatures cannot blame Me; but the blame rests on them alone.

First Book of Adam and Eve, 13:13-19

When the sixth-day second Adam was given dominion over Paradise, Satan was asked to bow before this Adam much like he was brought before Yahushuah and asked to honor His dominion. The Lord would test Satan this time to see whether he and his hosts would serve as ministering spirits to humanity or not. Like before, He again—in pride— refused, and instead of serving the Lord's highest creatures decided to plot against them. He had already been exiled to the lower heavens and wanted Adam and Eve to join him on the fallen Earth. In tempting her to eat of the forbidden fruit, Lucifer caused both to lose their immortal light vestures. For this he was cursed by the Lord, stripped of his heavenly apparel, and transformed into the likeness of an alien-dragon-reptilian-looking being. The subsequent fall of Adam and Eve resulted in humanity's loss of immortality and beginning of the Second World Age, the age of flesh. During this 7,000 year cycle we would incarnate in flesh as fallen angels and learn through the knowledge of good and evil just what a world would look like without the sovereign rule of our Father Yahweh and His Son, Yahushuah Savior Messiah. During this age all would be allowed to determine for self just what focus is important in pursuing the experience of duality in this world.

> And when the prince of the lower order of angels saw what great majesty had been given unto Adam, he was jealous of him from that day, and he did not wish to worship him. And he said unto his hosts, Ye shall not worship him, and ye shall not praise him with the angels. It is meet that ye should worship me, because I am fire and spirit; and not that I should worship a thing of dust, which hath been fashioned of fine dust.
>
> And the Rebel meditating these things would not render obedience to God, and of his own free will he asserted his independence and separated himself from God. But he was—swept away out of heaven and fell, and the fall of himself and of all his company from heaven took place on the Sâtânâ because he turned aside [from the right way],

and Shêdâ because he was cast out, and Daiwâ because he lost the apparel of his glory. And behold, from that time until the present day, he and all his hosts have been stripped of their apparel, and they go naked and have horrible faces. And when Sâtânâ was cast out from heaven, Adam was raised up so that he might ascend to Paradise in a chariot of fire.

The Cave of Treasures

The whole reason the Second World Age and 7,000 years of satanic rule upon the wilderness of the lower visible Earth came into being was to specifically accommodate the rebellion of Lucifer and deception of Adam and Eve. This world of duality would specifically serve as proving grounds for the First World Age spirits, who would now incarnate into the flesh and, being given free will, seal their fate by choosing to serve either good or evil. Those rebel angels exiled from heaven during the First World Age were stripped of their beautiful, bright natures and heavenly countenance, and—like Lucifer—transformed into serpent, reptilian, dragon, alien-like beings. They are forms of darkness though they still have power to shape-shift and can assume the likeness of even an angel of light. The watchers that descended during the age of Jared were human spirit beings with supernatural attraction and heavenly form, which the daughters of Cain found irresistible.

> Then the angel went from Adam and seized Satan at the opening of the cave, and stripped him of the pretense he had assumed, and brought him in his own hideous form to Adam and Eve; who were afraid of him when they saw him. 14 And the angel said to Adam, This hideous form has been his ever since God made him fall from heaven. He could not have come near you in it; he therefore transformed himself into an angel of light.
>
> The First Book of Adam and Eve, Ch. 28:13-14

Then God sent His Word unto Adam, saying, Adam, that figure is the one that promised thee the Godhead, and majesty; he is not favourably disposed towards thee; but shows himself to thee at one time in the form of a woman; another moment, in the likeness of an angel; on another occasions, in the similitude of a serpent; and at another time, in the semblance of a god; but he does all that only to destroy thy soul.

The Second Book of Adam and Eve, 3:15-16

Woe to you and your house, for the greatest of evils has befallen the race of The Children of God and it is defiled. The heritage of Kadamhapa is lost. The fetid flow defiling the woman results from the incompatible intermingling, but it is not all, for sicknesses and diseases are also generating from the ferments of the impure implantation.

Kolbrin Bible

FORBIDDEN FRUIT

Many find the Genesis 3 tale of humanity's fall difficult to understand. Most believe that eating of the tree of the knowledge of good and evil had something to do with a piece of fruit. Others believe that the fruit represents something deeper, more seductively connotative, than what most people are willing to admit. Was the forbidden fruit even a fruit at all, and what were the two trees in the garden? Could the two trees be representative of Yahushuah (Tree of Life) and Lucifer (Tree of knowledge of good and evil)? Maybe through the tale of the forbidden fruit the Lord was preserving truth for this time and disguising in parable form the true accounting of what happened in Paradise from those who were simply incapable of discernment.

It's my contention that the fruit, the two trees, and even the garden may hold multiple meanings and, as such, can be construed in a variety of ways. My personal take on the story is that Genesis 3 symbolically represents the loss of immortality and the bright natures that the Lord had adorned and clothed Adam, Eve, and even the rebel angels with prior to their fall. Called a vesture of light, eating of the forbidden fruit led to the loss of this light state of being, fall from grace, and banishment to a region whereby they would fulfill the prophecies put forth by the Lord in chapter three of Genesis, dealing with life in the flesh. The curse of the tree is the curse of taking on flesh form; loss of their bright nature would lead them into flesh incarnation, and it would be in the flesh that they would be deceived into performing an act of sexual lust, that also representative of the eating of the forbidden fruit, would justify their fall from grace and banishment from the kingdom.

Deciphering the story this way also helps one explain why it was that He specifically told Eve that she would, after eating of the fruit from this certain tree, now conceive a child when prior she had neither understanding of nor thought for sexual interaction. The eating of the forbidden fruit, in my opinion, veils not only the loss of immortality but also the seduction of Eve and experience of carnality, which led to the birth of Cain as the firstborn son of the devil. For those that are not aware of my previous work where I expound upon these ideas, please check out my fourth book, *Lucifer, Father of Cain*, for details on the premise of this notion.

I surmise that, based on the sum total of scripture, that the Tree of the Knowledge of Good and Evil was not only associated with Lucifer but also a certain vine that Lucifer had planted in the Lord's paradise. A little known Dead Sea manuscript called the Genesis Apocryphon relates the tale of a drowned, post-flood world and describes Noah's disembark from the ark to take what would be his first steps upon a renewed Earth. The land was smitten in disarray as roots, herbs, seedlings, and remnant vines were everywhere disheveled and uprooted upon the ground. Noah first built an altar to the Lord in honor of his family's deliverance, then goes about replanting what he could find in hopes that it would replenish itself in natural abundance and seasonal growth. When he came across the grape vine, Noah recognized it as the 'tree by which Adam fell from grace.' Hesitant to replant the vine, Noah admonishes the Lord in prayer for guidance as he had great respect for its ability to cause folly in humans and did not want to replant something that would cause later repercussions for him and his family.

Did the vine really have some role to play in Adam and Eve's loss of immortality and fall from grace? And if it did have a part to play, what role was specific to the fall, and how did Lucifer utilize it to make them susceptible to punishment and banishment from the kingdom? Those are the questions that plagued my mind initially when I came across these particular passages as they are also associated with another story that most have never heard about, which I will bring forth soon in this chapter.

If the vine had a part to play in causing Adam and Eve's banishment from Paradise, Noah was adamant to not incur the Lord's wrath by replanting it for the folly of future generations. He wanted to be careful not to make the same mistakes as his previous ancestors and so prayed about it before proceeding forward. The Lord then answered him and told him that, whereas the vine had once been a condemnation to humanity, it would now serve as a blessing.

> And I said, I pray thee show me which is the tree which led Adam astray. And the angel said to me, It is the vine, which the angel Sammael planted, whereat the Lord God was angry, and He cursed him and his plant, while also on this account He did not permit Adam to touch it, and therefore the devil being envious deceived him through his vine. And I Baruch said, Since also the vine has been the cause of such great evil, and is under judgment of the curse of God, and was the destruction of the first created, how is it now so useful? And the angel said, Thou askest aright. When God caused the deluge upon earth, and destroyed all flesh, and four hundred and nine thousand giants, and the water rose fifteen cubits above the highest mountains, then the water entered into paradise and destroyed every flower; but it removed wholly without the bounds the shoot of the vine and cast it outside. And when the earth appeared out of the water, and Noah came out of the ark, he began to plant of the plants which he found.
>
> But he found also the shoot of the vine; and he took it, and was reasoning in himself, What then is it? And I came and spake to him the things concerning it. And he said, Shall I plant it, or what shall I do? Since Adam was destroyed because of it, let me not also meet with the anger

of God because of it. And saying these things he prayed that God would reveal to him what he should do concerning it. And when he had completed the prayer which lasted forty days, and having besought many things and wept, he said: Lord, I entreat thee to reveal to me what I shall do concerning this plant. But God sent his angel Sarasael, and said to him, Arise, Noah, and plant the shoot of the vine, for thus saith the Lord: Its bitterness shall be changed into sweetness, and its curse shall become a blessing, and that which is produced from it shall become the blood of God; and as through it the human race obtained condemnation, so again through Jesus Christ the Immanuel will they receive in Him the upward calling, and the entry into paradise.

Know therefore, O Baruch, that as Adam through this very tree obtained condemnation, and was divested of the glory of God, so also the men who now drink insatiably the wine which is begotten of it, transgress worse than Adam, and are far from the glory of God, and are surrendering themselves to the eternal fire. For (no) good comes through it. For those who drink it to surfeit do these things: neither does a brother pity his brother, nor a father his son, nor children their parents, but from the drinking of wine come all evils, such as murders, adulteries, fornications, perjuries, thefts, and such like. And nothing good is established by it.

Baruch 3:8-17

The correlation between the vine and the tree of the knowledge of good and evil has also been cited by the highly prized, protected, and only recently revealed manuscript called the Kolbrin Bible, released May 31, 2006. This text also details the events leading to the fall of Adam and Eve and what role the vine played in that transgression. The story begins with Eve, being in attendance at a moon festival, when a concoction brewed from the grapes of this vine was passed about in a chalice among the assembly of worshipers gathered there for ritual. The potion was so intoxicating that those who drank of it lost consciousness, only to wake up hours later. Once revived, those that had partook in the ritual become keenly aware of awkward aches and pains, which they associated to a violation, which had occurred to them while unconscious. The sensations they felt were a sign that the "abominable thing" had been done to them, meaning that they must have endured rape by some entity or spirit unknown to them. Confused, Eve left the moon festival and returned home, where she enticed Adam to also swill some remnants of this beverage. Adam declined until Eve was able to use her womanly wiles to implore him to drink. She then drank the rest and again succumbed to the stupor induced by the concoction.

When they awake, they realize that their bodies had been violated in a sexual manner, as both experienced pains unlike any they've ever known prior. The tale of Maeva and Dadam seems to allude to, as the tale of Baruch, some role played by the vine in the fall of humanity and rape of Eve. Perhaps the Tree of the Knowledge of Good and Evil is symbolic of both the vine and Lucifer. While many may still deny that the eating of the forbidden fruit had any hidden sexual connotation, the following story seems to verify that a sexual act was partially to blame for the fall and banishment of humanity from paradise. Intoxication could have lead to their loss of consciousness, and loss of consciousness could have left both Adam and Eve susceptible to spiritual violation from what we are not told, but based on myriad scriptures we can infer it was Satan and his minions. This story also seems to confirm that Cain was not a child of Adam's but a consequence of the rape that Eve endured while under the influence of this vine.

> About the land of The Children of God was the wasteland where Yoslings, called The Children of Zumat, which means They Who Inherit Death, dwelt. Amongst these, Namtenigal, the wily hunter, was the most wise and cunning; he alone was unafraid of The Children of God and

he alone dared enter the Gardenland. In the days when Estartha was teaching, Namtenigal often came to hear her words and The Children of God were not displeased, for teaching the wild men about them was a duty with which they had been charged. Namtenigal, therefore, participated in their rites but could not partake of the elixir from the Gwinduiva, because this was forbidden. While it gave health and strength to The Children of God, safeguarding them from the sicknesses of the Yoslings, if given to others it caused a wasting away. It was also altogether forbidden for any of The Children of God to mate with the Yoslings, for this was deemed to be the most unforgivable of sins. Now, the wily one learned much from Estartha and in the fullness of time brought his own son to her and he became as her son, living in her house and forsaking the ways of his people. Estartha called him Lewid the Lightbringer, for it was her intention that he should be taught the ways of those who walked in light, that he might in time enlighten his own people.

Lewid grew up tall and handsome, he was quick to learn and became wise. He was also a man of the chase, strong and enduring, a hunter of renown. But there were times when the call of his people was strong, then he would go out furtively into the night to indulge in their dark rituals. Thus he became knowledgeable in the ways of the flesh and in the carnal indulgences of the body.

Dadam became a servant of the Sacred Enclosure where the misty veil between the realms could be penetrated, for all those having the blood of Aruah had twinsight, an ability to see wraiths and sithfolk, ansis and spiritbeings, all the things of the Otherworld, not clearly but as through a veil.

Beside the place called Gisar was a pleasant parkland with trees of every kind and a stream, also thickets of flowering bushes and all manner of plants growing lushly. It was the custom of Maeva to wander there in the sunshine and Lewid also went there; so it came about that they met among the trees. Maeva knew the man but had shunned him in the past, now she saw he was handsome, possessed of many attractions, so her foot was stayed and she did not run away.

As the days passed they dallied longer together and Lewid talked of things Maeva had not heard before. She felt a stirring in her blood but did not respond or heed his temptations, because of the things which were forbidden. So Lewid went to the Moonmother, wise woman of the Yoslings, and telling of his desires beseeched her to help him. The Moonmother gave him two apples containing a vile substance which they had drawn through their stalks; this Lewid gave to Maeva who then became helpless in his hands. They met again after this, for Maeva became enamoured towards Lewid, but it happened that she became ill with a strange sickness and was afraid. Then Dadam became ill and Lewid also, and Lewid said to the woman, You must obtain the pure essences from within the Sacred Enclosure, and Setina, the Moonmother, will prepare an elixir which will cure us. This he said because none of his kind had ever been able to obtain the Sacred Substances, though they had always coveted what had been denied them. Now, because of her frailty, the woman was pliable in his hands and Lewid seized the opportunity. To achieve his ends Lewid gave Maeva a potion which had been prepared by the Moonmother and she administered this to Dadam and those with him, by guile and deceit, so that they fell asleep. While they slept Maeva stole from the Sacred Substances and took them to Lewid who gave them to the Moonmother, and she made a brew. Part of this was given to Maeva and the rest was drunk by the Yoslings, from their awful ankital during their night rites. When the morning came they were all smitten with grievous pains, and before the sun set that day all the Yoslings were stricken with a sickness such as they had not known before.

Maeva took what had been given to her and finding Dadam laid low in his bed gave him a draught from her vessel, though she had to use womanly wiles to get him to drink it. She drank the remainder and they both slept. But when they awoke in the morning both were suffering pains and this was something they had not known before. Dadam said to the woman, What have you done, for what has happened to us cannot be unless the things which are forbidden have been done. The woman replied, Lord, I was tempted and I fell, I have done that which is forbidden and unforgivable. Dadam said, I am bound by duty to do certain things, but first let us go into the Gisar to the place called Bethkelcris, where I will seek enlightenment. So they went there together and stood before the shrine beneath the Tree of Wisdom.

There they were filled with an inflowing vision, seeing themselves as they were and as they should have been, and they were ashamed. He because he had not followed the proper path of a man and she because of her falsity. There, in the reflecting mist, the contamination of the woman was revealed, and the man's heart shriveled within him like a flower licked by flame.

Then they saw a great Spiritbeing materializing in the reflecting mist and he said to them, Woe to you and your house, for the greatest of evils has befallen the race of The Children of God and it is defiled. The heritage of Kadamhapa is lost. The fetid flow defiling the woman results from the incompatible intermingling, but it is not all, for sicknesses and diseases are also generating from the ferments of the impure implantation. (Maeva was pregnant with Cain.)

Dadam said, The fault is with the woman, wherefore should I suffer? The Spiritbeing replied, Because you two are now as one the conkerworms of disease and sickness strike both equally, but you shall not again defile this place. Henceforth, the misty veil becomes an impenetrable barrier severing our two realms from each other, so they can no longer be easily spanned. Between us there will now be no means of communication.

Kolbrin

The Lord warned Adam to avoid the tree of the knowledge of good and evil and to not eat or drink anything sacrificed unto idols. This beverage was created during a full moon festival, which honored pagan gods and made those who drank of it susceptible to demonic influence. This beverage may have caused both Adam and Eve to pass out, leaving their bodies exposed to the carnal advances of whatever forces frequented those pagan moon festivals. The story does not inform us as to who took advantage of them while they were intoxicated and while there is no certainty as to who was responsible for their sexual violation, we can infer from other stories that it was Satan and his rebel angels. One of the most intriguing aspects of the Kolbrin revelation is the allusion that Eve was impregnated by an *impure seed* as a result of being violated by some unnatural force. This violation resulted in her pregnancy with Cain.

I have been asked by many of my radio listeners as to whether I believe that the fruit, which caused Adam and Eve to fall, was imbued with any psychedelic or psychotropic properties characteristic of certain plants, especially those utilized by Native shamans in opening and accessing spiritual worlds. The fruit that caused the spiritual fall of sixth-day Adam and Eve was spiritual in nature in that it affected their immortality, stripping them of their bright natures, and causing their fall from grace. This fruit was not an earthly fruit.

The text from the Nag Hammadi codices, as well as the story of Maeva and Dadam from the Kolbrin Bible, does allude to the visionary capacity of the second fruit eaten by Adam and Eve after their fall and transformation to flesh. This fruit did heighten their consciousness, granting them access to knowledge that made them realize situation, story, and circumstance. What the initial fruit was that caused the fall to Earth, we cannot yet conclude; however, we do know that it resulted in their opening up and tapping into experiences they were not yet ready for, the consequences for which led to life within human flesh.

In my opinion, the second fruit eaten on the eighth day—after Adam and Eve assume flesh form—has a better chance of being a type a teacher or power plant. A fruit of this nature could indeed expand consciousness, which the texts say made them aware of their fallen state, and that they were living among devils and demons bent on persecuting them and their progeny. While this scenario seems a possibility, I do not believe a fruit is necessary or required for the Lord to open His creatures' minds to whatever information He would have them know.

I do believe that there is a transcendent component to the ritualized techniques utilized by native medicine peoples initiated into their spiritual practices. However, my concern is what portals they open and what kind of ancestor spirits are being invited in to possess the participants of such ritual. The Father warns our Hebraic ancestors of having involvement with divination, familiar spirits, enchantments, herbs, roots, or ritual that could open one up to demonic influence. The fallen angels have, since and before the inception of modern humanity on this planet, sought to lead astray cultures and peoples pursuing secrets and doctrines that could lead them into depravity, judgment, and condemnation. Thus the necessity of adherence to the commandments.

"The fetid flow defiling the woman results from the incompatible intermingling, but it is not all, for sicknesses and diseases are also generating from the ferments of the impure implantation" (Kolbrin).

Cain was not a child of Adam but the son of Samael, the angel of death, which is another name for Satan, who was also blamed for planting the vine. The *Kebra Nagast,* an ancient Ethiopic Holy Book, details Adam's lineage from Seth to Christ, excluding both Cain and Abel from Adam's genealogy. The reason both are left out of Adam's genealogy is because Cain was not a child of Adam's but of Samael, Satan, the angel of death. Abel was excluded because he was killed by his brother Cain, and bore no progeny to continue his seed. One quote, which ties Cain to Lucifer undeniably and which confirms 1 John 3:12, is a recently discovered passage referenced from the Nag Hammadi codices, which says this:

> He who has been created is beautiful, but you would <not> find his sons noble creations. If he were not created, but begotten, you would find that his seed was noble. But now he was created (and) he begot. What nobility is this? First, adultery came into being, afterward murder. And he was begotten in adultery, for he was the child of the Serpent. So he became a murderer, just like his father, and he killed his brother. Indeed, every act of sexual intercourse which has occurred between those unlike one another is adultery.
>
> The Gospel of Philip

Notice first the reference to he whom was created. This created one is Lucifer and describes his being a direct creation of the Creator when He brought forth the angels. Then it says that if he were not created, but begotten (born of woman), that his children might have been noble because they would have been natural creatures born of the procreative processes innate within all those that are the seed of woman. The next line is the giveaway for those with eyes to see. It says that the one that was created begot; this created one is Lucifer who became Satan the adversary. He begot when he seduced Eve and impregnated her with Cain. Cain's birth was the consequence of adultery, which then led to the murder of Abel by Cain, the wicked one of Lucifer. This often-overlooked passage also confirms Matthew 13, which says, "He who sows the good seed is the Son of Man. The field is the world, the good seeds are the sons of the kingdom, but the tares are the sons of the wicked one. The enemy who sowed them is the devil, the harvest is the end of the age, and the reapers are the angels." I will later cover thoroughly and in more detail the many scriptures I have found that also verify this accounting. However, before moving on, I will touch upon Genesis 4:1, the verse many reference to discredit this possibility.

When the Hebrew people were taken into exile by the Babylonians, they remained there for seventy years and, being assimilated into their culture, lost touch with their original teachings and language. As they learned new languages, necessity required they translate their holy books into two different languages of the time, Palestinian and Aramaic. These translations, called Targums, were read side by side with the original Hebrew Torah in the synagogues for those who no longer understood Hebrew. Careful study of these first CE language translations reveals a far different interpretation for Genesis as related by the 1611 King James Version of the Bible.

The older versions of the Biblical Pentateuch include exclusions to Genesis 3, 4, and 5 that seem to clarify that Cain truly was a child of Satan, the devil. Another thing of interest within the Targums is that the serpent that seduced Eve was called Sammael. Sammael is one of the names that the Gnostics used for the blind god Yaldaboath, whom many people teach is Yahweh of the Old Testament. The assertion that Yahweh is Yaldaboath of the codices is absolutely wrong and I believe presented in this way so as to discredit the Gnostic texts and prevent any serious research of them. I ask you please to study everything with an open mind and to not trust any human's interpretation on what they think something says or is supposed to mean. Study everything as one would the Old and New Testament and take it before the Lord in discernment; He is and always will be final authority for all things.

> And the woman beheld Sammael, the angel of death, and was afraid; yet she knew that the tree was good to eat, and that it was medicine for the enlightenment of the eyes, and desirable tree by means of which to understand. And she took of its fruit, and did eat; and she gave to her hus-

band with her, and he did eat. And the eyes of both were enlightened, and they knew that they were naked, divested of the purple robe in which they had been created. And they saw the sight of their shame, and sewed to themselves the leaves of figs, and made to them cinctures...

And the Lord God brought the three unto judgment; and He said to the serpent, Because thou hast done this, cursed art thou of all the cattle, and of all the beasts of the field: upon thy belly thou shalt go, and thy feet shall be cut off, and thy skin thou shalt cast away once in seven years; and the poison of death shall be in thy mouth, and dust shalt thou eat all the days of thy life. *And I will put enmity between thee and the woman, and between the seed of thy son, and the seed of her sons; and it shall be when the sons of the woman keep the commandments of the law, they will be prepared to smite thee upon thy head; but when they forsake the commandments of the law, thou wilt be ready to wound them in their heel...*

And Adam knew his wife Eve, who had desired the Angel; and she conceived, and bare Cain; and she said, I have acquired a man, the angel of the Lord...

Palestinian Targum Genesis 3:6, 3:15, 4:1

And Adam knew Hava his wife, who had desired the Angel; and she conceived, and bare Kain; and she said, I have acquired a man, the Angel of the Lord. And she added to bear from her husband Adam his twin, even Habel.

Targum Onkelos, Genesis 4:1

"And Adam knew his wife Eve, who was pregnant by the Angel Sammael, and she conceived and bare Cain; and he was like the heavenly beings, and not like the earthly beings, and she said, I have acquired a man, the angel of the Lord."

Targum of Jonathan, Genesis 4:1

This is the book of the genealogy of Man. In the day that the Lord created man, in the likeness of the Lord He made him. Male and female He created them, and blessed them in the name of His Word; and He called their name Man in the day they were created. And Adam lived a hundred and thirty years, and begat Sheth, who had the likeness of his image and of his similitude: for before had Hava born Kain, who was not like to him; and Habel was killed by his hand. And Kain was cast out; neither is his seed genealogized in the book of the genealogy of Adam. But afterwards there was born one like him, and he called his name Sheth. And the days of Adam after he begat Sheth were eight hundred years, and he begat sons and daughters.

Palestinian Targum, Genesis 5:1

Notice that chapter five of Genesis from the Targum's specifies Kain as not being of the genealogical line of Adam and that Hava or Eve birthed him prior to giving birth to Sheth, who was of the similitude and likeness of Adam. Kain's line is detailed in Genesis four, which, according to the Targum's, begins with the seduction of Hava by Sammael, the angel of death. Traditional KJV readers believe that Genesis 4:1 references Cain's birth to Adam: "And Adam knew Eve his wife; and she conceived, and bare Cain, and said, I have gotten a man from the LORD." (KJV)

What is interesting about the commentary from the various translations are that the additions cite Habel as being a twin born to Adam after Cain's conception and that Adam was responsible only for siring Abel. Another asserts Samael as being the father of Cain, who resembled the likeness of the heavenly beings and not earthly beings. Cain's birth can only be clarified, in my opinion, with the insight of the Targum's. Sammael is one of the three names of Yaldaboath, the demiurge that the Gnostics say rules over this world. Just to further illustrate that this story was known to the Early Christians, I will utilize another story which also illustrates this fact but in a different light, one which focuses primarily on the fact that Adam had found his wife Eve already pregnant with Cain before having ever known her in any carnal way.

> XIII. I Now it was the sixth month with her, and behold Joseph came from his building, and he entered into his house and found her great with child. And he smote his face, and cast himself down upon the ground on sackcloth and wept bitterly, saying: With what countenance shall I look unto the Lord my God and what prayer shall I make concerning this maiden? For I received her out of the temple of the Lord my God a virgin, and have not kept her safe. Who is he that hath ensnared me? Who hath done this evil in mine house and hath defiled the virgin? Is not the story of Adam repeated in me? For as at the hour of his giving thanks the serpent came and found Eve alone and deceived her, so hath it befallen me also. And Joseph arose from off the sackcloth and called Mary and said unto her O thou that wast cared for by God, why hast thou done this? Thou hast forgotten the Lord thy God. Why hast thou humbled thy soul, thou that wast nourished up in the Holy of Holies and didst receive food at the hand of an angel? 3 But she wept bitterly, saying: I am pure and I know not a man. And Joseph said unto her: Whence then is that which is in thy womb? and she said: As the Lord my God liveth, I know not whence it is come unto me.

> Protevangelium of James

In this first century text, Joseph states that the story of Adam had been repeated in him, meaning that Adam too found his wife pregnant with a child he had no idea from whence it came. Like Joseph, who returned home to find Mary pregnant, so too had Adam found Eve already pregnant with Cain. Both were confused as to what had happened; yet we know that Mary was blessed to be chosen as receptacle for the glory of our Savior, while Eve was seduced and impregnated with Cain.

The devil planted a reed in the middle of paradise. And in one spit he made the serpent, whom he commanded to live in the reed. In such a way the devil concealed his evil design so they might not know his trickery... However, the devil slipped into the body of the evil serpent and seduced the angel who was in the form of a woman and he spread over her head the powerful desire of sin, and he satiated Eve with his bodily desire while he attended to the serpent's tail (suggests the penis). That is why the humans are called the children of the devil and children of the serpent, because they serve the desire of the devil, who is their father, and will serve it to the consummation of this century.

The Gospel of the Secret Supper

But a very horrible snake craftily deceived them to go to the fate of death and receive knowledge of good and evil. But the woman first became a betrayer to him. She gave, and persuaded him to sin in his ignorance. He was persuaded by the woman's words, forgot about his immortal creator, and neglected clear commands. Therefore, instead of good they received evil, as they had done. And then they sewed the leaves of the sweet fig tree and made clothes and put them on each other. They concealed their plans, because shame had come upon them. The Immortal became angry with them and expelled them from the place of immortals. For it had been decreed that they remain in a mortal place, since they had not kept the command of the great immortal God, and attended to it.

Sibylline Oracles, Book 1

PRISON PLANET

Humanity must grasp again the memory of how it was that we fell from grace to be clothed in flesh and subject to death. The most important piece of wisdom anywhere relevant to our current displacement from heaven and the Father is understanding how the fall led humanity to a state of being stripped of our former bright nature and glory as immortal beings. The world had not remained in a wholesome, innocent state because Adam of Paradise and his wife, Eve, were deceived only nine hours after their initial creation. The Lord had to accommodate Lucifer's rebellion and the seduction of Eve before completing the ordering of creation in what should have been blessing and goodness. He would, therefore, manifest the Second World Age as a solution to verify the loyalties of all those souls that would incarnate into this visible, material realm. Here, free will would be allowed to reign along with the experience of duality in both good and evil expression for what would be only a short time. This Second World Age would exist for only 7,000 years as we the Elohim spirits of the First World Age incarnate into flesh and are tried by life and lesson.

> At the third hour of the day Adam and Eve ascended into Paradise, and for three hours they enjoyed the good things thereof; for three hours they were in shame and disgrace, and at the ninth hour their expulsion from Paradise took place.
>
> Cave of Treasure

And there were fruit trees in the garden better than that one. But the wicked Satan did not keep his faith and had no good intent towards Me, that although I had created him, he considered Me to be useless, and sought the Godhead for himself; for this I hurled him down from heaven so that he could not remain in his first estate—it was he who made the tree appear pleasant in your eyes, until you ate of it, by believing his words. Thus have you transgressed My commandment, and therefore I have brought on you all these sorrows.

For I am God the Creator, who, when I created My creatures, did not intend to destroy them. But after they had sorely roused My anger, I punished them with grievous plagues, until they repent. But, if on the contrary, they still continue hardened in their transgression, they shall be under a curse forever.

First Book of Adam and Eve 6:6-10

Prior to the fall, Adam and Eve inhabited paradise with the various angels assigned to attend its glorious space. After the fall, they assumed Earthly bodies of flesh and then fulfilled all the prophecies declared in Genesis 3, namely that they would hunger, thirst, work, procreate, and eventually die. The Lord had originally intended Adam and Eve to be clothed in immortality, but because of the deception of Satan, and their desire to be as gods with knowledge of good and evil, the Lord was forced to cast them out of Paradise, placing them here upon the lower Earth in the Cave of Treasures.

Yahweh separated the feminine from Adam so that death should come to him by his wife, as He knew that Lucifer would attempt to seduce Eve. The fall was an integral part of the Lord's desire to create another world, a proving ground of sorts, whereby all would be tried by the persecutions of those fallen angels who were given dominion over the Earth.

"And God created that sea of his own good pleasure, for He knew what would come of the man He would make; so that after he had left the garden, on account of his transgression, men should be born in the earth" (The Apocalypse of Adam, 1:4).

Already banished to the lower Earth, Satan desired to exact revenge against Yahushuah for casting him from the upper heavens, but having no power against the Lord, he decided on plotting the fall of sixth day Adam and Eve. He wanted their children and all those who would be born of the flesh to be subject to a world under his dominion for the short time the Father and the Son would allow him rule. Satan would accomplish this task by assuming the shape of the serpent to enter the Lord's Paradise.

This serpent is not a snake as we know snakes today but considered by some scriptures to be the wisest and most beautiful of all creatures then found upon the earth. Before the Lord cursed it, this serpent was a type of dragon enchanter, a magician clever enough to trick others into committing sin. Eve was seduced by this Nachash, and eating of the forbidden fruit set the stage for what would be the beginning of the Second World Age.

"And the serpent said unto the woman, Ye shall not surely die: For God know that in the day ye eat thereof, then your eyes shall be opened, and ye shall be as gods, knowing good and evil" (Genesis 3:4-5, KJV).

When Yahweh questioned Adam and Eve about their nakedness, He was commenting on their feeble attempts to hide what was the loss of their bright natures that they, thanks to Lucifer, were now devoid of. Their initial awareness of being naked was their recognition that they had lost the light with which they had originally been clothed.

> And he said, Who told thee that thou wast naked? Hast thou eaten of the tree, whereof I commanded thee that thou shouldest not eat? And the man said, The woman whom thou gavest to be with me, she gave me of the tree, and I did eat. And the LORD God said unto the woman,

What is this that thou hast done? And the woman said,
The serpent beguiled me, and I did eat.

Genesis 3:11-13 (KJV)

Many claim that angels cannot have sex with humankind because of a passage that stated that angels were not created to be given in marriage, and that is true; however, those that fell and willingly took on the flesh assumed form as spirit men that are and were capable of fornication with earth women. Proof that angels had fornicated with humankind early in our history can be confirmed from myriad sources, yet I will use two: the *Book of Enoch* and the *Genesis Apocryphon*. Both verify the accounting of angelic interdiction into the affairs of and direct procreation with humanity.

Lamech, the son of Enoch, knew about and was warned by his father, about the watchers, and their incursion upon the world of humanity. Upon the birth of his son, Noah, who had an extremely bright nature, Lamech was greatly distressed that his wife, too, had been impregnated by a fallen watcher. He doubted Noah was his son and confronted Batenosh, his wife in accusation. She assured him that she had not been with anyone but him, but still uncertain Lamech summoned the ghost of his father Enoch, so as to inquire through him whether Noah was truly his child or one born of the watchers. Enoch revealed to him that Noah was indeed his son and that the Lord would soon judge the world for the incursion of the watchers upon the daughters of humanity. It was during his grandfather Jared's lifetime that the watchers rebelled against the Lord and challenged Him to place them into flesh form, which birthed a race of cannibalistic giants upon the unsuspecting world.

The consequence of this led to the global deluge and the wiping out of all flesh from the face of the Earth. Post deluge, Yahweh would restore harmony and order through Noah and his family as they were the last remaining of the children of Adam that had retained purity in their generations. Noah's line was the only remnant of humans on the earth that had avoided mixing with the contaminated DNA of the fallen watchers and the hybrid giants. Through Noah's children Yahweh would repopulate and replenish the Earth in restored goodness and harmony. This story proves that prior to Lamech, as Genesis 6 claims, the fallen angels had already interbred with humanity.

> Then I considered whether the pregnancy was due to the Watchers and Holy Ones, or (should be ascribed) to the Nephil[im], and I grew perturbed about this child. Then I Lamech, became afraid and went to Batenosh, [my] w[ife ... saying, Dec]lare [to me] by the Most High, by the Lord of Greatness, by the E[ternal] King [whether the child comes from the] heavenly beings! Everything will you truthfully tell me, whether [... ...] you will tell me without lies: is this [... ... swear] by the Eternal King until you speak truthfully to me and not with lies [...].
>
> Then Batenosh my wife spoke with me forcefully. [She we]pt and said, O my brother and master, recall for yourself my pregnancy [... ...] marital relations, and my breath within its sheath (?). (Can) I truthfully [tell you] everythin[g?] [... ...] then I was perturbed even more. When Batenosh my wife noticed that my face had changed (its) expression [... ...] then she gained control of her emotion(s) and spoke with me. She said to me, O my master and [brother, recall for yourself] my pregnancy. I swear to you by the Great Holy One, by the Ruler of Hea[ven] that this seed is yours, that this pregnancy is from you, that from you is the planting of [this] fruit [and that it is] not from any alien, or from any of the Watchers, or from any heavenly bein[g. Why has the appearance] of your face changed like this upon you? And (why) is it disfigured, and your spirit dejected like this?

> The Genesis Apocryphon, Column 2

As related previously, the tree of knowledge of good and evil was and is, in my opinion, symbolic of both Lucifer and the grape vine from which the Kolbrin Bible says an intoxicating beverage had been formulated. This beverage caused a powerful stupor to overcome each, leaving them susceptible to rape by Satan and his demon angels. The Genesis 3 account veils a prophecy that would be fulfilled once Adam and Eve are transformed into flesh bodies on the eighth day. The Lord had already foreseen what would happen to all three now that Adam and Eve would also join Lucifer and his angels in being born on a strange planet and in a fallen state. After Eve takes on physical form, she is raped and impregnated by Lucifer with his firstborn child, Cain. This unholy sexual union began the 7,000-year cycle of the Second World Age, for why truly would the Lord condemn anyone to death for simply eating a piece of fruit? Yahweh foresaw what would happen to each of them once all had been transformed into flesh. That is why He told Eve that the consequences of her actions with Lucifer would result in labor and pained child birth.

"Unto the woman he said, I will greatly multiply thy sorrow and thy conception; in sorrow thou shalt bring forth children; and thy desire shall be to thy husband, and he shall rule over thee" (Genesis 1:6, KJV).

Eve lusted after the beauty of the tree and, having desired it, ate of its fruit, symbolically meaning two things—that she lost her angelic, bright-natured, immortal state of being and that she was impregnated by Satan with Cain, who would be the firstborn son of the devil and the seed line that he would use to war against the seed of the woman. The statements in Genesis 3 are prophetic in nature and relate to the eighth day when they would be transformed into fleshly Earth bodies. Eve, who was still a virgin, had never birthed any children and did not know the pain of childbirth, is told by God in this verse that she would now, as the result of her fornication with Lucifer, bear children in pain and that her desire would be for Adam, which is the lustful call to procreate, the blooming of sexuality in mortal humans.

And unto Adam he said, Because thou hast hearkened unto the voice of thy wife, and hast eaten of the tree, of which I commanded thee, saying, Thou shalt not eat of it: cursed is the ground for thy sake; in sorrow shalt thou eat of it all the days of thy life; Thorns also and thistles shall it bring forth to thee; and thou shalt eat the herb of the field; In the sweat of thy face shalt thou eat bread, till thou return unto the ground; for out of it wast thou taken: for dust thou art, and unto dust shalt thou return.

Genesis 3:17 (KJV)

Yahweh told Adam before banishment from the kingdom that whereas in paradise the ground gave fruit and bounty freely of itself, upon the lower Earth he would now have to work the ground to bring forth food and the sustenance they would need to replenish the strength of their earthly bodies and those of their children. He also told them both specifically that, as mortal beings, they and their children would eventually have to succumb to death. Before the fall, they knew not mortality, thirst, hunger, cold, heat, darkness, night, nor death. The Second World Age began with the generations of Adam through Seth and Lucifer through Cain.

Eve, who would be progenitor of both lines, would be called the mother of all living, and yet Adam, because he was not the father of Cain or his line, is not called the father of all living. Adam's firstborn son, Abel—who became the first soul to succumb to death once in bodily incarnation—would be replaced by Seth, who would sire the generations of Adam.

"When Eve was still with Adam, death did not exist. When she was separated from him, death came into being. If he enters again and attains his former self, death will be no more" (The Gospel of Phillip).

And on the morning of the forty-third day, they came out of the cave, sorrowful and crying. Their bodies were lean, and they were parched from hunger and thirst, from fasting and praying, and from their heavy sorrow on account of their transgression. And when they had come out of the cave they went up the mountain to the west of the garden. There they stood and prayed and besought God to grant them forgiveness of their sins. And after their prayers Adam began to beg God, saying, O my Lord, my God, and my Creator, You commanded the four elements* to be gathered together, and they were gathered together by Thine order.

Then You spread Your hand and created me out of one element, that of dust of the earth; and You brought me into the garden at the third hour, on a Friday, and informed me of it in the cave. Then, at first, I knew neither night nor day, for I had a bright nature; neither did the light in which I lived ever leave me to know night or day. Then, again, O Lord, in that third hour in which You created me, You brought to me all beasts, and lions, and ostriches, and fowls of the air, and all things that move in the earth, which You had created at the first hour before me of the Friday.

And Your will was that I should name them all, one by one, with a suitable name. But You gave me understanding and knowledge, and a pure heart and a right mind from you, that I should name them after Thine own mind regarding the naming of them. O God, You made them obedient to me, and ordered that not one of them break from my sway, according to Your commandment, and to the dominion which You had given me over them.

But now they are all estranged from me. Then it was in that third hour of Friday, in which You created me, and commanded me concerning the tree, to which I was neither to go near, nor to eat thereof; for You said to me in the garden, 'When you eat of it, of death you shall die.' And if You had punished me as You said, with death, I should have died that very moment. Moreover, when You commanded me regarding the tree, I was neither to approach nor to eat thereof, Eve was not with me; You had not yet created her, neither had You yet taken her out of my side; nor had she yet heard this order from you.

Then, at the end of the third hour of that Friday, O Lord, You caused a slumber and a sleep to come over me, and I slept, and was overwhelmed in sleep. Then You drew a rib out of my side, and created it after my own likeness and image. Then I awoke; and when I saw her and knew who she was, I said, 'This is bone of my bones, and flesh of my flesh; from now on she shall be called woman.' It was of Your good will, O God, that You brought a slumber in a sleep over me, and that You immediately brought Eve out of my side, until she was out, so that I did not see how she was made; neither could I witness, O my Lord, how awful and great are Your goodness and glory. And of Your good-will, O Lord, You made us both with bodies of a bright nature, and You made us two, one; and You gave us Your grace, and filled us with praises of the Holy Spirit; that we should be neither hungry nor thirsty, nor know what sorrow is, nor yet faintness of heart; neither suffering, fasting nor weariness.

But now, O God, since we transgressed Your commandment and broke Your law, You have brought us out into a strange land, and have caused suffering, and faintness, hunger and thirst to come over us. Now, therefore, O God, we pray you, give us something to eat from the garden, to satisfy our hunger with it; and something wherewith to quench our thirst. For, behold, many days, O God, we have tasted nothing and drunk nothing, and our flesh is dried up, and our strength is wasted, and sleep is gone from our eyes from faintness and crying.

First Book of Adam and Eve 34:1-19

Then God looked again at Adam and his crying and groaning, and the Word of God came to him, and said to him:— O Adam, when you were in My garden, you knew neither eating nor drinking; neither faintness nor suffering; neither leanness of flesh, nor change; neither did sleep depart from thine eyes. But since you transgressed, and came into this strange land, all these trials are come over you.

First Book of Adam and Eve 35:1-2

For seducing Eve and causing the fall of the Lord's most beloved creatures, Yahweh condemned Satan to feed off the dust of the Earth, which metaphorically represents his need to feed on the flesh and blood of humanity. Once the most beautiful of all angels, Satan in his transformed state is now recognized as many different embodiments: the ancient dragon which drew one third of the stars of heaven, a feathered serpent reptilian, hybrid fish god, and even the many names associated to him as a wraith or demon which possesses physical flesh, assuming personas as he moves in and out of body, people, and lifetime to achieve the goals of the New World Order.

"And the LORD God said unto the serpent, Because thou hast done this, thou art cursed above all cattle, and above every beast of the field; upon thy belly shalt thou go, and dust shalt thou eat all the days of thy life" (Genesis 3:14, KJV).

> Then Adam and Eve came out at the mouth of the cave, and went towards the garden. But as they went near it, before the western gate, from which Satan came when he deceived Adam and Eve, they found the serpent that became Satan coming at the gate, and sorrowfully licking the dust, and wiggling on its breast on the ground, by reason of the curse that fell on it from God. And whereas before the serpent was the most exalted of all beasts, now it was changed and become slippery, and the meanest of them all, and it crept on its breast and went on its belly. And whereas it was the fairest of all beasts, it had been changed, and was become the ugliest of them all.
>
> Instead of feeding on the best food, now it turned to eat the dust. Instead of living, as before, in the best places, now it lived in the dust. And, whereas it had been the most beautiful of all beasts, all of which stood dumb at its

beauty, it was now abhorred of them. And, again, whereas it lived in one beautiful home, to which all other animals came from elsewhere; and where it drank, they drank also of the same; now, after it had become venomous, by reason of God's curse, all beasts fled from its home, and would not drink of the water it drank; but fled from it.

The First Book of Adam and Eve 17:1-6

In Genesis 3:15 we are presented with the prophecy of the coming war between the children of Adam and the children of Satan. In Genesis 4 we are given a detailed accounting of the children of Cain and his blood line as they are left out of the Genesis 5 accounting of the children of Adam through Seth. Understanding that there are two bloodlines on the earth will help one to understand why—throughout the Old Testament, New Testament, and lost forgotten books of scripture—the Lord commands the children of Adam to avoid intermarrying with the children of Cain. Unless one understands that Cain originated out of the devil's loins one would not understand why it is that evil is perpetuated in such abundance in this world. There is literally a seed line dedicated to the worship of Lucifer and evil just as there is a seed line dedicated to God and good. Those born of Cain's line are more apt to bring forth evil and are more susceptible to following the abominable ways of Satan and his dedication to self-destruction. Speaking to the serpent, the Lord said, "I will put enmity between thee and the woman, and between thy seed and her seed. It shall bruise thy head, and thou shalt bruise his heel" (Genesi 3:15, KJV).

From the very beginning of the fall of Adam and Eve, Satan would wage a perpetual war against their descendants for what would be dominion of the Earth. Genesis 3:15 very literally confirms that Satan indeed has his own seed line. This line also foretells the birth of Yahushuah Savior Messiah through the line of Seth. The two seed lines would battle against one another for 7,000 years, and through this warring all would come to know the experience of both good and evil. Once one understands what was behind the fall and how it led to the prophecies revealed in Genesis 3, one will understand why it was that the Lord told Adam, "But of the fruit of the tree which is in the midst of the garden, God hath said, Ye shall not eat of it, neither shall ye touch it, lest ye die" (Genesis 2:3, KJV).

Some claim that Yahweh lied when he told this to Adam because Adam did not immediately die; however, most do not understand that Adam and Eve would not fulfill this prophecy as human, angelic, bright-nature beings. It was not until they were re-crafted into earthly flesh bodies and upon ending their mortal life spans that they in fact did as Genesis 2:3 and 2:17 foretold. Besides, we know that one day is as a thousand years unto the Lord and that both Adam and Eve died before they reached a thousand years of age.

> Then came the Word of God to Adam, and said to him:— O Adam, look at that garden of joy and at this earth of toil, and behold the garden is full of angels, but look at yourself alone on this earth with Satan whom you obeyed. Yet, if you had submitted, and been obedient to Me, and had kept My Word, you would be with My angels in My garden. But when you transgressed and obeyed Satan, you became his guests among his angels, that are full of wickedness; and you came to this earth, that brings forth to you thorns and thistles.
>
> First Book of Adam and Eve 56:1-4

ABANDON HOPE ALL YE THAT ENTER HERE

Once Adam and Eve fall from grace, their bodies are transformed into flesh. In this form they would be tested in duality, learning the ways of good from the angels of the Lord assigned to minister to them and evil from Satan and his minions who would hold dominion over the lower visible Earth until the end of days and second coming of Yahshuah Savior Messiah.

> Then God, the ruler of the Aeons and the powers, divided us in wrath. Then we became two Aeons. And the glory in our hearts left us, me and your mother Eve, along with the first knowledge that breathed within us. And glory fled from us; not from this Aeon from which we had come forth, I and Eve your mother. But knowledge entered into the seed of great Aeons. For this reason I myself have called you by the name of that man who is the seed of the great generation or from whom it comes. After those days the eternal knowledge of the God of truth withdrew from me and your mother Eve. Since that time we learned about dead things, like men.
>
> The Apocalypse of Adam

Humanity must grasp again the memory of how it was that we fell from grace to be clothed in flesh and subject to death. The most important piece of wisdom anywhere relevant to our current displacement is understanding how the fall lead humankind to a state of being stripped of our former bright nature. The fall condemned humanity to be born of the flesh upon the Earth while inhabiting the planet with the condemned rebel angels and the fallen watchers. Because the Lord exalts Adam above the angels who abandoned their first estate, the archons set a course to wage war on the descendants of Adam and Eve, fulfilling the prophecy of Genesis 3:15.

"Know you and understand concerning this Satan, that he seeks to deceive you and your descendants after you" (First Book of Adam and Eve, 29).

For only in understanding the fall can one grasp how we came to be on the Earth with Satan and his minions. It is important to acknowledge evil for only in accepting that the fallen angels are haughty, proud, arrogant, and unwilling to repent can one understand the kind of evil that is present even unto this day upon the world stage, and how determined they are to not leave one of the sons of men to inherit the ordinances they abandoned in leaving their first estate.

Even with the severity of their condemnation the fallen ones promise only to escalate murder against the children of Adam and Eve. Yahushuah, however, in His infinite wisdom would devise a plan to restore those angels that would incarnate into flesh during the Second World Age. Salvation would be brought to Adam, Eve, and their righteous descendants while condemnation would await those angels who abandoned their first estate, preferring evil to good.

> And He made Adam in His own image and likeness, so that He might remove Satan because of his pride, together with his host, and might establish Adam—His own plant—together with the righteous, His children, for His praises. For the plan of God was decided upon and decreed in that He said, I will become man, and I will be in everything which I have created, I will abide in flesh. And in the

days that came after, by His good pleasure there was born in the flesh of the Second Zion the second Adam, Who was our Savior CHRIST.

Kebra Nagast 1

The plan of salvation would require the Lord adorning flesh Himself, and after dying on the cross He would assert His authority over death and how he is the author of eternal life to those who believe upon Him. He is returning again this time to assume His Judgment seat where He will send out His angels as reaper for the harvest. Those that are ready will inherit everlasting life and serve the Lord where the rebel angels once had opportunity to, and those that aren't shall, along with the angels that denied Him, be cast into outer darkness.

> Then Satan said to Adam, Do you think that when I have promised one something that I would actually deliver it to him or fulfill my word? Of course not. For I myself have never even thought of obtaining what I promised. Therefore I fell, and I made you fall by that for which I myself fell; and with you also, whosoever accepts my counsel, falls thereby. But now, O Adam, because you fell you are under my rule, and I am king over you; because you have obeyed me and have transgressed against your God. Neither will there be any deliverance from my hands until the day promised you by your God. Again he said, Because we do not know the day agreed on with you by your God, nor the hour in which you shall be delivered, for that reason we will multiply war and murder on you and your descendants after you. This is our will and our good pleasure, that we may not leave one of the sons of men to inherit our orders in heaven. For as to our home, O Adam, it is in burning fire; and we will not stop our evil doing, no, not one day nor one hour. And I, O Adam, shall set you on fire when you come into the cave to live there.

The first Book of Adam and Eve 57:5-10

The war against God has been ongoing since even before the dawn of humanity upon this planet. While most have little understanding of how evil entered the world stage, those who do their homework will easily find ample texts to confirm that indeed the fallen angels have always rebelled against and disregarded the commandments of our Lord, so much even that they willing abandoned their positions in the heavens to interject themselves into the affairs of humanity. The Lord warned us about the rebel angels and their proclivity toward evil; that is why the first two commandments deal directly with the fallen ones and those who worship them. Lucifer has always sought some way to interfere with the fate and destiny of humans. His plan has always been to wage war egregiously against the Lord and his highest creatures. His hope was that he could somehow thwart judgment by preventing the birth of the Messiah.

Having fallen also, Adam and Eve attempted a last-ditch effort to beseech the Lord for forgiveness, hoping He would allow them to remain in Paradise. The Father instead sent the Word to implore them to follow the commandments and instructions. He would provide—as guide—for life. So long as they adhered to His directions, Yahweh Elohim would send His only begotten Son, Yahushuah, to enter the flesh exactly 5,500 years after their banishment to lead them back into paradise. With strengthened heart both were then exiled to the wilderness of the lower Earth.

> But the Lord turned to Adam and said: 'I will not suffer thee henceforward to be in paradise. And Adam answered and said, Grant me, O Lord, of the Tree of Life that I may eat of it, before I be cast out. Then the Lord spake to Adam, Thou shalt not take of it now, for I have commanded the cherubim with the flaming sword that turneth (every way) to guard it from thee that thou taste not of it; but thou hast the war which the adversary hath put into thee, yet when thou art gone out of paradise, if thou shouldst keep thyself from all evil, as one about to die, when again the

Resurrection hath come to pass, I will raise thee up and then there shall be given to thee the Tree of Life.

The Apocalypse of Moses 28-29

God said to Adam, I have ordained on this earth days and years, and you and your descendants shall live and walk in them, until the days and years are fulfilled; when I shall send the Word that created you, and against which you have transgressed, the Word that made you come out of the garden, and that raised you when you were fallen.

First Book of Adam and Eve, 31

For 5,500 years the souls of humanity would be confined in Sheol until that time when Yahushuah Savior Messiah, as promised, would enter the flesh, die upon the cross, descend into hell, and lead the righteous born of Adam and Eve back into Paradise. This is the first resurrection as spoken about in Revelation. When Yahushuah ascended unto His glory, all of the souls of the patriarchs were also resurrected and taken up to paradise with Him, where New Jerusalem awaits us even now.

Then came the Word of God to Adam, and said to him:— O Adam, as to what you said, 'Bring me into a land where there is rest,' it is not another land than this, but it is the kingdom of heaven where alone there is rest. But you can not make your entrance into it at present; but only after your judgment is past and fulfilled. Then will I make you go up into the kingdom of heaven, you and your righteous descendants; and I will give you and them the rest you ask for at present.

And if you said, 'Give me of the Water of Life that I may drink and live'—it cannot be this day, but on the day that I shall descend into hell, and break the gates of brass, and bruise in pieces the kingdoms of iron. Then will I in mercy save your soul and the souls of the righteous, to give them rest in My garden. And that shall be when the end of the world is come.

And, again, in regards to the Water of Life you seek, it will not be granted you this day; but on the day that I shall shed My blood on your head* in the land of Golgotha**. For My blood shall be the Water of Life to you at that time, and not to just you alone, but to all your descendants who shall believe in Me; that it be to them for rest forever.

The Lord said again to Adam, O Adam, when you were in the garden, these trials did not come to you. But since you transgressed My commandment, all these sufferings have come over you. Now, also, does your flesh require food and drink; drink then of that water that flows by you on the face of the earth.

The First Book of Adam and Eve 42:1-11

Those born into the flesh would languish under the authority of death and the dominion of Satan until the 7,000 years were fulfilled and the Second World Age completed. Yahushuah would, as prophesied, enter the flesh, be born of a virgin, and serve as the sacrificial lamb for that year's Feast of Passover.

In fulfilling His role, the Son would then grant a total forgiveness of sins to all, offering salvation even to the Canaanite bloodlines, which now include the Illuminati and pagan nations that have been excluded from the blessings of Hebraic Israel. Clearing the slate for the past deeds of humanity, Christ presented to each of us individually a chance to aspire again to salvation and eternal rest He so graciously extends to each of us no matter which seed-line we were born into. Many born into the Illuminati, Kainite, Luciferian bloodlines have resigned themselves to accept their family's lot without hope of ever being able to change for themselves the path fated for them.

Considered unredeemable, some believe that, because of Illuminati ties, one cannot inherit the kingdom. Know, however, that Christ died on the cross for all of us and that even the most evil and vile of humans, if truly desiring repentance, can and will be grafted into the family of Christ. We are each called now to serve as foot washers to one another so that, in His example, we should be found worthy to escape all those things coming upon the earth, which will make men's hearts fail them.

On that day, when every knee shall bow and every tongue confess that Christ is judge and Lord, it will be our own choices within this life— the choices, thoughts, actions, and deeds we committed while in the flesh—that will convict us before Him. Use what one has left of time and life to glorify the Lord and kingdom. We are determining with each moment, each thought, and each choice whom we wish to serve and even whether we wish to serve at all. Our choices are individual, and yet we are co-creators of our personal fate and destiny, and as such we must assume responsibility for our part in the creation of our realities and the manifestation of our lives.

> And Thou knowest how Thy Watchers, the fathers of these spirits, acted in my day: and as for these spirits which are living, imprison them and hold them fast in the place of condemnation, and let them not bring destruction on the sons of thy servant, my God; for these are malignant, and 6 created in order to destroy… And He said: Let the tenth part of them remain before him, and let nine parts descend into the place of condemnation.' And one of us He commanded that we should teach Noah all their medicines; for He knew that they would not walk in uprightness, nor strive in righteousness. And we did according to all His words: all the malignant evil ones we bound in the place of condemnation and a tenth part of them we left that they might be subject before Satan on the earth.
>
> The Book of Jubilees, 10

THE WATCHER
REBELLION

I have cited passages from long-forgotten books and deciphered codices that have only recently been released to provide clarity on this most intriguing subject of Old Testament Lore—the fallen angels, archons, principalities, and rulers of darkness not of this world. It is important to understand that even though Lucifer and one third of the Angels were cast out of the heavens on the second day, another group of angels descended willingly from their celestial abode to reside here upon the Earth during the age of Jared, Enoch's father. This group of 200 angels brought additional evil into the world and aligned themselves with those angels that fell during Lucifer's first rebellion. This second incursion of angels is what leads to the birth of the giants of Genesis 6 or the men of renown.

How and why the watcher rebellion happened and what this has to do with explaining the strangeness of the world we now live in makes for quite an intriguing story. I will connect myths long forgotten to a specific chapter of a little known book called the Kebra Nagast to unlock this tale and relate how the watchers provoked the anger of the Most High. After Lucifer seduced Eve, some of the Lord's angels, in secret envy, rushed to report on Adam's transgression and their fall from grace. Jealous that the Lord had appointed Adam dominion over the third heaven of paradise, and not understanding why the Lord would so love such an inferior creation, the watchers ridiculed Adam's shortcomings and substandard nature.

> And there were certain angels with whom God was wroth—now He, the Knower of the heart knew them— and they reviled ADAM, saying, Since God hath shown love to him He hath set us to minister unto him, and the beasts and creeping things, and the fish of the sea, and the birds of the air, and all fruits, and the trees of the field, and the heavens and the earth also; and He hath appointed the heavens to give him rain, and the earth to give him fruits. And the sun and the moon also hath He given him, the sun to give him light by day and the moon to give him light in the night season.
>
> He hath fashioned him with His fingers, and He hath created him in His own image, and He hath kissed him and breathed upon him the spirit of life; and He saith unto him, 'My son, My firstborn, My beloved.' And He hath set him in a garden to eat and enjoy himself without sickness or suffering, and without toil or labour, but He hath commanded him not to eat from one tree. And being given all these things by God, ADAM hath transgressed and eaten of that tree, and he hath become hated and rejected, and God hath driven him out of the Garden, and from that time ADAM hath abandoned his hope, for he hath transgressed the commandment of his Creator.
>
> Kebra Nagast 100

Attempting to rouse trouble for Adam, some of the watchers inform the Lord that even after He had brought all things into subjection to His human creations, both Adam and Eve transgress the only commandment He gave when placing them in Paradise. Even after warning Adam to abstain from any contact with the Tree of Knowledge of Good and Evil, Lucifer, both interact with and are seduced by him. This single transgression would results in their banishment from paradise and loss of immortality. They would be forced now to incarnate into bodies of flesh, in which they would have to sustain their physical natures with actual labor in gathering the sustenance they would need to continue living.

> And God answered the angels who reviled ADAM in this wise, and He said unto them, Why do ye revile ADAM in this wise? For he is flesh, and blood, and ashes and dust. And the angels answered and said unto Him, May we declare before Thee the sin of ADAM? And God said unto them, Declare ye (his sin), and I will hearken unto you, and I Myself will answer you in respect of ADAM My servant. For God had worked on behalf of ADAM. And God said, I created him out of the dust, and I will not cast away that which I have fashioned. I brought him forth out of non-existence, and I will not make My handiwork a laughingstock for his enemies.
>
> Kebra Nagast 100

Those angels that were jealous of Adam laid reviling accusation against him and tempted the Lord with question as to whether He had made the right decision in creating Adam. Their contempt leads them to challenge their own loyalties as they requested the Lord to transform them also into bodies of flesh.

> And those angels said, Praise be unto Thee, O Lord. For Thou, the Knower of hearts, knowest that we have reviled ADAM because he hath transgressed Thy commandment that he was not to eat of one tree after Thou hadst made him lord over everything which Thou hast created, and hadst set him over every work of Thy hands. And if Thou hadst not told him, and if Thou hadst not commanded him not to eat of one tree there would have been no offence (on his part); and if he had eaten because of a lack of food there would have been no offence (on his part). But Thy word made him to know, and Thou didst say, 'As surely as thou eatest of this tree thou shalt die.' And he, after

hearing this, made bold and ate. Thou didst not let him lack sweet fruits to eat from the Garden, and Thou didst not let him lack one to comfort him and a companion like unto himself. And these things we say and make known unto Thee, and we have revealed unto Thee how he hath transgressed Thy commandment.

Kebra Nagast 100

The Lord defended Adam and Eve and addressed the envy of the watchers by declaring that He created them (the watchers) out of air and fire to be angels with purpose only to serve Him. He said that, should He have created them from the four elements, they would have transgressed even worse than that of Adam and Eve. Declaring their superior nature, they accept the challenge and implore the Lord to allow their transformation into bodies of flesh. Before transforming them, however, He gave them fair warning to remain true and to not go the way of evil in embracing flesh form. Should they go the route of Lucifer and ditch all faith in goodness they, too, would suffer the wrath of those who abandoned their first estate. He wanted the watchers to know that, given free will they, too, could and would place their own souls at risk for condemnation in following the path of those Angels that rebelled with Lucifer in his attempt to assert his own throne above the glory of God. Only in understanding the consequences of their decisions would the Lord allow their descent to the Earth.

> And the Merciful One and the Lover of mercy answered them on behalf of ADAM, and said unto them, You have I created out of fire and air with the one intent (that ye should) praise (Me). Him have I created of twice as many elements as you—of dust and water, and of wind and fire; and he became (a being) of flesh and blood. And in him are ten thoughts (or, intentions), five good, and five bad. And if his heart inciteth him to good, he walketh with good intent; and if the Devil seduceth him, he walketh with him on an evil path.

As for you, ye have no other object in your minds but praise of Me, with the exception of that arrogant one who produced evil, and became an evil being, and was driven forth from your assembly. And now, why do ye magnify yourselves over ADAM? If ye were as he is, and I had created you of water and dust, ye would have been flesh and blood, and ye would have transgressed My commandment more than he hath done, and denied My word. And the angels said unto Him, Praise be unto Thee, O Lord! Far be it from us! We will not transgress Thy commandment, and we will not oppose Thy word; for we are spiritual beings for life, and he is a creature of dust (doomed) to folly. And now try us well, and put us to the test so that Thou mayest know whether we are able to keep Thy word.

And when they had vaunted themselves in this manner God, the Lover of men, said unto them, If now ye go astray so far as this in transgressing My word, the wrong will be upon your own heads, (for) JAHANNa.m. (or, hell), and fire, and sulphur, and fervent heat, and whirlwind shall be your habitation until the Great Day: ye shall be kept in chains which can neither be loosened nor broken for ever.

But if ye keep truly My word, and ye do My commandment, ye shall sit upon My right hand and upon My left. For everyone who hath conquered is mighty, and he who is conquered shall be overpowered. Now SATAN hath no power whatsoever, for he hath only what he maketh to germinate in the mind; and he cannot grasp firmly, and he cannot perform anything, and he cannot beat, and he cannot drag, and he cannot seize, and he cannot fight; he can only make thoughts to germinate silently in the mind. And him who is caught by the evil mind he prepareth for destruction; and if (a man) hath conquered the evil mind he findeth grace and hath a reward which is everlasting. And to you, according to what ye wish, there shall be upon you the mind of a man and the body of a man. But take good heed to yourselves that ye transgress not My word and break not My commandment; and defile not ye yourselves with eating, or drinking, or fornication, or with any other thing whatsoever; and transgress ye not My word.

And straightway there were given unto them with His word flesh, and blood, and a heart of the children of men. And they were content to leave the height of heaven, and they came down to earth, to the folly of the dancing of the children of CAIN with all their work of the artisan, which they had made in the folly of their fornication, and to their singings, which they accompanied with the tambourine, and the flutes, and the pipes, and much shouting, and loud cries of joy and noisy songs.

And their daughters were there, and they enjoyed the orgies without shame, for they scented themselves for the men who pleased them, and they lost the balance in their minds. And the men did not restrain themselves for a moment, but they took to wife from among the women those whom they had chosen, and committed sin with them. For God hath no resting-place in the hearts of the arrogant and those who revile, but He abideth in the hearts of the humble and those who are sincere.

And He spake in the Gospel, saying, Woe be unto those who make themselves righteous, and despise their neighbours. And again He saith, God loveth the humble, and He holdeth lightly those who magnify themselves. And straightway God was wroth with them, and He bound them in the terror of SHEÔL until the day of redemption, as the Apostle saith, He treated His angels with severity. He spared them not, but made them to dwell in a state of judgement, and they were fettered until the Great Day. The word of God conquered, Who had fashioned ADAM in His likeness (or, form), and those who had reviled and made a laughingstock of ADAM were conquered. And the daughters of CAIN with whom the angels had companied conceived, but they were unable to bring forth their children, and they died. And of the children who were in their wombs some died, and some came forth; having split open the bellies of their mothers they came forth by their navels.

And when they were grown up and reached man's estate they became giants, whose height reached unto the clouds; and for their sakes and the sakes of sinners the wrath of God became quiet, and He said, My spirit shall only rest on them for one hundred and twenty years, and I will destroy them with the waters of the Flood, them and all sinners who have not believed the word of God. And to those who believed the word of their fathers, and did His Will, no injury came from the waters of the Flood.

Kebra Nagast, 100

According to Enoch, 200 angels descended upon Mt. Ermon and agreed to take of themselves wives from the daughters of man. They made mutual imprecations agreeing in pact to commit to the course of interfering with the affairs of humanity. They knew that their decision to fornicate with Earthly women would essentially amount to an unpardonable sin from which there was no turning back. Regardless, they agreed to assume this path and to deal with the consequences of it.

It was their invasion that leads to the birth of an abominable race of bloodthirsty, human-flesh-eating giants that became known as the men of renown for uncanny size and semi-divine like abilities.

And it came to pass when the children of men had multiplied that in those days were born unto them beautiful and comely daughters. And the angels, the children of the heaven, saw and lusted after them, and said to one another: 'Come, let us choose us wives from among the children of men and beget us children.' And Semjaza, who was their leader, said unto them: 'I fear ye will not indeed agree to do this deed, and I alone shall have to pay the penalty of a great sin.' And they all answered him and said: 'Let us all swear an oath, and all bind ourselves by mutual imprecations not to abandon this plan but to do this thing.' Then sware they all together and bound themselves by mutual imprecations upon it. And they were in all two hundred; who descended in the days of Jared on the summit of Mount Hermon, and they called it Mount Hermon, because they had sworn and bound themselves by mutual imprecations upon it.

The Book of Enoch, 6:1-7

Once upon the Earth, the fallen watchers join Satan and his minions in meddling into the affairs of humanity. Their intercession led to every evil abomination being loosed upon the world stage. After the birth of their hybrid children, the fallen watchers, along with the rebel angels, set to task establishing themselves as gods to be worshiped like unto the Most High.

They were the ones responsible for the founding of many of the early post-flood civilizations such as Atlantis, Sumer, Babylon, Egypt, and Indian empires. Their access to heavenly wisdom and knowledge of stars, planets, and harvests made it easy to ascertain control over human populations and areas. By limiting the amount and depth of knowledge available, they had an easy time of controlling and manipulating what essentially became reality for the masses. Their own they would educate through priestly rites of initiation and limited enrollment into secretive mystery schools.

This allowed them to control the flow of information and what was available as education to the elect and masses. Control of knowledge and educational systems easily enabled them to guard and maintain who would or wouldn't bid their will in serving their interests against our own. They were and are responsible for having lead humanity wayward throughout all the generations of humankind, duping many cultures and peoples into worshiping false idols. The main goal of their polytheistic teaching structure has been and always will be to distort the true prophecies and knowledge of the one true God and how He has established a plan for creation through the coming and second coming of Yahushuah Savior Messiah. Not only are they attempting to keep people from knowing about their

Creator, they are also hiding anything that is associated to His Son and the deliverance of salvation unto the children of this world born of woman. Their wish is to hide the revelation of the End Times judgment and take with them to the pits as many flesh-incarnated souls as possible.

Kingdoms and kingship were fostered as ways to enslave peoples to the desire and whims of the elect who, more often than not, serve the bidding of the rebel angels. Since the Tower of Babel attempt, Lucifer has been deceiving the peoples of the world into setting up one world order or global governmental type system in which to oppress the masses. The rebel angels have never had trouble finding those willing to serve evil. Since ancient times a select few have been confided with hidden knowledge and granted special privilege. Certain initiates have been utilized by the fallen ones to predict seasons, equinoxes, eclipses, and other celestial phenomenon as a way to maintain the celebration of certain festivals and times of year. The prediction of celestial events was utilized to trick the masses into supporting the often Luciferian blood rites. The divine right of kings was installed as way of centralizing power into the hands of those whom had been selected by them to rule with impunity the extent of their conquered world. The Illuminati families serving the fallen ones are dedicated to enslaving the masses and controlling us through trade, commerce, government, politics, and even religion. Yahweh tolerates their attempt to illustrate to the rest of the world why He alone is worthy of being worshiped as the Most High God.

Without His just guidance and lawful compassion to rule over the universes, the natural order would be one of chaos and suffering in which righteousness, justice, law, order, peace, and harmony could not exist because of the prevalence of humanity to be led astray in committing evil. The band of watchers that abandoned their estate are the sons of God, spoken of in the Book of Enoch.

This same story confirmed by Genesis:

And it came to pass, when men began to multiply on the face of the earth, and daughters were born unto them, That the sons of God saw the daughters of men that they were fair; and they took them wives of all which they chose. And the Lord said, My spirit shall not always strive with man, for that he also is flesh: yet his days shall be an hundred and twenty years. There were giants in the earth in those days; and also after that, when the sons of God came in unto the daughters of men, and they bare children to them, the same became mighty men which were of old, men of renown. And GOD saw that the wickedness of man was great in the earth, and that every imagination of the thoughts of his heart was only evil continually. And it repented the Lord that he had made man on the earth, and it grieved him at his heart.

Genesis 6:1-6 (KJV)

The same story from the *Book of Jubilees*:

And it came to pass when the children of men began to multiply on the face of the earth and daughters were born unto them, that the angels of God saw them on a certain year of this jubilee, that they were beautiful to look upon; and they took themselves wives of all whom they chose, and they bare unto them sons and they were Giants.

And lawlessness increased on the earth and all flesh corrupted its way, alike men and cattle and beasts and birds and everything that walks on the earth all of them corrupted their ways and their orders, and they began to devour each other, and lawlessness increased on the earth and every imagination of the thoughts of all men (was) thus evil continually. And God looked upon the earth, and behold it was corrupt, and all flesh had corrupted its orders, and all that were upon the earth had wrought all manner of evil before His eyes.

The Book of Jubilees 5:1-2

It is of utmost importance that every seeker delve into the details of this one story, for in understanding it one will recognize its relationship to ancient mythology, the origins of evil, and how that evil came to be *reality* for humanity. It is absolutely essential to understand who the fallen watchers were and how their meddling led to the introduction of all abomination on the world stage. In order for one to understand where we are now and where we are going, one must comprehend this ancient tale with all of its implications to understand what humanity will soon be dealing with again as the Lord predicted that as it was in the days of Noah, so shall it be in the days of the second coming of the Son of Man.

> For owing to these three things came the flood upon the earth, namely, owing to the fornication wherein the Watchers against the law of their ordinances went a whoring after the daughters of men, and took themselves wives of all which they chose: and they made the beginning of uncleanness. And they begat sons the Naphidim, and they were all unlike, and they devoured one another: and the Giants slew the Naphil, and the Naphil slew the Eljo, and the Eljo mankind, and one man another. And every one sold himself to work iniquity and to shed much blood, and the earth was filled with iniquity. And after this they sinned against the beasts and birds, and all that moves and walks on the earth: and much blood was shed on the earth, and every imagination and desire of men imagined vanity and evil continually.
>
> The Book of Jubilees 7:21

Unless one understands this single aspect of our ancient past, one will be left in a quandary trying to explicate how evil came into the world and how we—as creatures and a race—got to be where we are now. And while most would exclude stories of giants as nothing other than child's lore, skeletons of six-fingered, six-toed giants with double sets of teeth have been found all over the planet and have been alluded to throughout the oral traditions of all cultures living across the globe.

These ancient tales cite how giants came into being, who their parents are, and how their evil deeds led directly to the Lord wiping out all flesh in deluge. Most Christians still do not understand that the flood was brought upon the world by the Lord as judgment to wipe the Earth clean of abominable human-eating giants. Most people cannot tell you why the flood was allowed as judgment by the Lord and why it was that He established a new covenant with Noah in which He strictly forbid the consumption of any flesh that had blood within it.

> And all the others together with them took unto themselves wives, and each chose for himself one, and they began to go in unto them and to defile themselves with them, and they taught them charms and enchantments, and the cutting of roots, and made them acquainted with plants. And they became pregnant, and they bare great giants, whose height was three thousand ells: Who consumed all the acquisitions of men. And when men could no longer sustain them, the giants turned against them and devoured mankind. And they began to sin against birds, and beasts, and reptiles, and fish, and to devour one another's flesh, and drink the blood. Then the earth laid accusation against the lawless ones.
>
> The Book of Enoch, 7

A little known Pseudipigraphal book called *The Book of the Baruch* not only discusses the results of the deluge and its ravages upon land, it even mentions in total number how many from the various giant tribes perished in the flood of Noah's day.

The different translations number the giant dead as being different sums, yet these scriptures taken together show just how numerous their numbers were and how the deluge and their presence upon the globe are tied directly together. Most Christians still assume it was the wickedness of humanity, which ominously set the tone for the flood, yet this is unfounded as the following scripture will show.

> And the angel said to me, Rightly you ask me. When God made the flood upon the earth, he drowned every firstling, and he destroyed 104 thousand giants, and the water rose 20 cubits above the mountains, and the water entered into the garden, bringing out one shoot from the vine as God withdrew the waters.
>
> Baruch 3:10, Slavonic

> And the angel said, Rightly you ask: when God caused the Flood over the earth and destroyed all flesh and 409,000 giants, and the water rose over the heights 15 cubits, the water entered Paradise and killed every flower, but it removed the sprig of the vine completely and brought it outside.
>
> Baruch 4, Greek

Once the planet cried out for respite from the incursion of the watchers, blame is ascribed to various angels who took part in the second rebellion, and punishment was to be exacted upon them and their seedline. Without the disclosure of the Book of Enoch we would not have detail of this incursion nor to whom would we ascribe the evil we see even today upon the world stage. That is why I recommend to all truth seekers to, in the least, read various extra-biblical books before placing judgment upon their authenticity or relevance. It takes much study to fill in the pieces of the jigsaw puzzle that is truth and that, in seeking, one will be lead to discernment and wisdom. Matthew 7:8 instructs, "Seek and ye shall find. Knock and the door shall be opened. For every one that asketh receiveth; and he that seeketh findeth; and to him that knocketh it shall be opened."

> And Azâzêl taught men to make swords, and knives, and shields, and breastplates, and made known to them the metals of the earth and the art of working them, and

bracelets, and ornaments, and the use of antimony, and the beautifying of the eyelids, and all kinds of costly stones, and all colouring tinctures. And there arose much godlessness, and they committed fornication, and they were led astray, and became corrupt in all their ways.

Semjâzâ taught enchantments, and root-cuttings, Armârôs the resolving of enchantments, Barâqîjâl, (taught) astrology, Kôkabêl the constellations, Ezêqêêl the knowledge of the clouds, Araqiêl the signs of the earth, Shamsiêl the signs of the sun, and Sariêl the course of the moon. And as men perished, they cried, and their cry went up to heaven.

The Book of Enoch 8:1-2

The rebel angels and fallen watchers are the so-called ancient astronauts that roamed the Earth and solar system in pre-deluge days as the pantheon of myriad gods worshiped by the Greeks, Romans, Egyptians, Hindi, and other cultures, which revered multiple gods. The reason that mythology, no matter which part of the world it is from, always relates stories about pagan gods—and their often rape or abduction of human women or men—is because, like the alien abduction phenomena of the modern day era, these things are still, as in our ancient past, happening today.

How can anyone justify such behavior as being linked to so-called higher beings? Should these beings truly be gods, would not they behave and act in accordance to the same laws and ordinances that the Most High has provided to humanity through the gospel and work of the prophets? Why then would Zeus, the so-called father of the gods, find it necessary to repeatedly rape Earthly woman when he is supposed to be some kind of supreme being? Why would a supreme being need to have anything to do with carnal lust or physical procreation at all?

It is the interaction of these fallen angels as pagan gods that leads to the teaching of all sorts of abomination upon the Earth. Their sin is so great that once the Lord does judge them, He will no longer allow them to supplicate His authority in prayer. As a consequence of their intrusion He will not forgive them and even took Enoch from among the children of men to be a witness unto their transgressions. The fallen watchers before the creation of humanity had free reign to do as they wished upon the Earth.

And then Michael, Uriel, Raphael, and Gabriel looked down from heaven and saw much blood being shed upon the earth, and all lawlessness being wrought upon the earth. And they said one to another: 'The earth made without inhabitant cries the voice of their cryingst up to the gates of heaven. And now to you, the holy ones of heaven, the souls of men make their suit, saying, Bring our cause before the Most High.' And they said to the Lord of the ages: 'Lord of lords, God of gods, King of kings, and God of the ages, the throne of Thy glory (standeth) unto all the generations of the ages, and Thy name holy and glorious and blessed unto all the ages!

Thou hast made all things, and power over all things hast Thou: and all things are naked and open in Thy sight, and Thou seest all things, and nothing can hide itself from Thee. Thou seest what Azazel hath done, who hath taught all unrighteousness on earth and revealed the eternal secrets which were (preserved) in heaven, which men were striving to learn: And Semjaza, to whom Thou hast given authority to bear rule over his associates. And they have gone to the daughters of men upon the earth, and have slept with the women, and have defiled themselves, and revealed to them all kinds of sins. And the women have borne giants, and the whole earth has thereby been filled with blood and unrighteousness.

And now, behold, the souls of those who have died are crying and making their suit to the gates of heaven, and their lamentations have ascended: and cannot cease because of the lawless deeds which are wrought on the earth. And Thou knowest all things before they come to pass, and Thou seest these things and Thou dost suffer them, and Thou dost not say to us what we are to do to them in regard to these.

The Book of Enoch, 9:1-11

Most people will dismiss these passages as fairy tale or make-believe, not wanting to look into the literal interpretation of these stories and what that might entail for seekers of truth. Most cannot even begin to fathom that angels could somehow rebel against their sovereign Lord and take wives for themselves from among the daughters of men, and yet that is the story conveyed by the underlying truth that connects all of the gospels. Many people cite this passage from Matthew 22:30, "For in the resurrection they neither marry, nor are given in marriage, but are as the angels of God in heaven," when trying to discredit the possibility that angels can have sex with women, but remember that, according to the Kebra Nagast, the Watchers implored the Lord to allow them to take on bodies of flesh, making such copulation a possibility. Even after promising to uphold their virtue, the Watchers lusted after the daughters of humanity, for which the Lord would instruct His angels to place them in darkness and force them to watch the destruction of their seed until the time of the end when they would be loosed again upon the world with the Antichrist.

They would, at the end of days, suffer the same death as the angels, which revolted during the Lucifer rebellion. For their transgression they are not allowed to implore the Lord with prayer and so ask Enoch to pray to Him on their behalf. The Lord said of Enoch's supplication, "They should pray on behalf of humans and not humans pray on behalf of them."

Though this knowledge may seem more fantasy than reality, anyone who remotely entertains the possibility that there was a rebellion of angels against the authority of the Most High—and that these rebel angels may have sired a race of giant, super beings known as men of renown—will recognize that this possibility goes a long way in explaining the vast amounts of archaeological phenomena, which modern science still cannot yet explain. Archeologists are now discovering remnants of civilizations that appeared suddenly, post deluge, out of seeming nothingness to be established in all parts of the vast world with similar pyramidal traits aligned to constellations, and at a time when humans are thought to have had no advanced technologies. These megalithic structures were not made by the ancestors of humanity, but by the hybrid children of the fallen angels—the giants of old— which is further confirmation of the gospel.

The fact that a race of giants existed sometime in our ancient past does seem to fit the remaining archaeological evidence. There are even modern-day reports of giants still living in the land within Afghanistan, surrounding mountainous region, Patagonia, remote regions of South America, and especially within the interiors of the Earth. Barry Chamish, a secular journalist from Israel, wrote and documented reports of giants landing in Israel from 1986-1999. He published his articles and eyewitness accounts in a 2010 book entitled The Return of the Giants. In his book, Barry cites the numerous articles he wrote while working as an investigative journalist during these years. His book asserts that many Isreali citizens not only reported incidents dealing with either UFO craft or with the 7-foot, round-faced giants cited as occupying them, but that scientific specimens and samples were taken and analyzed every step of the way to confirm the sightings. I interviewed Barry about his experience and book, one can find it here for more information: http://www.blogtalkradio.com/fallenangelstv/2010/07/17/barry-chamish—return-of-the-nephilim

Barry's work verifies that UFOs are associated with giants and that they are indeed returning. In "Are Giants Returning to the Holy Land?" he claims,

I have had extensive conversations with the contactees and there is much in common with their stories. That is fit subject for a separate lecture. In short, all were the same age, all were white-collar workers, three have been haunted since their encounters telepathically, all their men slept through the encounters, two women had mysterious pregnancies, etc. But the core commonality is that these women did not know each other and separately described the same seven-foot tall, bald, round-faced giants.

And if absolute proof that giants were about in Israel was needed, it came in December in the village of Yatzitz, twelve miles east of Rishon Letzion. The giants had opened a new axis after Kadima, a triangle of twenty miles linking Rishon Letzion, Holon and Yatzitz.

Herzl Casatini, the village security chief, and his friend Danny Ezra were sharing conversation when they heard an explosion and felt Ezra's house shake. Herzl opened the door and stood face to face with a nine-foot tall creature in metallic clothes, whose face was hidden in 'a haze.' He shut the door and called the police. They arrived and discovered deep boot tracks in the hard mud. The tracks sank 35 centimeters into the ground, meaning whoever made them had to have literally weighed a ton. Thinking there might have been a terrorist incursion, the army was called in. Military trackers were totally stumped. The tracks carried on for eight kilometers. The heel dug in only five centimeters, meaning that whatever made the tracks was walking almost on tip-toes—if you can call it walking. Sometimes the distance between tracks was twelve feet, meaning the intruder was a world-record-holding broad jumper, weighing about a ton.

The Yatzitz incident confirmed, even to the deepest skeptics, that giants were indeed sighted and they left proof that was nearly impossible to dispute. The best the Israeli authorities could come up with to explain the tracks was they were left by an unknown cult. It would have to be very unknown for records of cults whose ceremonies include dressing as giants and leaving miles of unidentifiable tracks are undoubtedly quite rare.

Finally I will share another credible sighting, which occurred in Voronezh, Russia. First reported in America, October 11, 1989, by the St. Louis Dispatch, the incident was originally published by the Russian newspaper TASS. According to the article, on September 27, 1989, at 6:30 P.M, eyewitnesses reported stories of as many as three different nine-foot tall, three-eyed aliens emerging from a UFO type craft that had landed on the outskirts of the city. Witnesses even spoke about a robot accompanying one of the aliens. Testimony included an entire group of schoolchildren as well as police officers.

The story continues with the school children gathering for a game of soccer when a faint pink glow descended from the skies and landed. They saw a "three-eyed alien about 10-feet tall, clad in silvery overalls and bronze-colored boots and wearing a disk on his chest... A boy screamed with fear, but when the alien gazed at him, with eyes shining, he fell silent, unable to move. Onlookers screamed, and the UFO and the creatures disappeared."

How would primitive cultures have the ability to construct such large structures and use blocks of stone, some weighing in excess of 200 tons for construction when even our modern-era heavy construction equipment cannot lift even one of these stones? Who, if not the rebel angels—with assistance from the fallen Watchers—was responsible for jumping the gun on evolution and bringing from heaven to Earth knowledge of organized society and civilization?

Knowledge about the rebel angels and the enormity of their giant children can explain how many ancient sites were constructed in megalithic fashion when modern technology to this day cannot match or even equal their feats of accomplishment. Enoch tells us that it was the fallen watchers who brought to Earth knowledge of how the mysteries of heaven worked. In utilizing their knowledge, they conspired amongst themselves to rule the world, propping themselves up as the gods to be served in worship.

That is why there is a specific commandment by the Most High not to worship idols or bow to foreign gods. I knew that I must write this book now as many people new to these stories may not have the time to sift through the wealth of information flooding in with the New Age, and being readily persuaded could risk damning their souls to hell following false doctrines. Those who follow the self serving path of Satan, or who are led astray by paganism to worship the idol gods or fallen angels, will join them in condemnation when the Lord returns for judgment.

Having researched for the past two decades much of what is available, as far as ancient mythologies and religions, my hope is to provide elucidation where one might be confused trying to make sense of the current revelations coming out from individuals like Zecharia Sitchin, Michael Tsarion, and others who espouse that the Annunaki, aliens, or ancient astronauts genetically manipulated our race and that these extra-terrestrials are our gods.

While I agree that, yes, Annunaki have been and are currently trying to alter humanity genetically, I will contest that those manipulations were never for the advancement or betterment of humankind and that their experiments have only served to dumb down humanity, making us easier to manage and control. I attest that their manipulations have only been to oppress the human race at every step in our evolution and that, in keeping us oppressed, they could themselves manage control of the planet and its resources.

The fact that humanity still denies their existence, even in the face of insurmountable evidence, verifies how successful they have been at concealing their presence from the masses. Regardless, soon all the peoples of the world will be forced not only to acknowledge their presence, but to discern as to whether their presence is malevolent or benevolent to our own existence.

And he made a plan with his powers. He sent his angels to the daughters of men, that they might take some of them for themselves and raise offspring for their enjoyment. And at first they did not succeed. When they had no success, they gathered together again and they made a plan together. They created a counterfeit spirit, who resembles the Spirit who had descended, so as to pollute the souls through it. And the angels changed themselves in their likeness into the likeness of their mates (the daughters of men), filling them with the spirit of darkness, which they had mixed for them, and with evil. They brought gold and silver and a gift and copper and iron and metal and all kinds of things. And they steered the people who had followed them into great troubles, by leading them astray with many deceptions. They (the people) became old without having enjoyment. They died, not having found truth and without knowing the God of truth. And thus the whole creation became enslaved forever, from the foundation of the world until now. And they took women and begot children out of the darkness according to the likeness of their spirit. And they closed their hearts, and they hardened themselves through the hardness of the counterfeit spirit until now.

The Apocryphon of John

The rebel angels through the elect and divine right of rule were able to institute a variety of kingdoms and kingships throughout the world, in which they established their own hybrid seed lines as vicars to the 'gods.' They did this as a way of manipulating conflict and as a way of fomenting wars using the ancient Luciferian strategy of divide and rule. In discerning truth one must be especially careful to not be misled when studying the historical accounts of those cultures that were under the influence of the fallen Watchers established early in Earth history. Those civilizations always depicted those from heaven who came to the Earth as deliverers of wisdom and bringers of civilization. Many of these civilizations were organized with the purposeful intent of confusing the masses so as to be able to hide the truth about the Son of God, and the salvation the Messiah would and did bring to the world. Many of the cultures that were reseeded by beings from the heavens post deluge ended up being involved in some way with human sacrifice, blood rituals, and sometimes even cannibalism. More often than not, those cultures and civilizations—which were established by either Lucifer or the fallen angels—were pervasively involved in what Yahweh termed as "abominable behavior."

"And thou shalt not let any of thy seed pass through the fire to Molech, neither shalt thou profane the name of thy God: I am the LORD" (Leviticus 18:21, KJV).

> When thou art come into the land which the LORD thy God giveth thee, thou shalt not learn to do after the abominations of those nations. There shall not be found among you any one that maketh his son or his daughter to pass through the fire, or that useth divination, or an observer of times, or an enchanter, or a witch, Or a charmer, or a consulter with familiar spirits, or a wizard, or a necromancer.
>
> Deuteronomy 18:9-11 (KJV)

The Pseudipigraphal and apocryphal texts are the scriptural foundation by which one can fully elucidate the vague account of Genesis 6 and the fallen angel interdiction into the affairs of humanity. There are literally multiple passages from multitudinous sources that reveal the same story as the one related by Enoch. Without knowledge of who the fallen watchers were and how the behavior of their giant children ties in with the global deluge, we would simply have no way of comprehending the ancient world around us. And we definitely would not understand who and what forces were and are responsible for the evil found in the world then, now, and until the harvest at the end of days.

At the time of the judgment the righteous elect will receive the gift of everlasting life and replace the rebel angels fated for destruction that held not their first estate but decided instead to "go a whoring after the daughters of men." Without the clarity of Enoch exposing the actions of the Fallen Watchers, humanity would be left in a serious dilemma trying to explicate why God would allow evil to come about naturally as part of the universal order. The Book of Enoch tells us that evil is wholly unnatural, that those responsible for that evil had been allotted only a certain time to exist, and that once this period of time had passed the Lord would send his Son Yahushuah Savior Messiah to judge the sins of the world. While many seekers may consider this revelation too *new age* or fanciful to have a basis in reality, the New Testament hints at this same story:

> I will therefore put you in remembrance, though ye once knew this, how that the Lord, having saved the people out of the land of Egypt, afterward destroyed them that believed not. And the angels which kept not their first estate, but left their own habitation, he hath reserved in everlasting chains under darkness unto the judgment of the great day. Even as Sodom and Gomorrha, and the cities about them in like manner, giving themselves over to fornication, and going after strange flesh, are set forth for an example, suffering the vengeance of eternal fire. Likewise also these filthy dreamers defile the flesh, despise dominion, and speak evil of dignities...
>
> Raging waves of the sea, foaming out their own shame; wandering stars, to whom is reserved the blackness of darkness for ever. And Enoch also, the seventh from Adam, prophesied of these, saying, Behold, the Lord cometh with ten thousands of his saints, To execute judgment upon all, and to convince all that are ungodly among them of all their ungodly deeds which they have ungodly committed, and of all their hard speeches which ungodly sinners have spoken against him.

> Jude 1:6-9, 13-15

For if God spared not the angels that sinned, but cast them down to hell, and delivered them into chains of darkness, to be reserved unto judgment; And spared not the old world, but saved Noah the eighth person, a preacher of righteousness, bringing in the flood upon the world of the ungodly; And turning the cities of Sodom and Gomorrha into ashes condemned them with an overthrow, making them an ensample unto those that after should live ungodly; And delivered just Lot, vexed with the filthy conversation of the wicked: (For that righteous man dwelling among them, in seeing and hearing, vexed his righteous soul from day to day with their unlawful deeds;) The Lord knoweth how to deliver the godly out of temptations, and to reserve the unjust unto the day of judgment to be punished.

2 Peter 2:5-9 (KJV)

"For we wrestle not against flesh and blood, but against principalities, against powers, against the rulers of the darkness of this world, against spiritual wickedness in high places" (Ephesians 6:12).

THE REALITY OF
THE RULERS

Most individuals raised in the modern world have minimal, if any, contact with what is the considered the supernatural or divine. Most are raised in worlds where people pursue life through the daily grind of school, work, family, and simple survival of the fittest. Today, many have a hard enough time just trying to feed self and family or draw money enough to pay monthly bills. Most do not have the luxury of time necessary to seek God in a meaningful way. Survival has taken precedence over all other pursuits in life, and without time to seek truth or God, pursuit of the mystical is relegated to a secondary priority, if given any priority at all. Life being the way it is, many will never seek the kingdom or understand the larger questions for our being here on this planet and at this special time.

Please know that I in no way am belittling or judging how others choose to live out their lives; I am simply trying to make a point that the superficial things that consume the focus of so many cannot redeem one's spirit for entrance into the kingdom of heaven. Salvation for those that do their homework is the whole reason for our being in the flesh at this time. That is why I feel it's important for all of us to take up the cross as much as possible, placing the Lord first and foremost in life to what degree one can, and—in true repentance—cry out to the Lord in a way that transforms one to a holy way of life in which Christ can then inhabit the temple of our flesh. What most do not realize is that our bodies are woven into a multi-dimensional matrix where the invisible and visible worlds overlap, allowing us to interact with invisible and visible beings. This world is a plane of trial and tribulation where those fortunate to incarnate into flesh would, through lifetime, decide by action, thought, and behavior just what inheritance will await them at the end of days when the Lord returns to harvest the spirits of those angels and humanity that rebelled against Him. As fallen sons of God, we are inheritors of this temporal world as a result of our ancestors fall into flesh. Here one must realize that, as entrapped spiritual beings, we live amongst devils and demons under the rule of Satan.

We are merely visitors to this world of material illusion where economics, wealth, assets, and money thwart justice and the rule of law. In this world Satan gives his perverted authority to those whom he wishes, usually choosing cold-blooded and sadistic individuals from the Kainite hybrid lines he sired into being to rule and oppress the sons of Seth. Called the Grail or Merovingian lines, the descendants claim kinship to Cain, Ham, Tubal-Cain, and Canaan; they are they whom Satan appoints to occupy various thrones, titles, presidencies, and prime-ministerships. Those that are the most sadistic, cruel, cold-hearted, and ready to commit evil are appointed the arbiters of power and control for the tentacles of the New World Order. Even today, most of the kings and queens of this world are blood-related descendants of the line of Cain. They are the synagogue of Satan that "say they are Jews but are not" that the Lord speaks about in Revelation 2:9 and 3:9. They are the Rothschild power behind Zionism and the controllers of modern-day Israel, a nation which proudly displays on its flag, the seal of Solomon—the six pointed star of Saturn, Kronos, or Satan.

It's important to understand that the enmity between the seed of the serpent and the seed of the woman is an ancient war of a spiritual nature fought between the angels of Yahweh and the angels of

Lucifer, and that we wrestle not against flesh and blood but powers principalities: the rulers of darkness that are not of this world. The eye at the top of the Illuminati pyramid, the unseen hand behind the tentacles of the New World order, the force for who kings, queens, presidents, and prime ministers dance on a string—is Lucifer the puppet master, Oz behind the scenes controlling the show and out-come for his own demented self pleasure. It's my opinion that the antichrist also, though a system, will be an inter-dimensional being of supernatural ability possessed directly by the spirit of Lucifer as Abbaddon, Apollyon. He will return with Niburu, the Wormwood of Revelation 8, and direct the wrath of the locust army as it devas-tates and destroys those not written into the Book of Life. Whether this invasion is of the Nordic giant-humanoid type, dragon-reptoid-alien-fish type, or predator-insect-locust-breathe-fire-sting-in-their-tails type of alien, we won't know until the event horizon, yet I pray daily that the Lord count all of us worthy enough to not be here for the return of the Nephilim and Niburu.

To understand what we are dealing with in our modern world as the alien abduction phenomena, seekers must understand the full meaning and implications of Genesis 6, which discusses the fallen angels mating with the daughters of Cain and creating a race of giants as this phenomenon is repeated over and over throughout the world's religions and mythologies.

"For we wrestle not against flesh and blood, but against principali-ties, against powers, against the rulers of the darkness of this world, against spiritual wickedness in high places" (Ephesians 6:12, KJV).

> On account of the reality of the authorities, (inspired) by the spirit of the father of truth, the great apostle—referring to the authorities of the darkness—told us that our con-test is not against flesh and blood; rather, the authorities of the universe and the spirits of wickedness. I have sent this (to you) because you inquire about the reality of the authorities. Their chief is blind; because of his power and

his ignorance and his arrogance he said, with his power, It is I who am God; there is none apart from me.

When he said this, he sinned against the entirety. And this speech got up to incorruptibility; then there was a voice that came forth from incorruptibility, saying, You are mistaken, Samael—which is, god of the blind. And this (is the reason) that you will fight against the powers, because they do not have rest like you, since they do not wish that you be saved.

The Letter of Peter to Phillip

According to the word of the Lord, we know that the visible realms were preceded by the invisible realms and that all things material had their basis in pure energy, which is the Great Spirit, Great Mystery, or Father of us all. To better explain the splintering off of the visible worlds from the invisible, I will relate the story of Sophia and her fall according to the Gnostic texts. This will help the reader understand how these teachings tie into and fit with all of the other available texts out there, including the Old and New Testament, Apocryphal, and Psuedipigraphal writings.

Then the apostles worshiped again saying, Lord, tell us: In what way shall we fight against the archons, since the archons are above us? Then a voice called out to them from the appearance saying, Now you will fight against them in this way, for the archons are fighting against the inner man. And you are to fight against them in this way: Come together and teach in the world the salvation with a promise. And you, gird yourselves with the power of my Father, and let your prayer be known. And he, the Father, will help you as he has helped you by sending me. Be not afraid, I am with you forever, as I previously said to you when I was in the body. Then there came lightning and thunder from heaven, and what appeared to them in that place was taken up to heaven.

The Letter of Peter to Phillip

Many biblical researchers have never heard of Sophia-Pistis and as such cannot make sense of the stories related by the Nag Hammadi codices. It is important to note that these teachings come directly from Yahushuah to the twelve apostles after His resurrection when, as Christ, He returned to teach the mysteries of heaven before departing in ascension. These teachings are considered the newest New Testament apocrypha and cover mysteries, secrets, and insights that were, as then, mostly untouched by earlier gospels and teachings. Yahushuah even says within these codices that whereas He had used parables to impart wisdom before, He would now speak plainly and with precision to His disciples about inheriting the kingdom of the Father. In the next few chapters I will relate the gnostic story of creation according to the Nag Hammadi codices to illustrate what happened during the time and space between the creation of the heavenly realms and the lower realms.

> Mary said to him: Holy Lord, where did your disciples come from, and where are they going, and (what) should they do here? The Perfect Savior said to them: I want you to know that Sophia, the Mother of the Universe and the consort, desired by herself to bring these to existence without her male (consort).
>
> But by the will of the Father of the Universe, that his unimaginable goodness might be revealed, he created that curtain between the immortals and those that came afterward, that the consequence might follow ... [BG 118:] ... every aeon and chaos—that the defect of the female might <appear>, and it might come about that Error would contend with her. And these became the curtain of spirit. From <the> aeons above the emanations of Light, as I have said already, a drop from Light and Spirit came down to the lower regions of Almighty in chaos, that their molded forms might appear from that drop, for it is a judgment on him, Arch-Begetter, who is called 'Yaldabaoth'.

That drop revealed their molded forms through the breath, as a living soul. It was withered and it slumbered in the ignorance of the soul. When it became hot from the breath of the Great Light of the Male, and it took thought, (then) names were received by all who are in the world of chaos, and all things that are in it through that Immortal One, when the breath blew into him. But when this came about by the will of Mother Sophia—so that Immortal Man might piece together the garments there for a judgment on the robbers—<he> then welcomed the blowing of that breath; but since he was soul-like, he was not able to take that power for himself until the number of chaos should be complete, (that is,) when the time determined by the great angel is complete.

The Sophia of Jesus Christ

And when these things had come to pass, then Pistis came and appeared over the matter of chaos, which had been expelled like an aborted fetus—since there was no spirit in it. For all of it (chaos) was limitless darkness and bottomless water. Now when Pistis saw what had resulted from her defect, she became disturbed. And the disturbance appeared, as a fearful product; it rushed to her in the chaos. She turned to it and blew into its face in the abyss, which is below all the heavens.

And when Pistis Sophia desired to cause the thing that had no spirit to be formed into a likeness and to rule over matter and over all her forces, there appeared for the first time a ruler, out of the waters, lion-like in appearance, androgynous, having great authority within him, and ignorant of whence he had come into being. Now when Pistis Sophia saw him moving about in the depth of the waters, she said to him, Child, pass through to here, whose equivalent is 'yalda baoth'.

On The Origin of the World

Who was and is Pistis-Sophia? According to Yahushuah, Pistis Sophia is the sacred daughter, bride, consort, and feminine aspect of the androgynous holy child Christ. Some texts say that she descended from the thirteenth aeon, chasing the false light of Lucifer the fallen cherub, Prince of the air and Lord of the earth. It is also said that, in her motherly nature, she desired to bring forth a child. Her desire became so insatiable that Sophia births for herself an abomination, an aborted fetus of a being that came to be known as Yaldaboath. After her fall, she was established as the veil between the higher authorities and the angels of the twelve constellations of this dimensional reality.

> And the Sophia of the Epinoia, being an aeon, conceived a thought from herself and the conception of the invisible Spirit and foreknowledge. She wanted to bring forth a likeness out of herself without the consent of the Spirit,—he had not approved—and without her consort, and without his consideration. And though the person of her maleness had not approved, and she had not found her agreement, and she had thought without the consent of the Spirit and the knowledge of her agreement, (yet) she brought forth. And because of the invincible power which is in her, her thought did not remain idle, and something came out of her which was imperfect and different from her appearance, because she had created it without her consort. And it was dissimilar to the likeness of its mother, for it has another form. And when she saw (the consequences of) her desire, it changed into a form of a lion-faced serpent.
>
> And its eyes were like lightning fires which flash. She cast it away from her, outside that place, that no one of the immortal ones might see it, for she had created it in ignorance. And she surrounded it with a luminous cloud, and she placed a throne in the middle of the cloud that no one might see it except the holy Spirit who is called the mother of the living. And she called his name Yaltabaoth.—The Apocyphon of John

After the natural structure of the immortal beings had completely developed out of the infinite, a likeness then emanated from Pistis (Faith); it is called Sophia (Wisdom). It exercised volition and became a product resembling the primeval light. And immediately her will manifested itself as a likeness of heaven, having an unimaginable magnitude; it was between the immortal beings and those things that came into being after them, like [...]: she (Sophia) functioned as a veil dividing mankind from the things above.

On the Origin of the World

When light and darkness separated, two opposing sets of ruling authorities come into being. Satan as Yaldaboath was leader of the lower angels, which when brought into being did not realize that there was an invisible hierarchy—that far surpassed them in greatness—hidden everywhere above and around them. Whether he lied or deceived those angels under his control, the text does not say, yet we know that he was granted authority over the fallen ones and that the Bible states that this authority was given to Satan as the fallen cherub Lucifer. He even tempted the Lord with offering of the entirety of the world if He would just give reverence to him.

What is most interesting about Yaldaboath, however, is that the codices attest his being leader of a certain class of angels called the seraphim. The seraphim were a serpent-reptilian-dragon-like race of angels that rebelled with Satan. The reason I mention this is because a lot of so-called experts on the Gnostic texts claim that the Gnostic community as a whole believe that Yaldaboath is Yahweh of the Old Testament.

I believe that this lie is being perpetuated by the same forces that so long ago stripped so much of what is now called apocryphal or pseudepigrapha books out of what was then the canon of our Bible. The rulers have always tried to keep knowledge from the masses so that truth can be hidden and reality determined by the same aforementioned controllers. The goal for the Illuminati, as in the past, is to keep seekers from delving into this information, and prevent any study of it. The Gnostic texts, for those that read them, refer many times to the fact that the angels serving Yaldaboath are indeed the Seraphim Angels. We know that the Seraphim Angels, according to the Bible, fell with and served under the cherub Lucifer, verifying that they are both the same being.

> But Yaldabaoth possessed a multitude of faces, adding up to more than all of them, so that when he is in the midst of the seraphim, he could masquerade in front of them all at will. He shared with them (portions) from his fire. Because of the power of the glory which dwells in him from the light of his Mother. He became Lord over them. Because of that, he called himself God, and he was not obedient to the place from which he had come.
>
> On The Origin of the World

> But it came to pass in course of time the evil voice (Satan) encompassed the earth about with serpents that spake like men and angels, and the serpents made friends with All Evil, Father of Anra'mainyus; and the women of the tribes of A'su went and tempted the first men, the I'hins, whereby there was born into the world evil offspring.
>
> The Lord's Fifth Book

Having fallen, Sophia was established as a veil between the higher firmament of the invisible, imperishable realms of light and the lower, visible firmament of perishability until that time when the male aspect of the Christ, Yahushuah, returns to restore her to full authority. Most of the gnostic texts say that Sophia matter is the mother of Yaldaboath, also called Sakla (blind god) and Samael (angel of death). Yaldaboath, Satan, and Lucifer, are all names of the same being and refer to the same story.

According to the codices, Yaldaboath was not witness to the higher realms coming into being but, as first ruler of the lower visible realms, created a host of demonic forces which mirrored in duality the heavenly kingdom. Infused by the power that Sophia surrendered in bringing him to existence as the first child of the lower order, he believed and announced himself "god."

> Sophia taketh the lion-faced power of Self-willed for the true Light. It came to pass then thereafter that she looked below and saw his light-power in the parts below; and she knew not that it is that of the triple-powered Self-willed, but she thought that it came out of the light which she had seen from the beginning in the height, which came out of the veil of the Treasury of the Light. And she thought to herself: I will go into that region without my pair and take the light and thereout fashion for myself light-æons, so that I may go to the Light of lights, which is in the Height of heights.
>
> This then thinking, she went forth from her own region, the thirteenth æon, and went down to the twelve æons. The rulers of the æons pursued her and were enraged against her, because she had thought of grandeur. And she went forth also from the twelve æons, and came into the regions of the chaos and drew nigh to that lion-faced light-power to devour it. But all the material emanations of Self-willed surrounded her, and the great lion-faced light-power devoured all the light-powers in Sophia and cleaned out her light and devoured it, and her matter was thrust into the chaos; it became a lion-faced ruler in the chaos, of which one half is fire and the other darkness,— that is Yaldabaoth, of whom I have spoken unto you many times. When then this befell, Sophia became very greatly exhausted, and that lion-faced light-power set to work to take away from Sophia all her light-powers, and all the material powers of Self-willed surrounded Sophia at the same time and pressed her sore.
>
> Pistis Sophia 31

We are told by Yahushuah that Pistis Sophia descended toward Yaldaboath, attempting to retrieve the light that went out of her in birthing him and all matter into being. She thought that if she could seize her power that she could return to the height of heights to be reunited with the light of lights, which she had willingly departed. Being caught in the lower realms, she finds herself persecuted by Yaldaboath as he attempts to pilfer all of her power and establish his own authority among the lower angels. It's my opinion that Yaldaboath is the Lucifer that Yahushuah witnessed fall like lightning from heaven, and whether or not his mind was stripped clean like humanity's when he fell, he forgot about the authorities above him, or in arrogance he simply denies them; those that come to be under his authority are ignorant of those above them and readily accept Satan as a god, bowing to his rule.

> And I was in that region, mourning and seeking after the light which I had seen in the height. And the guards of the gates of the æons searched for me, and all who remain in their mystery mocked me. But I looked up unto the height towards thee and had faith in thee.
>
> Now, therefore, O Light of lights, I am sore pressed in the darkness of chaos. If now thou wilt come to save me,—great is thy mercy,—then hear me in truth and save me. Save me out of the matter of this darkness, that I may not be submerged therein, that I may be saved from the emanations of god Self-willed which press me sore, and from their evil doings. Let not this darkness submerge me, and let not this lion-faced power entirely devour the whole of my power, and let not this chaos shroud my power.
>
> Hear me, O Light, for thy grace is precious, and look down upon me according to the great mercy of thy Light. Turn not thy face from me, for I am exceedingly tormented. Haste thee, hearken unto me and save my power.
>
> Pistis Sophia

This is the first archon who took a great power from his mother. And he removed himself from her and moved away from the places in which he was born. He became strong and created for himself other aeons with a flame of luminous fire which (still) exists now. And he joined with his arrogance which is in him and begot authorities for himself.

Apocryphon of John

Having been cast out of the higher realms and having created a whole host of lower order demons, Yaldaboath considers himself the god of all. He then, with his demons, further oppresses Sophia, attempting to steal the spark of divine light in her, which is the Father. Yaldaboath, like a vampire, slowly drained her of her light until she began to feel that she would be extinguished from existence altogether and, desperate to repent, called upon the light of lights, pleading the Father to send His Son Christ to redeem her of her fallen state.

This ruler, by being androgynous, made himself a vast realm, an extent without limit. And he contemplated creating offspring for himself, and created for himself seven offspring, androgynous just like their parent. And he said to his offspring, It is I who am god of the entirety.

The Hypostasis of the Archons

But Yaltabaoth had a multitude of faces, more than all of them, so that he could put a face before all of them, according to his desire, when he is in the midst of seraphs. He shared his fire with them; therefore he became lord over them. Because of the power of the glory he possessed of his mother's light, he called himself God. And he did not obey the place from which he came. And he united the seven powers in his thought with the authorities which were with him.

Apocryphon of John

And they were completed from this heaven to as far up as the sixth heaven, namely that of Sophia. The heaven and his earth were destroyed by the troublemaker that was below them all (Destruction of Tiamat). And the six heavens shook violently; for the forces of chaos knew who it was that had destroyed the heaven that was below them. And when Pistis knew about the breakage resulting from the disturbance, she sent forth her breath and bound him and cast him down into Tartaros. Since that day, the heaven, along with its earth, has consolidated itself through Sophia the daughter of Yaldabaoth, she who is below them all.

On the Origin of the World

MANUSCRIPT B

Fragment 1

(9) [... 1 saw Watchers]

(10) in my vision, the dream-vision. Two (men) were fighting over me, saying ...

(11) and holding a great contest over me. I asked them, 'Who are you, that you are thus empo[wered over me?' They answered me, 'We]

(12) [have been em]powered and rule over all mankind.' They said to me, 'Which of us do yo[u choose to rule (you)?' I raised my eyes and looked.]

(13) [One] of them was terr[i]fying in his appearance, [like a serpent, [his] cl[oa]k many-colored yet very dark...

(14) [And I looked again], and ... in his appearance, his visage like a viper, and [wearing ...]

15) [exceedingly, and all his eyes ...]

Fragment 2

(1) [... em]powered over you ...

(2) [I replied to him,] 'This [Watcher,] who is he?' He answered me, 'This Wa[tcher ...]

(3) [and his three names are Belial and Prince of Darkness] and King of Evil.' I said, 'My lord, what dom[inion ...?']

(4) ['and his every way is darkened, his every work da[rk]ened. In Darkness he ...

(5) [Yo]u saw, and he is empowered over all Darkness, while I [am empowered over all light.]

(6) [... from] the highest regions to the lowest I rule over all Light, and over al[1 that is of God. I rule over (every) man]

Testament of Amram

FLYING FIERY SERPENTS

Recently one of my Bulgarian listeners, Alexander Beatus, sent to me an interesting text that has not even yet been released to Western culture in English translation. Dr. Stephen Guide, in his series entitled *The Thracian Script Decoded Books One through Four*, deciphered the ancient Thracian hieroglyphic writing system, which he claims precedes Sumerian cuneiform by 1,000 to 1,500 years. In decoding this script we are introduced to the first post-flood civilization established after the biblical deluge of Noah's day. He also reveals a text written by a Thracian king named Sitarih (i.e., Sitalkes/Sitalk) dated 424-431 Bc called *The Book of Atam and Eua*. My new friend Alexander has taken it upon himself to translate this book into English and, having known about my keen interest in ancient texts, asked me to look it over to see what I thought.

As I read through, to my surprise I found in this very ancient text that the serpent in paradise, the *nachash* of Genesis 3 that everybody equates to being a simple snake, is referred to as being a flying snake, a winged serpent, and the guardian of the Tree of the Knowledge of Good and Evil. This reference led me to take a closer examination of the word *nachash* and its uses in context to other serpentine references found throughout the word. I discovered that the word *nachash* (naw-khash) has special relationship to the flying fiery serpents mentioned in Isaiah, the dragons of Arabia as mentioned in 2 Esdras 15, and the cockatrice also mentioned in Isaiah. The cockatrice, according to Wikipedia, is a legendary creature that is essentially a two-legged dragon with a rooster's head. It is also related to the pheonix of egyptian mythology and the basilisk, which is depicted as king of the serpents, an upright serpent being with power to kill by fright and able to breathe fire.

> There is the same power also in the serpent called the basilisk. It is produced in the province of Cyrene, being not more than twelve fingers in length. It has a white spot on the head, strongly resembling a sort of a diadem. When it hisses, all the other serpents fly from it: and it does not advance its body, like the others, by a succession of folds, but moves along upright and erect upon the middle. It destroys all shrubs, not only by its contact, but those even that it has breathed upon; it burns up all the grass too, and breaks the stones, so tremendous is its noxious influence.

> The Natural History

The reference in the *Book of Atam and Eua* to the nachash as being a winged serpent or phoenix-like creature also lead me to look deeper into the word saraph, or seraph, which in Sanskrit means "reptile" with plural seraphim meaning "an order of angelic being." Saraf, saraph, and seraph are all singular forms of the word seraphim, which also means "burning ones" and is synonymous with the word nachash, or serpent translated into English from the Hebrew. Dr. Henery M. Morris confirms in his book *The Genesis Record* that some scholars like myself assert nachash originally meant upright, shining creature and that the word is associated with an angel or divine being who was also an enchanter.

It's important to understand that when we speak about the nachash, saraph, or seraphim that we address the distinctions between a snake and this supposed serpentine being. The serpent mentioned in Genesis 3 was a very special type of reptile in that this creature stood upright, was endowed with reason, and had the ability to communicate with Eve in language and dialogue. Not only was this nachash endowed with these certain traits, it is also mentioned as being the most cunning of the Lord's creatures in its ability to beguile or seduce others into committing sin. The serpent depicted in the garden was more like the basilisk than a snake and was associated also to seraphim, the six-winged celestial angels that had once served before the face of the Lord, but being led in rebellion by Lucifer became those rebel angels which lost their first estate during the prior rebellion and war in heaven, which occurred during the First World Age. These angels were later joined by the fallen Watchers that fell during the time of Jared, which occurred after the creation of modern day Adam and Eve and advent of the Second World Age. The seraphim angels are the nachash, dragon angels that were banished from the upper heavens by Michael and the cherubim. This order of angels is also cited in the Book of Enoch as being the drakones (δρακονεσ serpents).

In Hebrew nachash is translated "shine" as in the shine of brass, or "whisper" like in the subtle chanting of an incantation or conjuring of enchantment. The nachash was not and is not a literal snake, especially in the sense of a snake that has no arms and legs and moves about on its belly; this Nachash was, in a literal sense, a shining enchanter capable of shrewd (smooth or slick) behavior that he utilized in deceiving Eve. I firmly believe that this nachash was as suggested, an angel diviner or enchanter who, as guardian of the tree of the knowledge of good and evil, beguiled Eve into initially eating the forbidden fruit. It was only after the seduction of Eve and her sharing sin with Adam that this serpent was then placed on its belly, meaning that it had prior been able to walk upright before the curse, which stripped it of its limbs. In his curse upon the serpent, the Lord also condemned this nachash to then feed off of the dust of the earth. I believe this dust is symbolic of the dust that Adam's physical body was made from—ashes to ashes, dust to dust—and that what the Lord was alluding to in this particular passage was the fact that these dragon lords not only feed on the flesh and blood of humanity, but also demand from those that worship them the sacrifice of inno-cent human victims that they then also feed upon in frenzied ritual any time the blood of innocents is shed upon the Earth.

> Aye, when the blood was offered, forth came they to dwell among men. In the form of man moved they amongst us, but only to sight where they as are men. Serpent-headed when the glamour was lifted but appearing to man as men among men. Crept they into the Councils, taking forms that were like unto men. Slaying by their arts the chiefs of the kingdoms, taking their form and ruling o'er man. Only by magic could they be discovered. Only by sound could their faces be seen. Sought they from the kingdom of shadows to destroy man and rule in his place.
>
> Emerald Tablet 8

In studying the roots of serpent worship around the world, one will find the same story being related worldwide. Those cultures that worshiped the fallen angels as a pantheon of gods were often the ones that received high knowledge and instruction on elevating their civilization from beings that were reported as holding serpentine form, much like Quetzlcoatl and Kulkulcan. The feathered serpent is just one of the embodiments of the ancient nachash.

The roots of serpent worship precede the flood and even the creation of modern humanity upon this planet. Post flood it was the descendents of Ham, specifically the Canaanites, that were respon-sible for the re-institution of serpent worship, idolatry, and rever-ence of these fallen beings guised as the benefactors and providers of humanity post-flood.

> And he found a writing which former (generations) had carved on the rock, and he read what was thereon, and he transcribed it and sinned owing to it; for it contained the teaching of the Watchers in accordance with which they used to observe the omens of the sun and moon and stars

in all the signs of heaven. 4. And he wrote it down and said nothing regarding it; for he was afraid to speak to Noah about it lest he should be angry with him on account of it.

Jubilees 8

One can read about and trace the roots of serpent worship and idolatry to the earliest post-flood civilizations in a book called *Worship of the Serpent Traced through the World and Its Traditions Referred to the Events in Paradise,* written by John Bathurst Deane and published in 1860, for more information on the things that I have and will be mentioning here.

The nachash are the fallen angels known to us as the seraphim. They are the dragons of old, which kept not their first estate and who also established idolatry as a way to usurp the worship of the only true God, the Most High, and Creator of us all. This deception would serve to not only lead the world astray but would feed Satan and the fallen ones with the veneration they so lavishly desire in their pursuit to be as gods themselves. Idolatry as spoken of in the Wisdom of Solomon is the root of all confusion and sin. Unless one understands that idolatry is associated to the worship of these dragon lords as gods, and that this worship is directly associated to the beguiling of Eve by the nachash of Genesis 3, one would not know why the Lord hates idolatry as an institution and why the first two commandments of the ten commandments has to do with idolatry and the worship of foreign gods in placing others before Him.

Another incident of particular interest associated with the nachash is a rebellion mentioned as having taken place during the Exodus from Egypt under the leadership of Moses and Aaron by the children of Ham who, like the people of Egypt, worshiped serpents as their gods. The Egyptian gods, like the pagan gods of other nations, were the hybrid demigods born from the copulation of angels with the daughters of men. In the earliest days of our ancestors, the fallen ones appointed themselves rule over the vast cultures and civilizations that were then springing up world-wide; they were the ones that spawned the hybrid royal lines celebrated throughout all pagan nations and religions as the overseers of humanity. Those that look into these connections will find that the Egyptian gods, as well as the pharaohs that ruled over Egypt, are often depicted as partially serpentine or are depicted with serpents relating their association to and reverence for the nachash of Genesis 3.

The children of Ham, for their rebellion, were punished by the reptilian beings that they had then worshiped. For such trespass the Lord allowed the nachash that they worshiped to punish them much like that which will be repeated with the return and release of the locust army to be unveiled with the release of the four angels from the river Euphrates at the end of days. The locust army will, at that time, serve as a repeat of this particular incident in that they will also be released to punish those that still worshiped these serpent beings as the returning Annunaki star gods.

The serpents that were sent against the children of Ham as punishment were not snakes in the traditional sense of the word as the nachash of Genesis 3 was also not a simple snake. The serpents of the locust army will also not be simple snakes but will be supernatural beings utilized by the Lord to punish those not written into the Book of Life as a repeat of what happened during the Exodus.

> In return for their foolish and wicked thoughts, which led them astray to worship irrational serpents and worthless animals, thou didst send upon them a multitude of irrational creatures to punish them, that they might learn that one is punished by the very things by which he sins. For thy all-powerful hand, which created the world out of formless matter, did not lack the means to send upon them a multitude of bears, or bold lions, or newly created unknown beasts full of rage, or such as breathe out fiery breath, or belch forth a thick pall of smoke, or flash terrible sparks from their eyes; not only could their damage

exterminate men, but the mere sight of them could kill by fright.

Wisdom of Solomon 11

Notice in this passage that Solomon speaks of these serpentine beings as being able to breathe out fire and belch forth a thick pall of smoke and that these beings also have the ability to send forth sparks from their eyes in such a capacity that they can even exterminate men by the mere sight of their frightening appearance. The locust army of Revelation 9 is also described:

> Out of their mouths issued fire and smoke and brimstone. By these three was the third part of men killed, by the fire, and by the smoke, and by the brimstone, which issued out of their mouths. For their power is in their mouth, and in their tails: for their tails were like unto serpents, and had heads, and with them they do hurt. And the rest of the men which were not killed by these plagues yet repented not of the works of their hands, that they should not worship devils, and idols of gold, and silver, and brass, and stone, and of wood: which neither can see, nor hear, nor walk: Neither repented they of their murders, nor of their sorceries, nor of their fornication, nor of their thefts.

Revelation 9

Notice that at the end of days the locust army will be sent by the Lord to torment those excluded from salvation that are not written into the Book of Life. This will include the lines of Cain who are the children of the devil that are the hierarchy of the New World order, led by the hybrid blood royal elites. They are those whom shall suffer the anguish of wanting to die but are not allowed to. It is my contention that just as the children of Ham were punished by the fiery serpents during the tribulation of the Exodus, the children of Cain—who rule on the thrones of the world today—will also be punished by these same serpent-locust beings. The locust army of

SONS OF GOD

Joel 2 and Revelation 9 are released with the loosening of the four angels who were long ago bound in the river Euphrates.

These supernatural beings were detained for specific time and reason, and when the day of the Lord is at hand these star-gods will unveil themselves as the saviors, benefactors, and creators of what will be a devastated and destroyed humanity eager for global resolution. The antichrist will be one of these supernatural beings able to offer up global resolutions to solve our planetary ails. Whether the antichrist unveils himself as a physical flesh human or literally as a supernatural dragon-giant-like being, we won't know until that day and that hour; however, I do believe that the locust army will return with the unveiling of the false Christ.

The big lie that deceives even the most elect, should it be possible, is that these beings are our creators and benefactors when, throughout the duration of human history, they have worked to deceive and lead astray the children of Adam and even sought to prevent the birth of the messiah through the woman's seed. The word has warned us since time immemorial that this would be the end game for these beings and their antichrist. In fact, the sign of Revelation 12, "And there appeared a great wonder in heaven; a woman clothed with the sun, and the moon under her feet, and upon her head a crown of twelve stars: And she being with child cried, travailing in birth, and pained to be delivered" is a sign to the fallen ones that their time is up. This asrologcal sign is a celestial phenomena which will occur September 23, 2017, and is also a warning to humanity that the locust army would soon return to bring great destruction such as has not been known since the destruction of the First World Age.

In the next part of this chapter I would like to introduce the reader to important insight from a South African Zulu sangoma named Credo Mutwa, born July 21, 1920, to a Christian father and Zulu mother. At the age of fourteen, Credo was initiated by one of his grandfather's daughters, a sangoma herself taught by Credo's grandfather, an elder in traditional African wisdom.

He has conducted a few very profound interviews with David Icke and Rick Martin which, taken in tangent, provided profound insight into the ancient history of this planet and its interactions with the ancient reptilian race I term the nachash. In his traditional knowledge, Credo alludes to Satan as being a serpent, an enchanter much like the nachash as described in Genesis 3 and Wisdom of Solomon. In his tribal tongue the nachash are called the Chitauri or Chitauli, which means "the dictators, the ones who tell us the law." Referred to as Jabulon in his tradition, Satan is—according to his people—the king of the Chitauli who, like the basilisk or Medusa of Greek mythology, possesses the power to kill humans by sight. Indoctrinated into legends, mythologies, and ancient traditions, we are not privy to hear the knowledge that Credo retains, which—if delved into—will confirm the biblical account of these ancient dragon beings having been here long before modern humanity's presence upon this planet.

But, when the Chitauri arrived in Africa they told our people that they were gods and that they were going to give us human beings great gifts on one conditon. We had to worship them and accept them as our creators. Some told our people that they were our elder brothers and that this Earth had produced them generations ago. And they said they had come back to the green womb of their mother and that they were going to make us into gods.

Jabulon, sir, is a very strange god. He is supposed to be the leader of the Chitauli. He is a god, to my great surprise, which I find certain groups of White people, especially, worshipping. We have known about Jabulon for many, many centuries, we Black people. But I am surprised that there are White people who worship this god, and these people, amongst them are people whom many have blamed for all the things that have happened on this Earth, namely, the Freemason people. We believe that Jabulon is the leader of the Chitauli. He is the Old

One. And one of his names, in the African language, sir, is Umbaba-Samahongo-the lord king, the great father of the terrible eyes-because we believe that Jabulon has got one eye which, if he opens it, you die if he looks at you.

Before human beings were created on this planet, there had existed a very wise race of people known as the Imanyukela. These people had come from the constellation known to white people as Orion, and they had inhabited our earth for thousands and thousands of years. And that before they had left our earth to return once more to the sacred Spider constellation, they made a great evacuation under the earth, beneath the Ruwensory Mountains-the Mountains of the Moon. And deep in the bowels of Mother Earth, the Imanyukela built a city of copper buildings. A city with a wall of silver all around it. A city built at the huge mountain of pure crystal. The mountain of knowledge. The mountain from which all knowledge on earth comes. And a mountain to which all knowledge on earth ultimately returns.

No matter where you go in Africa, no matter how deep into the interior of the dark continent you tread, you will find very ancient stories which are incredibly similar. You will find African tribes and races who will tell you that they are descendants from gods who came out of the skies thousands of years ago. Some, however, say that theses gods came to them from the sea in magical boats made out of reeds or wood or copper or even gold. In some cases these gods and goddesses are described as beautiful human beings whose skins were either bright blue or green or even silver. But most of the time you will find it being said these great gods, especially the ones that came out of the sky were non human, scaly creatures, which lived most of the time in mud or in water. Creatures of an extremely frightening and hideously ugly appearance. Some say that these creatures were like crocodiles, with crocodile like teeth and jaws, but with very large round heads. Some say that these creatures are very tall beings with snake like heads, set on long thin necks, very long arms and very long legs. There are those that tell us that these gods who came from the skies traveled through the land in magical boats made of bright metal, silver, copper or gold. Boats which had the ability to sail over water or even to fly through the sky like birds.

Throughout Africa we are told that these mysterious beings taught human beings many things. They taught human beings how to have laws, knowledge of herbal medicine, knowledge of arts and knowledge of the mysteries of creation and the cosmos as a whole. We are told that some of these gods had the ability to change their shapes at will. They had the ability to assume the shape and the appearance of any creature that there is on earth whenever they had good reason to do so. A sky god could even turn itself into a rhinoceros and elephant or even a stork, a sky god could even turn itself into a rock or even a tree.

In Africa these mysterious gods are known by various names, in West Africa, in the land of the Bumbara people these amphibian or reptilian sky gods are known as Zishwezi. The word zishwezi means either the swimmers or the divers or the gliders. It was said that these sky gods could dive from above the clouds down to the top of a mountain whenever they felt like it, they could also take deep dives into the bottom of the ocean and from there fetch magical objects and then bring them to the shore, placing them at the feet of the astonished black people.

In the land of the Dogon people we find the famous Nommo, a race of reptilian or amphibian beings who were said to have come from the Sirius star to give knowledge and religion to the black people of Dogon. ...One is told that when the Nommo arrived from the sky in their fantastic sky ship, there were several of them, thirteen or fourteen of them. And they created a lake around their sky ship and every morning they used to swim from their sky ship to the shores of the lake and there preach to the people who assembled in large numbers around the lake. It is said that before the Nommo departed, returning with a great noise back to their home star, they first chose one of their number, killed it and cut its body up into little pieces and then gave these pieces to the assembled people to eat in the first sacrificial ritual of its kind on earth. When the people had eaten the sacred flesh of the star creature and drunk its blood mixed with water, the Nommo took the lower jaw of their creature and by some incredible fact of magic brought the whole creature back to life again. We are told that this is the way that the Nommo taught our people that there is no death and that behind every death there shall be a resurrection.

In the Americas, in South and Central America mostly, the feathered serpent is called Quetzlcoatl, and amongst my people, the Zulus, we find belief in a serpent called Yndlondlo. The Yndlondlo is said to be a huge mamba or a huge python, whose neck is covered in greyish blue feathers, like the feathers of a blue crane, and at the top of the serpents head grow three feathers. One green one, one red one and a white one which look like huge ostrich tail feathers. The Yndlondlo, like the (South) American Quetzlcoatl, is associated with God the Son.

Credo Mutwa

I would like to highlight a few things that Credo spoke about in this testimony. First notice that the Chitauri or Chitauli, like the Annunaki and Nephilim, are reptilian in nature and descend from the skies to the Earth to initiate formal contacts with pre-adamic human cultures still undeveloped in technology and organizational structure. The assistance of the fallen ones to primitive pre-adamic cultures became essential for the quick advancement and establishment for what became complex and highly organized societies. Fostering development, the fallen ones raised civilizations into ancient empires sophisticated in societal construction and complex civil planning. These pyramidal, ziggurat looking, megalithic type structures and cities of grand size were simultaneously established on every continent on the planet and by peoples science claims were supposedly working with only stone implements? It was fallen angelic knowledge and ability that propelled cultures to rise in quick advancement. The pre-adamic peoples who were fostered by the Annunaki, not knowing any better, accepted and worshiped them as their gods. Like Adam and Eve of paradise, the pre-adamic peoples could not comprehend the circumstances of the situation that they found themselves in, for why would anybody worship as god a being which demands blood ritual, victim sacrifice, and often cannibalistic behavior?

Another thing of keen interest, which Credo alludes to, is the group of occult elitist whom we've come to know as the Freemasons. He claims that some members of these secret societies not only know about the nachash, but also worship them, especially the ancient serpent known to Credo's people as Jabulon. This Jabulon is said to be king of the dragons and in possession of the ability to kill other creatures by sight. Jabulon is the great dragon that was cast out on the second day. He is the old serpent that Revelation 12:9 called "the Devil, and Satan, which deceiveth the whole world: he was cast out into the earth, and his angels were cast out with him."

Credo's, as well as other African oral traditions, especially that of the Dogon tribe, relate these beings as coming from Orion and having lived here on the planet prior to the appearance of modern-day humanity upon the Earth. Also mentioned are their construction of the underground cities and tunnel systems that lead to and interconnect various underground cities and bases claimed by many to be in existence. Credo says of the old gods that they were frightening in appearance and that they resembled crocodiles that walked upright and erect, much like the reference to the nachash of Genesis chapter 3. One can hear, in Credo's oral traditions and mythology, confirmation of this species of being as having existed as part of the natural world experience. Notice also that Credo suggests their use of magical boats and—like the Bible confirms—shape-shifting abilities.

And while modern-day humanity might consider the existence of such intelligent, reptilian like entities to be fringe lunacy, the underlying truth is these beings have been with us for a very long time.

Another intriguing aspect of Credo's testimony is that it aligns with the 36,000 BC testimony of Thoth, the Atlantean Priest-King, who described—in the Emerald Tablets of Thoth—how his people, the Atlanteans, had become involved with serpent-like, interdimensional beings. It was these beings, cited as the sons of Belial or sons of darkness, that taught them the ritual of star-gates and higher dimensional doorways, which resulted in their releasing uncontrollable cataclysm upon the world, which affects us even to this day. This interaction resulted in the destruction of what was then the golden age of Atlantis and its archipelago empire.

Of particular interest throughout the texts are the several passages referring to the dragon Annunaki angels as having the ability to possess bodies, absorb personalities, and even embody human world leaders and rulers in establishing their hidden rule over the children of men. It was the nachash that led the Atlanteans to their ultimate demise as a people and nation. Thoth gives us detail in this text that again confirms the esoteric reality of the dragon lords and how their ancient race preceded that of modern humanity.

These tablets also grant us insight into the historical destruction of Atlantis and how Thoth and his priesthood remnant were sent to the children of Khem to assist in the construction of the Great Pyramid of Giza. It would be his interdiction with the Egyptians, which would elevate their knowledge and capacity as a people increasing their stature within the world. There are few particular passages I'd like to highlight from these tablets to grant the reader further insight into what I have been discussing here.

> Great were my people in the ancient days, great beyond
> the conception of the little people now around me; know-
> ing the wisdom of old, seeking far within the heart of

infinity knowledge that belonged to Earth's youth. Wise were we with the wisdom of the Children of Light who dwelt among us. Strong were we with the power drawn from the eternal fire. And of all these, greatest among the children of men was my father, Thotmes, keeper of the great temple, link between the Children of Light who dwelt within the temple and the races of men who inhabited the ten islands. Mouthpiece, after the three, of the Dweller of Unal, speaking to the Kings with the voice that must be obeyed.

Grew I there from a child into manhood, being taught by my father the elder mysteries, until in time there grew within the fire of wisdom, until it burst into a consuming flame. Naught desired I but the attainment of wisdom. Until on a great day the command came from the Dweller of the Temple that I be brought before him. Few there were among the children of men who had looked upon that mighty face and lived, for not as the sons of men are the Children of Light when they are not incarnate in a physical body.

Chosen was I from the sons of men, taught by the Dweller so that his purposes might be fulfilled, purposes yet unborn in the womb of time. Long ages I dwelt in the Temple, learning ever and yet ever more wisdom, until I, too, approached the light emitted from the great fire. Taught me he, the path to Amenti, the underworld where the great king sits upon his throne of might. Deep I bowed in homage before the Lords of Life and the Lords of Death, receiving as my gift the key of Life. Free was I of the Halls of Amenti, bound not by death to the circle of life. Far to the stars I journeyed until space and time became as naught. Then having drunk deep of the cup of wisdom, I looked into the hearts of men and there found I greater mysteries and was glad. For only in the Search for Truth could my Soul be stilled and the flame within be quenched.

Down through the ages I lived, seeing those around me taste of the cup of death and return again in the light of life. Gradually from the Kingdoms of Atlantis passed waves of consciousness that had been one with me, only to be replaced by spawn of a lower star.

In obedience to the law, the word of the Master grew into flower. Downward into darkness turned the thoughts of the Atlanteans, until at last in his wrath arose from his Agwanti, the Dweller, (this word has no English equivalent; it means a state of detachment) speaking The Word, calling the power. Deep in Earth's heart, the sons of Amenti heard, and hearing, directed the changing of the flower of fire that burns eternally, changing and shifting, using the Logos, until that great fire changed its direction.

Over the world then broke the great waters, drowning and sinking, changing Earth's balance until only the Temple of Light was left standing on the great mountain on Undal still rising out of the water; some there were who were living, saved from the rush of the fountains.

Called to me then the Master, saying: Gather ye together my people. Take them by the arts ye have learned of far across the waters, until ye reach the land of the hairy barbarians, dwelling in caves of the desert. Follow there the plan that ye know of.

Gathered I then my people and entered the great ship of the Master. Upward we rose into the morning. Dark beneath us lay the Temple. Suddenly over it rose the waters. Vanished from Earth, until the time appointed, was the great Temple.

Fast we fled toward the sun of the morning, until beneath us lay the land of the children of Khem. Raging, they came with cudgels and spears lifted in anger seeking to slay and utterly destroy the Sons of Atlantis. Then raised I my staff and directed a ray of vibration, striking them still in their tracks as fragments of stone of the mountain. Then spoke I to them in words calm and peaceful, telling them of the might of Atlantis, saying we were children of the Sun and its messengers. Cowed I them by my display of magic-science, until at my feet they groveled, when I released them.

Long dwelt we in the land of Khem, long and yet long again. Until obeying the commands of the Master, who while sleeping yet lives eternally, I sent from me the Sons of Atlantis, sent them in many directions that from the womb of time wisdom might rise again in her children.

Long time dwelt I in the land of Khem, doing great works by the wisdom within me. Upward grew into the light of knowledge the children of Khem, watered by the rains of my wisdom. Blasted I then a path to Amenti so that I might retain my powers, living from age to age a Sun of Atlantis, keeping the wisdom, preserving the records.

Great grew the sons of Khem, conquering the people around them, growing slowly upwards in Soul force. Now for a time I go from among them into the dark halls of Amenti, deep in the halls of the Earth, before the Lords of the Powers, face to face once again with the Dweller.

Raised I high over the entrance, a doorway, a gateway leading down to Amenti. Few there would be with courage to dare it, few pass the portal to dark Amenti. Raised over the passage, I, a mighty pyramid, using the power that overcomes Earth force (gravity). Deep and yet deeper placed I a force-house or chamber; from it carved I a circular passage reaching almost to the great summit. There in the apex, set I the crystal, sending the ray into the Time-Space, drawing the force from out of the ether, concentrating upon the gateway to Amenti. (See The Great Pyramid by Doreal.)

Other chambers I built and left vacant to all seeming, yet hidden within them are the keys to Amenti. He who in courage would dare the dark realms, let him be purified first by long fasting. Lie in the sarcophagus of stone in my chamber. Then to reveal I to him the great mysteries. Soon shall he follow to where I shall meet him, even in the darkness of Earth shall I meet him, I, Thoth, Lord of Wisdom, meet him and hold him and dwell with him always.

Built I the Great Pyramid, patterned after the pyramid of earth force, burning eternally so that it, too, might remain through the ages. In it, I built my knowledge of Magic-Science so that it might be here when again I return from Amenti. Aye, while I sleep in the Halls of Amenti, my Soul roaming free will incarnate, dwell among men in this form or another. (Hermes, thrice-born.)

Emerald Tablet 1

The 1st Tablet begins with Thoth's testimony that he is one of the survivors of the destruction that sank Atlantis, one of the masses of the ten island archipelago empire. In Greek mythology, it is Poseidon—otherwise known as the Sumerian Enki—who takes a human spouse as wife, birthing into being the demigod Atlantean kings. Plato, in his work *Timaes*, speaks of the children of this line and their links to the god of the Sea, Poseidon.

The tale, which was of great length, began as follows: I have before remarked, in speaking of the allotments of the gods, that they distributed the whole earth into portions differing in extent, and made themselves temples and sacrifices. And Poseidon, receiving for his lot the island of Atlantis, begat children by a mortal woman, and settled them in a part of the island which I will proceed to describe...

In this mountain there dwelt one of the earth-born primeval men of that country, whose name was Evenor, and he had a wife named Leucippe, and they had an only daughter, who was named Cleito. The maiden was growing up to womanhood when her father and mother died. Poseidon fell in love with her, and had intercourse with her; and, breaking the ground, enclosed the hill in which she dwelt all round, making alternate zones of sea and land, larger and smaller, encircling one another; there were two of land and three of water, which he turned as with a lathe out of the center of the island, equidistant every way, so that no man could get to the island, for ships and voyages were not yet heard of. He himself, as he was a god, found no difficulty in making special arrangements for the center island, bringing two streams of water under the earth, which he caused to ascend as springs, one of warm water and the other of cold, and making every variety of food to spring up abundantly in the earth. He also begat and brought up five pairs of male children, dividing the island of Atlantis into ten portions: he gave to the first-born of the eldest pair his mother's dwelling and the surrounding allotment, which was the largest and best, and made him king over the rest; the others he made princes, and gave them rule over many men and a large territory.

And he named them all: the eldest, who was king, he named Atlas, and from him the whole island and the ocean received the name of Atlantic. To his twin-brother, who was born after him, and obtained as his lot the extremity of the island toward the Pillars of Heracles, as far as the country which is still called the region of Gades in that part of the world, he gave the name which in the Hellenic language is Eumelus, in the language of the country which is named after him, Gadeirus. Of the second pair of twins, he called one Ampheres and the other Evaemon. To the third pair of twins he gave the name Mneseus to the elder, and Autochthon to the one who followed him. Of the fourth pair of twins he called the elder Elasippus and the younger Mestor, And of the fifth pair be gave to the elder the name of Azaes, and to the younger Diaprepes. All these and their descendants were the inhabitants and rulers of divers islands in the open sea; and also, as has been already said, they held sway in the other direction over the country within the Pillars as far as Egypt and Tyrrhenia (Italy).

Plato, Timeas

Poseidon is known to many cultures by many names. It is my hope that in tying together the original story, one will realize that the mythologies all speak about this group of fallen angels and the hybrid children they sired unnaturally into world. Poseidon is Oannes, Kulkulkan, and Quetzlcoatl the hybrid fish god known worldwide as the feathered serpent who brought wisdom and knowledge to humankind. Uniting the world in trade, the Atlantean kings decided on conquering and enslaving the world in what would be their attempt to bring forth a new world order. Plato details this attempt to unify the empires of the world through war.

> Many great and wonderful deeds are recorded of your State in our histories; but one of them exceeds all the rest in greatness and valor; for these histories tell of a mighty power which was aggressing wantonly against the whole of Europe and Asia, and to which your city put an end. This power came forth out of the Atlantic Ocean, for in those days the Atlantic was navigable; and there was an island situated in front of the straits which you call the Columns of Heracles (the Strait of Gibraltar, known as the Pillars of Hercules): the island was larger than Libya and Asia put together, and was the way to other islands, and from the islands you might pass through the whole of the opposite continent which surrounded the true ocean; for this sea which is within the Straits of Heracles is only a harbor, having a narrow entrance, but that other is a real sea, and the surrounding land may be most truly called a continent. Now, in the island of Atlantis there was a great and wonderful empire, which had rule over the whole island and several others, as well as over parts of the continent; and, besides these, they subjected the parts of Libya within the Columns of Heracles as far as Egypt, and of Europe as far as Tyrrhenia (Italy). The vast power thus gathered into one, endeavored to subdue at one blow our country and yours, and the whole of the land which was within the straits; and then, Solon, your country shone forth, in the excellence of her virtue and strength, among all mankind; for she was the first in courage and military skill,

and was the leader of the Hellenes. And when the rest fell off from her, being compelled to stand alone, after having undergone the very extremity of danger, she defeated and triumphed over the invaders, and preserved from slavery those who were not yet subjected, and freely liberated all the others who dwelt within the limits of Heracles. But afterward there occurred violent earthquakes and floods, and in a single day and night of rain all your warlike men in a body sunk into the earth, and the island of Atlantis in like manner disappeared, and was sunk beneath the sea. And that is the reason why the sea in those parts is impassable and impenetrable, because there is such a quantity of shallow mud in the way; and this was caused by the subsidence of the island.

Plato, Critias

As we pick-up the ongoing tale of the Emerald Tablets, the story will elucidate more of the details of that day and age and why it led to the ultimate destruction of this fallen angel empire. The Tablets also provide minute detail into the strange nature and abilities of these beings when performing ritual magic to open star-gate portals and give greater clarity into the supernatural capacities of the Atlanteans because of their nephilim ties.

Long ages ago, the Suns of the Morning, descending, found the world filled with night. There in that past time began the struggle, the age old battle of darkness and Light. Many in that time were so filled with darkness that only feebly flamed the light from the night.

Some there were, masters of darkness, who sought to fill all with their darkness; sought to draw others into their night. Fiercely withstood they, the masters of brightness; fiercely fought they from the darkness of night. Sought they ever to tighten the fetters, the chains that bind man to the darkness of night. Used they always the dark magic, brought into man by the power of darkness; magic that enshrouded man's soul with darkness.

Banded together in as order, Brothers of Darkness, they through the ages, antagonists they to the children of men. Walked they always secret and hidden, found yet not found by the children of men. Forever they walked and worked in darkness, hiding from the light in the darkness of night. Silently, secretly, use they their power, enslaving and binding the souls of men.

Unseen they come and unseen they go. Man in his ignorance calls Them from below.

Dark is the way the Dark Brothers travel, dark with a darkness not of the night, traveling o'er Earth they walk through man's dreams. Power have they gained from the darkness around them to call other dwellers from out of their plane in ways that are dark and unseen by man. Into man's mind-space reach the Dark Brothers. Around it, they close the veil of their night. There through its life-time that soul dwells in bondage, bound by the fetters of the Veil of the night. Mighty are they in the forbidden knowledge, forbidden because it is one with the night.

Hark ye, O man, and list to my warning: be ye free from the bondage of night. Surrender not your soul to the Brothers of Darkness. Keep thy face ever turned toward the Light. Know ye not, O man, that your sorrow only has come through the Veil of the night? Aye, man, heed ye my warning: strive ever upward, turn your soul toward the Light. For well know they that those who have traveled far towards the Sun on their pathway of Light have great and yet greater power to bind with darkness the children of Light.

List ye, O man, to he who comes to you. But weigh in the balance if his words be of Light. For many there are who walk in Dark Brightness and yet are not the children of Light. Easy it is to follow their pathway, easy to fol-low the path that they lead. But yes, O man, heed ye my warning: Light comes only to him who strives. Hard is the pathway that leads to the Wisdom, hard is the pathway that leads to the Light. Many shall ye find, the stones in your pathway; many the mountains to climb toward the Light. Yet know ye, O man, to him that o'ercometh, free will he be of the pathway of Light. Follow ye not the Dark Brothers ever. Always be ye a child of the Light. For know ye, O man, in the end Light must conquer and darkness and night be banished from Light.

Listen, O man, and heed ye this wisdom; even as darkness, so is the Light.

When darkness is banished and all Veils are rendered, out there shall flash from the darkness, the Light.

Even as exist among men the Dark Brothers, so there exists the Brothers of Light. Antagonists they of the Brothers of Darkness, seeking to free men from the night. Powers have they, mighty and potent. Knowing the Law, the planets obey. Work they ever in harmony and order, freeing the man-soul from its bondage of night. Secret and hidden, walk they also. Known not are they to the children of men. Yet know that ever they walk with thee, showing the Way to the children of men. Ever have They fought the Dark Brothers, conquered and conquering time without end. Yet always Light shall in the end be master, driving away the darkness of night.

Aye, man, know ye this knowing: always beside thee walk the Children of Light.

Masters they of the Sun power, ever unseen yet the guardians of men. Open to all is their pathway, open to he who will walk in the Light. Free are They of Dark Amenti, free of the Halls where Life regins supreme. Suns are they and Lords of the morning, Children of Light to shine among men. Like man are they and yet are unlike. Never divided were they in the past. One have they been in Oneness eternal, throughout all space since the beginning of time. Up did they come in Oneness with the All One, up from the first-space, formed and unformed.

Emerald Tablet 6

Tablet 6 describes how the Atlanteans themselves began to divide into two main groups, the Sons of Darkness (or Belial) and the Sons of Light (or the Law). Both groups organize themselves in efforts to counter the others. The wars of the gods begins with further propagation of evil on the part of the Sons of Darkness who later, as the Sons of the Serpent, institute worship of the nachash. The Sons of Light prepare for the soon coming destruction of Atlantis and judgment from the Most High. The Atlanteans reach a point of perversion whereby, as scripture alludes, they abandoned their first estate breeding into the pre-adamic lines found on the Earth before the creation of modern humanity.

> Far in the past before Atlantis existed, men there were who delved into darkness, using dark magic, calling up beings from the great deep below us. Forth came they into this cycle. Formless were they of another vibration, existing unseen by the children of earth-men. Only through blood could they have formed being. Only through man could they live in the world.
>
> In ages past were they conquered by the Masters, driven below to the place whence they came. But some there were who remained, hidden in spaces and planes unknown to man. Lived they in Atlantis as shadows, but at times they appeared among men. Aye, when the blood was offered, forth came they to dwell among men.
>
> In the form of man moved they amongst us, but only to sight where they as are men. Serpent-headed when the glamour was lifted but appearing to man as men among men. Crept they into the Councils, taking forms that were like unto men. Slaying by their arts the chiefs of the kingdoms, taking their form and ruling o'er man. Only by magic could they be discovered. Only by sound could their faces be seen. Sought they from the kingdom of shadows to destroy man and rule in his place.
>
> But, know ye, the Masters were mighty in magic, able to lift the Veil from the face of the serpent, able to send

him back to his place. Came they to man and taught him the secret, the Word that only a man can pronounce. Swift then they lifted the Veil from the serpent and cast him forth from place among men.

Yet, beware, the serpent still liveth in a place that is open at times to the world. Unseen they walk among thee in places where the rites have been said. Again as time passes onward shall they take the semblance of men.

Called may they be by the master who knows the white or the black, but only the white master may control and bind them while in the flesh.

Emerald Tablet 8

Tablet 8 of the Emerald collection is, in my opinion, one of the most important texts anywhere having to do with the true nature of the nachash as intelligent reptilian beings. They, the tablets say, were called out of the great deep by earth-men delving into darkness seeking great power, and that these shadowy forces were conjured up prior to even the existence of Atlantis. It is noted that they entered our plane of existence and were able to somehow hold form only when the blood was offered through ritual or victim sacrifice. Thus the emphasis in pagan cultures on blood and the shedding of it.

They moved amongst us in the semblance of men, yet they were not men, but inter-dimensional beings reptilian in nature, serpent-headed and with unexplainable power to possess the identity of a person and—displacing the individual—assume full authority and free will over that being. Only by sight were they as men. Utilizing chameleon like capacity, the nachash were able to cloak themselves to our senses and perceptions, hiding their existence from humanity. Like shadows they were able to enter into the ranks of man. Could these reptilian beings, as hinted at by the Emerald Tablets, possess the royal bloodlines of today? Could they still inhabit the forms of rulers sitting on the thrones of the world? And if so, are they the

Bilderberger elite inhabiting the councils of men, making decisions for the masses of humanity based on what they see as best for us?

Not only does the most important story of humanity's loss of immortality and fall from grace have something to do with our ancestors' interaction with the nachash, it seems all cultures of the world cite ancient stories and mythologies that reveal our strange displacement from paradise and collective enslavement by beings that we are only now beginning to understand. Indeed all of the cultures of the world outside of the Hebrew Israelites worshiped these fallen angels as their collective pantheon of gods and goddesses.

> I will go before thee, and make the crooked places straight: I will break in pieces the gates of brass, and cut in sunder the bars of iron: And I will give thee the treasures of darkness, and hidden riches of secret places, that thou mayest know that I, the LORD, which call thee by thy name, am the God of Israel.
>
> Isaiah 45:2-3

SALVATION, HARVEST, AND THE PLAN OF REDEMPTION

Sophia's desire to bring forth child without approval of consort resulted in the separation of light from darkness and manifestation of Yaldaboath as the first ruler of the lower dual natured material world. This physical world would serve as a middle ground for the experience of light and darkness and intermingling of good and dreadful spirits. Sophia as veil represents the plane where light and darkness overlap, intermingling individual fate and destiny for those incarnating in flesh as part of the plan instituted by the Father to reconcile Sophia. His Son, Yahushuah, would accept the trial of flesh and also offer renewed opportunity to those angels that sat on the fence during the Lucifer rebellion and subsequent wars in heaven. Transformation into the physical would provide a proving ground of sorts for the Ophanim angels (the one third angels that made no choice during the First World Age to serve Him) to redeem their/our loyalties. Judgment on this world would also serve as condemnation for the one third of the insurgent angels and fallen Watchers that rebelled against His heavenly administration.

Some people equate Yaldoboath to being Yahweh, citing that the God of the Old Testament was evil because of His instruction to the

Israelites to spare no man, woman, or child when sending Joshua and the Hebrew peoples in to conquer the promised land of Canaan. What most do not realize is that Yahweh did so only because the land had prior been usurped by the children of Ham through the bastard child Canaan and was inhabited by the children of the Anak as a result of the Canaanites inter-breeding again with the children of the fallen Watchers, post flood. The land of Canaan was filled with giants who were the tribes of Anak or the Annunaki. That is the specific reason why the Lord instructed them to act in such brutal and decisive manner. Joshua and the invading Israelites would be utilized as tools for the eradication of these evil beings much like the flood was in purging the abomination that was the seed of Satan on this planet then. The summation of scripture is nothing more than the grand mythic tale of the birth, war, and battle for supremacy of earth and creation between these two seed-lines as each struggle against the other, as fortold in Genesis 3:15.

Yahweh, the unbegotten Father, is, was, and always will be the Lord of Creation as He is the fullness that contains all things within creation. He is the living and hidden God who sired, through His Son the Word, all created things. He allowed Sophia to bring forth Yaldaboath as part of a larger plan He had for the creation of the physical universe and the carnal aspect of world and humanity.

"The rulers thought that it was by their own power and will that they were doing what they did, but the Holy Spirit in secret was accomplishing everything through them as it wished" (The Gospel of Philip).

This world would verify to all why it is that creation needs a just and benevolent Creator God with all power to rule through might, justice, love, and law, for without such force or principle to maintain order, chaos, evil, death, violence, and destruction would lead all to non-existence. This temporary world would prove to the angels incarnating here as humanity just what kind of reality would be created should we be given free will to determine our own collective direction, fate, and destiny. The current state of the world is proof enough that without the Father and Son we cannot rule over planets much less universes. We as collective are being shown just what kind of a situation would be created and what kind of circumstances would come into existence without His supreme law, order, and harmony lording over all things, for without Him all would be brought to a violent end, which is exactly the lesson we are learning now.

Being the mother of matter, Sophia represents the veil where the visible and invisible merge where the seen and unseen cross over in dimensional reality that allows both the angels of the higher and the lower orders to interplay with one another. She represents the middle ground where both sets of angels can interact amongst one another through the vehicle of the flesh body and incarnation into this world. In this world, fate, destiny, and death would rule supreme over the flesh for the time that we would dwell within it. Sophia is also cited in the gnostic tradition as being the daughter of Barbelo and the feminine aspect of the Holy Spirit, Holy Child, and sister of Christ.

By the will of the Father she desired to birth visibility into manifestation separate from the higher light realms; it was that act of separation that brought Yaldaboath, the Demiurge, into being, granting him worlds to rule of his own. Just as the Lord knew Adam and Eve would fall from grace, so did He know that Sophia would fall for matter to be born and that Yaldaboath as Lucifer would assume the adversarial role in waging the angel wars.

Like Adam and Eve, Sophia was ashamed of her actions, and even though she was bidding the Father's intent, she attempted to cover up her deeds by casting Yaldaboath out of the heavens, concealing him in cloud and establishing for him a throne in the middle of the still unfolding visible universe. Yaldabaoth, which means "child," passed through here and received his name after having heard Sophia call to him once he came into being. Believing his own lie and denying any authority above him, he considered himself to be pre-existent and lord over the entirety of all he saw. What he did not know is that his reign and rule would be only temporary and for a short duration.

"Opening his eyes, he saw a vast quantity of matter without limit; and he became arrogant, saying, It is I who am God, and there is none other apart from me" (The Hypostasis of the Archons).

> Now the eternal realm (aeon) of truth has no shadow outside it, for the limitless light is everywhere within it. But its exterior is shadow, which has been called by the name 'darkness'. From it, there appeared a force, presiding over the darkness. And the forces that came into being subsequent to them called the shadow 'the limitless chaos'. From it, every kind of divinity sprouted up […] together with the entire place, so that also, shadow is posterior to the first product. It was <in> the abyss that it (shadow) appeared, deriving from the aforementioned Pistis. Then shadow perceived there was something mightier than it, and felt envy; and when it had become pregnant of its own accord, suddenly it engendered jealousy.
>
> Since that day, the principle of jealousy amongst all the eternal realms and their worlds has been apparent. Now as for that jealousy, it was found to be an abortion without any spirit in it. Like a shadow, it came into existence in a vast watery substance. Then the bile that had come into being out of the shadow was thrown into a part of chaos. Since that day, a watery substance has been apparent. And what sank within it flowed away, being visible in chaos: as with a woman giving birth to a child—all her superfluities flow out; just so, matter came into being out of shadow, and was projected apart. And it did not depart from chaos; rather, matter was in chaos, being in a part of it.
>
> On the Origin of the World

Having only short time to rule, the Lord brought Niburu into this solar system and by destroying Tiamat to create the new earth, established the planets in their new orbits and configuration to begin the next chapter of life focused on this planet, earth, which would be under Satan's rule. Time is established along with the constellations, zodiac, sun, moon, and stars to mark the passing of the season's cycles and years. The story of what happened next in the lower realms continues with the birth of seven androgynous beings, each representative of a particular planet and association to specific days of the week. With this solar system and time established, Yaldoboath created his own army of demonic forces to appoint as authorities over the lower visible firmament of this physical, fallen world.

These are the seven forces of the seven heavens of chaos. And they were born androgynous, consistent with the immortal pattern that existed before them, according to the wish of Pistis: so that the likeness of what had existed since the beginning might reign to the end. You will find the effect of these names and the force of the male entities in the Archangelic (Book) of the Prophet Moses, and the names of the female entities in the first Book of Noraia.

Now the prime parent Yaldabaoth, since he possessed great authorities, created heavens for each of his offspring through verbal expression—created them beautiful, as dwelling places—and in each heaven he created great glories, seven times excellent. Thrones and mansions and temples, and also chariots and virgin spirits up to an invisible one and their glories, each one has these in his heaven; mighty armies of gods and lords and angels and archangels—countless myriads—so that they might serve. The account of these matters you will find in a precise manner in the first Account of Oraia.

On The Origin of the World

His thoughts became blind. And, having expelled his power—that is, the blasphemy he had spoken—he pursued it down to chaos and the abyss, his mother, at the instigation of Pistis Sophia. And she established each of his offspring in conformity with its power—after the pattern of the realms that are above, for by starting from the invisible world the visible world was invented.

The Hypostasis of the Archons

The story of how we got to be here on this planet, and at this time, is the most incredible tale that could ever be imagined, and is the only interpretation I know that has the potential to answer all of the larger questions as to what this life, the one before, and the one hereafter is all about. In the next part of the book, I will discuss at length our collective fall into flesh and the transformation of our bodies from light to flesh on what was then the eighth day. Most do not understand how the conversion of our spiritual light bodies took place, why, or how it led to our entrapment and imprisonment within the flesh and this world.

What's more important is that most do not understand that humanity was forgiven the fall and granted instruction for life in the flesh so that we can later be redeemed. Know also that the Father, Son, and Holy Spirit worked to elevate us into remembrance once humanity awoke to the realization that we were bound in flesh on a planet surrounded by devils and demons. It's a misnomer to believe that we were just abandoned on this planet to live with Satan and his minions and that the Holy Trinity never worked to awaken Adam, Eve, and their descendants as to why they were fallen and how to return to their first estate. Those that do not understand this aspect of the elevation of humanity and how it also fits into the fall are grasping only part of the larger story and, as such, are not comprehending those scriptures that are tied to the second part of this teaching (the elevation), which most believe contradict what is revealed in traditional Old and New Testament scriptures as the fall. My hope is that, with this clarity, the reader will be able to understand the summation of all scripture everywhere in its totality.

After Sophia is established as the veil between the invisible and visible worlds, or spirit and matter, Yaldaboath's kingdom is unfolded as a counterfeit of the invisible and higher realms that existed prior to the unfolding of the lower worlds. Yaldaboath, believing nothing existed greater or prior to him, boasts of being the only god and challenged any higher authority to reveal itself, which Yahushuah then did by projecting an image of Himself as the first Adam and immortal image of humanity, shining gloriously upon the waters of the earth.

Embarrassed and frightened by the vision, Yaldaboath then acknowledged authorities above him, but being enamored by the beauty of the image he saw, was filled with a lust to capture its form. He then considers with his authorities, tactics as to how they might mold a counterfeit model of what they were witness to. Like a decoy, their intent is to lure to this world the beautiful spirit they saw reflected in the waters upon the earth.

Yaldaboath believes that if the spirit saw a molded form like itself that it might then descend to this world, and with luck they then might somehow capture it for their own benefit, enticing the beings above to this fallen world. What he did not realize, however, is that Yahushuah was guiding his plans for His own purpose and that He would allow Satan and his authorities a part in molding of the physical flesh bodies because it would be through these molded forms that judgment and salvation would come to being for all.

It would be through these bodies of flesh and modeled forms of clay that the Second World Age would begin with the birth of Cain. As the middle ground for flesh form, our bodies would contain both good and bad angels, the Watcher and a holy one, and come about as an agreement between the higher and lower angels.

> And so he dwells either in this world or in the resurrection or in the middle place. God forbid that I be found in there! In this world, there is good and evil. Its good things are not good, and its evil things not evil. But there is evil after this world which is truly evil—what is called the middle. It is death. While we are in this world, it is fitting for us

to acquire the resurrection, so that when we strip off the flesh, we may be found in rest and not walk in the middle. For many go astray on the way. For it is good to come forth from the world before one has sinned.

The Gospel of Philip

Mary said to him: Holy Lord, where did your disciples come from, and where are they going, and (what) should they do here? The Perfect Savior said to them: I want you to know that Sophia, the Mother of the Universe and the consort, desired by herself to bring these to existence without her male (consort). But by the will of the Father of the Universe, that his unimaginable goodness might be revealed, he created that curtain between the immortals and those that came afterward, that the consequence might follow ... [BG 118:] ... every aeon and chaos—that the defect of the female might <appear>, and it might come about that Error would contend with her. And these became the curtain of spirit. From <the> aeons above the emanations of Light, as I have said already, a drop from Light and Spirit came down to the lower regions of Almighty in chaos, that their molded forms might appear from that drop, for it is a judgment on him, Arch-Begetter, who is called 'Yaldabaoth'.

That drop revealed their molded forms through the breath, as a living soul. It was withered and it slumbered in the ignorance of the soul. When it became hot from the breath of the Great Light of the Male, and it took thought, (then) names were received by all who are in the world of chaos, and all things that are in it through that Immortal One, when the breath blew into him. But when this came about by the will of Mother Sophia—so that Immortal Man might piece together the garments there for a judgment on the robbers—<he> then welcomed the blowing of that breath; but since he was soul-like, he was not able to take that power for himself until the number of

chaos should be complete, (that is,) when the time determined by the great angel is complete.

The Sophia of Jesus Christ

Yaldaboath, also called Ariael (Lion of God) by the gnostic texts in
Thomas Heywood's book *Hierarchy of the Blessed Angels*, is presented
as an angel with authority over the element of fire and air—also
called the prince who rules over the waters as Earth's great Lord—
we know this being to be the Sumerian Enki—also known as Lord
of the Waters—which was a title associated with and attributed to
Oannes. It's my contention that all of these various and seemingly
disconnected embodiments all connect to Lucifer, the fallen cherub,
who after his fall became Satan, the adversary of Father Creator
and His only begotten Son, Yahushuah. Whereas some consider
Yaldaboath to be Yahweh, I equate the Gnostic Yaldaboath to the
Christian Satan and Islamic Iblis as all of these titles mean adversary, enemy of God, or something of similar designation.

So eager are the fallen ones to mold a being that would persuade
the image of the immortal human to descend to this world that
they accept and heed instruction from Yahushuah and Sophia as
to how mold an appropriate receptacle for the incarnation of light
beings upon the Earth. They hesitate only after being warned that
the being that they were molding into form would later result in the
incarnation of the true man whom would later trample upon their
worlds and fake authority.

Neither do they realize that the Father would send His Son later
to incarnate into one of these modeled forms and deliver salvation to
all those who would later find themselves trapped in the lower world
in one of their agreed upon forms. These eighth day molded forms
would serve as the vehicle by which the lower authorities would
condemn themselves while Adam, Eve, and all their descendants
would be restored to everlasting life and salvation through the Son.
The Father knew that once Adam and Eve were created into flesh

SONS OF GOD

form, Yaldaboath and the other lower authorities would sin against them, attempting to enslave them and their ancestors for the 7,000 years they would hold dominion of the earth.

Once the Father sent Christ to restore Pistis Sophia and her light, the agreed upon plan was initiated, and the lower authorities were shown how to mold flesh and blood human bodies. The eighth-day molded-flesh form then came about as an agreement by the Higher and Lower authorities as to what kind and type of body the fallen sixth-day Adam and Eve would incarnate into once banished from their former bright-natured selves. Whereas they had both once before been immortal angels, or sons of God, their new bodies would be mortal forms subject to fate and death.

"A prearranged plan came into effect regarding Eve, so that the modelled forms of the authorities might become enclosures of the light, whereupon it would condemn them through their modelled forms" (On the Origins of the World).

> And having created […] everything, he organized accord-
> ing to the model of the first aeons which had come into
> being, so that he might create them like the indestructible
> ones. Not because he had seen the indestructible ones, but
> the power in him, which he had taken from his mother,
> produced in him the likeness of the cosmos. And when he
> saw the creation which surrounds him, and the multitude
> of the angels around him which had come forth from him,
> he said to them, 'I am a jealous God, and there is no other
> God beside me.' But by announcing this he indicated to
> the angels who attended him that there exists another
> God. For if there were no other one, of whom would he
> be jealous?
>
> The Testimony of Truth

> Now when the heavens had consolidated themselves
> along with their forces and all their administration, the
> prime parent became insolent. And he was honored by

all the army of angels. And all the gods and their angels gave blessing and honor to him. And for his part, he was delighted and continually boasted, saying to them, I have no need of anyone. He said, "It is I who am God, and there is no other one that exists apart from me." And when he said this, he sinned against all the immortal beings who give answer. And they laid it to his charge.

On the Origin of the World

And he said, "If any other thing exists before me, let it become visible to me!" And immediately Sophia stretched forth her finger and introduced light into matter; and she pursued it down to the region of chaos. And she returned up to her light; once again darkness [...] matter.

The Hypostasis of the Archons

And when the light had mixed with the darkness, it caused the darkness to shine. And when the darkness had mixed with the light, it darkened the light and it became neither light nor dark, but it became dim. Now the archon who is weak has three names. The first name is Yaltabaoth, the second is Saklas, and the third is Samael. And he is impious in his arrogance which is in him. For he said, 'I am God and there is no other God beside me,' for he is ignorant of his strength, the place from which he had come.

Apocryphon of John

And Zoe (Life), the daughter of Pistis Sophia, cried out and said to him, You are mistaken, Sakla!—for which the alternative name is Yaltabaoth. She breathed into his face, and her breath became a fiery angel for her; and that angel bound Yaldabaoth and cast him down into Tartaros below the abyss.

The Hypostasis of the Archons

Then when Pistis saw the impiety of the chief ruler, she was filled with anger. She was invisible. She said, You are mistaken, Samael, (that is, blind god). There is an immortal man of light who has been in existence before you, and who will appear among your modelled forms; he will trample you to scorn, just as potter's clay is pounded. And you will descend to your mother, the abyss, along with those that belong to you. For at the consummation of your (pl.) works, the entire defect that has become visible out of the truth will be abolished, and it will cease to be, and will be like what has never been. Saying this, Pistis revealed her likeness of her greatness in the waters. And so doing, she withdrew up to her light.

On the Origin of the World

The Nag Hammadi codices are not understood well by those seeking to parallel them with the fall of Genesis 3 in the Old Testament. What people fail to realize is that these texts focus on humanity's story post-Fall, after our ancestors' banishment from paradise and placement upon the lower earth. The codices discuss what happened to Adam and Eve after having been transformed into their eighth day bodies, which were flesh and blood physical vessels similar to the bodies we inhabit today. This little known story is also important as it details how we ended up being on the Earth and in these physical incarnations. They also expound upon who the archons were, which too verified Adam and Eve falling into a world already inhabited by fallen angels. Because of the veil of forgetfulness, or cup of forgetting, the Lord would elevate their consciousness and heighten their awareness through the fruit of the Good. It was after partaking of this second fruit that they were able to comprehend where they had fallen from, and where they had fallen to. Without the insight of the codices it would be difficult to understand the fullness of the story that encompasses our banishment to this prison planet. Like the Books of Enoch, they shed light into the strange phenomena that was the rebel angels and nephilim of Genesis 6. They bring insight to a story that remains seemingly veiled even to this day.

And a voice came forth from the exalted aeon-heaven: 'The Man exists and the son of Man.' And the chief archon, Yaltabaoth, heard (it) and thought that the voice had come from his mother. And he did not know from where it came. And he taught them, the holy and perfect Mother-Father, the complete foreknowledge, the image of the invisible one who is the Father of the all (and) through whom everything came into being, the first Man. For he revealed his likeness in a human form. And the whole aeon of the chief archon trembled, and the foundations of the abyss shook. And of the waters which are above matter, the underside was illuminated by the appearance of his image which had been revealed. And when all the authorities and the chief archon looked, they saw the whole region of the underside which was illuminated. And through the light they saw the form of the image in the water.

Apocryphon of John

Declaring himself to be the only god, Yaldaboath blasphemes the authorities of those in the imperishable realms. For this deed, Father God would instruct Yahushuah as the light of lights to redeem Sophia through a plan to allow for the next creation or third creation of dust, flesh, and blood eighth-day Adam and Eve. Not believing that there was in existence already an immortal man of light, Yaldaboath arrogantly requests that those that are above him reveal themselves as proof of a higher existence than he. The higher authorities then made known their providence and shown down upon the waters of the earth—some texts say an image of Christ Himself, others that Christ filled Pistis Sophia with light reflecting her countenance upon the waters of the lower visible Earth.

Regardless of which it was, the lower authorities became enamored by the reflection of the divine upon the waters of the Earth. Understanding that there are, were gods that supplanted them in glory, the lower archons mocked Yaldaboath, realizing that the vision they were witness to must have been revealed by gods greater than themselves. Having conceded this revelation, Yaldaboath then declares that, "Should you not want to see our work destroyed by the 'God' reflected in the waters, 'Come let us make man in our image' as he desired to capture the image he had seen by creating a mate which might seduce it to the Earth." He, however, was only following the Father's will in creating what would be enclosures for light beings subject to form. The dark archons are then instructed on how to create a male form by which to attract the likeness of the heavenly vision of Pistis Sophia, or Yahushuah, that they saw reflected in the water. Yaldaboath would be tricked into surrendering the life giving breath given him by Sophia to a mud form of the fallen, earthly Adam.

> As incorruptibility looked down into the region of the waters, her image appeared in the waters; and the authorities of the darkness became enamored of her. But they could not lay hold of that image, which had appeared to them in the waters, because of their weakness—since beings that merely possess a soul cannot lay hold of those that possess a spirit—for they were from below, while it was from above. This is the reason why incorruptibility looked down into the region (etc.): so that, by the father's will, she might bring the entirety into union with the light.
>
> The Hypostasis of the Archons

> And having seen the likeness of Pistis in the waters, the prime parent grieved very much, especially when he heard her voice, like the first voice that had called to him out of the waters. And when he knew that it was she who had given a name to him, he sighed. He was ashamed on account of his transgression. And when he had come to know in truth that an immortal man of light had been existing before him, he was greatly disturbed; for he had previously said to all the gods and their angels, "It is I who am god." No other one exists apart from me. For he had been afraid they might know that another had been in

existence before him, and might condemn him. But he, being devoid of understanding, scoffed at the condemnation and acted recklessly. He said, "If anything has existed before me, let it appear, so that we may see its light."

And immediately, behold! Light came out of the eighth heaven above and passed through all of the heavens of the earth. When the prime parent saw that the light was beautiful as it radiated, he was amazed. And he was greatly ashamed. As that light appeared, a human likeness appeared within it, very wonderful. And no one saw it except for the prime parent and Pronoia, who was with him. Yet its light appeared to all the forces of the heavens. Because of this they were all troubled by it.

On the Origin of the World

The Lord answered me, "Listen, John, beloved of my Father, it is the ignorant who say, in their error, that my Father made these bodies of mud. In reality He created all the virtues of heaven through the Holy Spirit. But it is through their sin that they found themselves with mortal bodies of mud and were consequently turned over to death."

The Gospel of the Secret Supper

THE MOLDING OF EIGHTH-DAY DUST ADAM AND EVE

Creation unfolded in both a higher invisible and lower visible firmament with light ruling from above and shadow ruling the lower regions. Most people only understand one side of this story and so fail to grasp the details behind the heavenly fall of Lucifer and his demon angels and the fall of Adam and Eve, who also lose dominion of paradise and their bright natures to find themselves clothed in earthly flesh in the Garden of Eden on lower firmament of Earth surrounded by devils they fear in loathing.

For 7,000 years Satan would be allowed to test the souls of all the angels born into this world of flesh. Those that succeed in thwarting off his evil suggestions, having proven their righteous love and respect of the Lord, will inherit everlasting life at the second coming of Yahushuah. Most do not understand that there were two separate creations of Adam and Eve and that the fall condemned the Ophanim angels who, like the Laodician church of this age, rode the fence during the war in heaven to birth on the lower earth while inhabiting the planet with the condemned rebel angels. On the eighth day, Adam and Eve had their bodies transformed from one of a bright nature in that they were clothed in light to one of a carnal nature in that they would be transformed to earthly flesh form. The flesh forms that Adam and Eve would assume after the fall would come about as an agreement between the authorities of both the higher and lower worlds.

Fate and death also come about as an agreement between the forces of good and evil as each person incarnating into flesh would be imbued with both a spiritual body that, fashioned by the higher authorities, would direct the soul to redemption and a carnal spirit that, fashioned by the lower authorities, would lead the soul to destruction; both spirits are born with us as the conscience of human beings. This planet and this life are the middle ground where we determine our eternal fate by following the advice of either the angel of righteousness or unrighteousness. Some would term this aspect of self as conscience. One angel leads us on the narrow way, while the other leads us down the broad path of destruction. It's important for us to recognize that we have within us the capacity for both good and evil. The duality that is the Tree of the Knowledge of Good and Evil is the war in heaven that rages within each one of us even to this day. It is our choices that determine whether we follow the broad or narrow way that will present spirit and soul with chance for redemption or destruction. It's the choices we make daily which will determine whether we are deserving of salvation and eternal life or, like the fallen ones, have justice served through condemnation.

> I charged thee, saith he, in my first commandment to guard faith and fear and temperance. Yes, Sir, say I. But now, saith he, I wish to show thee their powers also, that thou mayest understand what is the power and effect of each one of them. For their effects are two fold. Now they are prescribed alike to the righteous and the unrighteous.
>
> Do thou therefore trust righteousness, but trust not unrighteousness; for the way of righteousness is straight, but the way of unrighteousness is crooked. But walk thou

in the straight [and level] path, and leave the crooked one alone.

For the crooked way has no tracks, but only pathlessness and many stumbling stones, and is rough and thorny. So it is therefore harmful to those who walk in it.

But those who walk in the straight way walk on the level and without stumbling: for it is neither rough nor thorny. Thou seest then that it is more expedient to walk in this way.

I am pleased, Sir, say I, to walk in this way. Thou shalt walk, he saith, yea, and whosoever shall turn unto the Lord with his whole heart shall walk in it.

Hear now, saith he, concerning faith. There are two angels with a man, one of righteousness and one of wickedness.

How then, Sir, say I, shall I know their workings, seeing that both angels dwell with me?

Hear, saith he, and understand their workings. The angel of righteousness is delicate and bashful and gentle and tranquil. When then this one enters into thy heart, forthwith he speaketh with thee of righteousness, of purity, of holiness, and of contentment, of every righteous deed and of every glorious virtue.

When all these things enter into thy heart, know that the angel of righteousness is with thee. [These then are the works of the angel of righteousness.] Trust him therefore and his works.

Now see the works of the angel of wickedness also. First of all, he is quick tempered and bitter and senseless, and his works are evil, overthrowing the servants of God. Whenever then he entereth into thy heart, know him by his works.

How I shall discern him, Sir, I reply, I know not. Listen, saith he. When a fit of angry temper or bitterness comes upon thee, know that he is in thee. Then the desire of much business and the costliness of many viands and drinking bouts and of many drunken fits and of various luxuries which are unseemly, and the desire of women, and avarice, and haughtiness and boastfulness, and whatsoever things are akin and like to these—when then these things enter into thy heart, know that the angel of wickedness is with thee.

Do thou therefore, recognizing his works, stand aloof from him, and trust him in nothing, for his works are evil and inexpedient for the servants of God. Here then thou hast the workings of both the angels. Understand them, and trust the angel of righteousness.

But from the angel of wickedness stand aloof, for his teaching is evil in every matter; for though one be a man of faith, and the desire of this angel enter into his heart, that man, or that woman, must commit some sin.

And if again a man or a woman be exceedingly wicked, and the works of the angel of righteousness come into that man's heart, he must of necessity do something good.

Thou seest then, saith he, that it is good to follow the angel of righteousness, and to bid farewell to the angel of wickedness.

This commandment declareth what concerneth faith, that thou mayest trust the works of the angel of righteousness, and doing them mayest live unto God. But believe that the works of the angel of wickedness are difficult; so by not doing them thou shalt live unto God.

Shepherd of Hermas, Mandate 6

The Shepherd of Hermas, for those that do not know, was considered inspired and included in the original eighty-book canon of the early church fathers. Though modern Christians have mostly forgotten about it, it also has valuable information contained within its passages for seekers of truth. Many do not understand that there were three creations of Adam and that our Lord Yahushuah as the Son of God was the first Adam, Adam of light pre-existent in spiritual perfection, and that it would be Him that would later incarnate as God in flesh through the immaculate conception of the virgin Mary.

He would be the immortal man that the archons fear would destroy their attempts and authority. He would be the long awaited and prophesied Holy One of Israel.

There is therefore now no condemnation to them which are in Christ Jesus, who walk not after the flesh, but after the Spirit. For the law of the Spirit of life in Christ Jesus hath made me free from the law of sin and death.

For what the law could not do, in that it was weak through the flesh, God sending his own Son in the likeness of sinful flesh, and for sin, condemned sin in the flesh:

That the righteousness of the law might be fulfilled in us, who walk not after the flesh, but after the Spirit. For they that are after the flesh do mind the things of the flesh; but they that are after the Spirit the things of the Spirit. For to be carnally minded is death; but to be spiritually minded is life and peace.

Because the carnal mind is enmity against God: for it is not subject to the law of God, neither indeed can be. So then they that are in the flesh cannot please God. But ye are not in the flesh, but in the Spirit, if so be that the Spirit of God dwell in you. Now if any man have not the Spirit of Christ, he is none of his.

And if Christ be in you, the body is dead because of sin; but the Spirit is life because of righteousness. But if the Spirit of him that raised up Jesus from the dead dwell in you, he that raised up Christ from the dead shall also quicken your mortal bodies by his Spirit that dwelleth in you.

Therefore, brethren, we are debtors, not to the flesh, to live after the flesh. For if ye live after the flesh, ye shall die: but if ye through the Spirit do mortify the deeds of the body, ye shall live. For as many as are led by the Spirit of God, they are the sons of God. For ye have not received the spirit of bondage again to fear; but ye have received the Spirit of adoption, whereby we cry, Abba, Father. The Spirit itself beareth witness with our spirit, that we are the children of God:

And if children, then heirs; heirs of God, and joint-heirs with Christ; if so be that we suffer with him, that we may be also glorified together. For I reckon that the sufferings of this present time are not worthy to be compared with the glory which shall be revealed in us. For the earnest expectation of the creature waiteth for the manifestation of the sons of God. For the creature was made subject to vanity, not willingly, but by reason of him who hath subjected the same in hope, Because the creature itself also shall be delivered from the bondage of corruption into the glorious liberty of the children of God.

For we know that the whole creation groaneth and travaileth in pain together until now. And not only they, but ourselves also, which have the firstfruits of the Spirit, even we ourselves groan within ourselves, waiting for the adoption, to wit, the redemption of our body.

Romans 8:1-23

Satan's temptation of sixth-day Adam and Eve resulted in humanity's fall and entrapment in flesh once Eve was split off from Adam. The third creation of Adam occurred on the eighth day in the wilderness of the lower Earth where Satan and his minions had already been banished. Many confuse the Genesis story of Adam's creation and subsequent fall with the Gnostic story of Adam's recreation and elevation. And though the stories seem similar, yet contradictory, they are two separate stories of events that take place in two separate areas of heaven and on two different days of creation. The fall occurred on the sixth day in Paradise, and the elevation took place on the eighth day on what was the destroyed Tiamat, which—after relocation to a new orbit—became the new earth, Ki, being ripe for the next chapter of life in this solar system.

It's important to make the distinction between both events in order to understand how these two pieces fit in with the totality of the scriptural timeline. The fruit of the knowledge of good and evil that lead to sixth day Adam's loss of immortality is not the same tree that leads to eighth day Adam's heightened awareness in the Gnostic story of the tree of good. It is difficult to grasp that indeed there are two separate occasions documented of Adam and Eve eating from a tree. The first time they eat of the fruit of Tree of the Knowledge of Good and Evil it led to their fall and condemnation and required birth and death. The second time they eat of the fruit it elevates their consciousness, awakening them to the realization as to where they have fallen to and among whom. This second partaking of the fruit of the Tree of Good leads to their awakening and realization that they were naked to knowledge of Spirit and God and that the gods around them were truly devils and demons.

"There are two trees growing in Paradise. The one bears animals, the other bears men. Adam ate from the tree which bore animals. He became an animal and he brought forth animals. For this reason the children of Adam worship animals" (Gospel of Philip).

I know it's difficult to understand this aspect of the creation story and how it relates together to the fall in forming the bigger picture of how we got to be here on this planet and in flesh form, yet the knowledge I am about to reveal will, if one allows it, explain how all of the stories fit together. This tale, once understood, also explains how the modeling of that eighth day earthly form would eventually lead to the condemnation of the fallen angels and the restoration of humanity to everlasting life and forever salvation.

It was not until I had read and delved into the Nag Hammadi codices that I myself began to discern what had happened to Adam and Eve after they were banished from paradise and were already fallen. I believe that this understanding is essential for making sense of the total story and how the fall and elevation interrelate. It's my belief that these codices shed light on new information, which—for the earnest truth seekers—can and does fill in gaps of knowledge that would otherwise remain ambiguous.

Transformed into a state of flesh, Adam realizes that he has been banished from paradise to find himself living in the same world as the fallen rebel angels. The interesting part of the next piece of the puzzle concerns the appearance of Eve. Whereas the first account of eating of the fruit led Eve to be seduced by Satan and resulted in the loss of their bright natures or vestures of light, the second eating of the fruit resulted in a spirit emissary being sent to Adam as Eve. It was in the form of Eve that Pistis-Sophia made Adam aware of where he had fallen from and how he got to be on the wilderness of the Earth. The Gnostic texts provide different accounts as to who the initial Eve was in assisting Adam; some say that it was Sophia, others her daughter Zoe (life), others Christ Himself.

The texts also cite Yahushuah as being the voice of the instructor that tempted them to eat of the second tree, the Tree of the Knowledge of Good and Evil and that this fruit, rather than condemn them to incarnation into the flesh, heightened their awareness of who they were prior to the fall, and made them aware of where they had come from, what this life would be about, and where to from there.

Part of the plan in elevating humanity was to trick Yaldaboath into giving the power he stole from Sophia initially to Adam. Another thing that people do not understand about the elevation of humanity is that when the Lord put the breath of life into Adam he was awakened to his spiritual nature, which greatly surpassed that of even the fallen angels. The Annunaki in the Sumerian texts cite the incredible appearance of this new being upon the planet and how its abilities surpass greatly even their own.

> A wonder of wonders it is,
>> in the wilderness by themselves to have come about!
>> Isimud was summoned.
>> Among the bulrushes in reed baskets I them found!
> he said.
>> Enlil the matter with graveness pondered,
>> with amazement his head he shook.
>> Indeed a wonder of wonders it is,

> a new breed of Earthling on Earth has emerged,
> A Civilized Man has the Earth itself brought forth,
> Farming and shepherding, crafts and toolmaking he can be taught!
> So was Enlil to Enki saying.
> Let us of the new breed to Anu word send!
> Of the new breed word to Anu on Nibiru was beamed.
> Let seeds that can be sown,
> let ewes that sheep become, to Earth be sent!
> So did Enki and Enlil to Anu the suggestion make.
> By Civilized Man let Anunnaki and Earthlings become satiated!
> Anu the words heard, by the words he was amazed:
> That by life essences one kind to another leads is not unheard of!
> to them words back he sent.
> That on Earth a Civilized Man from the Adamu so quickly appeared, that is unheard of!

Lost Book of Enki

One other thing of importance to mention here is that Adam and Eve, once banished, were not just abandoned to fend for themselves but were still cared for and nurtured by the angels of Yahushuah/Yahweh who worked to open their eyes and mind to the power and wisdom of the Holy Spirit. The Word and His angels have visited with them continually in protecting them from the demon rulers inhabiting and ruling over this realm.

Contrary to some beliefs, the fallen angels—even the Annunaki—cannot create or fashion life; they can only mold, manipulate, or counterfeit from creation that which already exists. The things they make are imitations, forgeries of what the Lord had previously fashioned into world. Only the Holy Trinity has power to endow matter with the spirit of life. The archons cannot imbue life or bring others back from the dead. After eating from the tree, Adam awakens to the realization that Eve is a heavenly angel sent to assist him in learning about the true Creator and the life he and his wife would live out in the flesh while in this fallen world.

> Then the authorities received the knowledge (gnosis) necessary to create man. Sophia Zoe—she who is with Sabaoth—had anticipated them. And she laughed at their decision. For they are blind: against their own interests they ignorantly created him. And they do not realize what they are about to do. The reason she anticipated them and made her own man first, was in order that he might instruct their modelled form how to despise them, and thus to escape from them.
>
> Now the production of the instructor came about as follows. When Sophia let fall a droplet of light, it flowed onto the water, and immediately a human being appeared, being androgynous. That droplet she molded first as a female body. Afterwards, using the body she molded it in the likeness of the mother, which had appeared. And he finished it in twelve months. An androgynous human being was produced, whom the Greeks call Hermaphrodites; and whose mother the Hebrews call Eve of Life (Zoe), namely, the female instructor of life.
>
> On the Origin of the World

The Nag Hammadi texts clarify that the archons are told how to fashion a body for Adam as a way of tricking Yaldaboath into imbuing the model they create with the life force Sophia surrendered to him when bringing him into being. To implement the plan of salvation, a delegation of angels is sent to Yaldabaoth to instruct him on how he might tempt and trap the vision he saw reflected in the water, enslaving all those born into human form. Yaldaboath would then transfer to the modeled form the light and power he stole from Sophia, so that in giving it to Adam children of light would be born of the flesh into this world until the restoration of Sophia, or matter, through the resurrection to take place at the end of days.

Now these through the will <...> The souls that were going to enter the modelled forms of the authorities were manifested to Sabaoth and his Christ. And regarding these, the holy voice said, Multiply and improve! Be lord over all creatures. And it is they who were taken captive, according to their destinies, by the prime parent. And thus they were shut into the prisons of the modelled forms until the consummation of the age.—On The Origin Of The world

And when the mother wanted to retrieve the power which she had given to the chief archon, she petitioned the Mother-Father of the All, who is most merciful. He sent, by means of the holy decree, the five lights down upon the place of the angels of the chief archon. They advised him that they should bring forth the power of the mother.

And they said to Yaltabaoth, 'Blow into his face something of your spirit and his body will arise.' And he blew into his face the spirit which is the power of his mother; he did not know (this), for he exists in ignorance. And the power of the mother went out of Yaltabaoth into the natural body, which they had fashioned after the image of the one who exists from the beginning. The body moved and gained strength, and it was luminous.

Apocryphon of John

And at that time, the prime parent then rendered an opinion concerning man to those who were with him. Then each of them cast his sperm into the midst of the navel of the earth. Since that day, the seven rulers have fashioned man with his body resembling their body, but his likeness resembling the man that had appeared to them.

His modelling took place by parts, one at a time. And their leader fashioned the brain and the nervous system. Afterwards, he appeared as prior to him. He became a soul-endowed man. And he was called Adam, that is, father, according to the name of the one that existed before him.

On the Origin of the World

Notice that the Adam created on the sixth day was made in the image of Yahushuah, the first Adam that existed before him, and that this sixth-day Adam was the image the archons saw reflected in the waters that the eighth-day fallen dust Adam would be formed and molded after. It's important to know that sixth-day Adam was created in the heavens above the earth and that the angels of both the higher and lower authorities were witness to his creation.

He was then taken up into paradise where he was protected from the evil that was occurring on the earth. The Lord then brought all creatures before him, and not finding another like him, decided upon making for him a helpmate, whom we've come to know as Eve. This Eve is the one that was seduced in Paradise by Lucifer who had to sneak in the guise of a serpent, having lost his former beauty, and it would be in this serpent form that he would tempt them to eat of the forbidden fruit. After eating this fruit, they would then be banished to the earth where the Second World Age would begin with the rape of Eve and birth of Cain.

> While Adam was listening to the speech of his Lord to him, and standing upon the place of Golgotha, all the creatures being gathered together that they might hear the conversation of God with him, lo! a cloud of light carried him and went with him to Paradise and the choirs of Angels sang before him, the cherubim among them blessing and the seraphim crying 'Holy!' until Adam came into Paradise. He entered it at the third hour on Friday, and the Lord, to Him be praise! gave him the commandment, and warned him against disobedience to it...
>
> When he and she ate the deadly fruit they were bereft of their glory, and their splendour was taken from them, and they were stripped of the light with which they had been clothed... After the clothing of fig-leaves they put on clothing of skins, and that is the skin of which our bodies are made, being of the family of man, and it is a clothing of pain.

KITAB AL-MAGALL

And in that moment the rest of the powers became jealous, because he had come into being through all of them and they had given their power to the man, and his intelligence was greater than that of those who had made him, and greater than that of the chief archon. And when they recognized that he was luminous, and that he could think better than they, and that he was free from wickedness, they took him and threw him into the lowest region of all matter.

Apocryphon of John

FALLEN ARCHONS

Infused with yearning to enslave those who would be birthed upon the Earth after the fall, the archons are led by Yahushuah to mold forms, which would serve as receptacles for the ensnaring of angelic souls. Having forgotten about their/our first estate, many would accept the trial of flesh and assume form in a carnal nature. That is the only reason that the powers agreed to assist in the molding of the eighth-day bodies of flesh. The Second World Age began with the rape of Eve, birth of Cain, and murder of Abel, the first casualty in an ancient war that predates even Genesis 3:15 and the enmity between the two seed lines. This war between the forces of good and evil is one that precedes the creation of humanity on this planet and originates with the rebellion in heaven that took place during the First World Age. And though many of us do not have remembrance of these past spiritual lives, the Lord refers to us in His Word when He mentions how He knew us before even the foundations of this world. "But we are bound to give thanks alway to God for you, brethren beloved of the Lord, because God hath from the beginning chosen you to salvation through sanctification of the Spirit and belief of the truth."—2 Thessalonica 2:13. I believe the whole reason why the Lord told us to know self is for us to come to realization that we are also fallen angels and that our actions in that prior spiritual life were such that incarnation in flesh would be required of us. Perhaps we, like Esau, rebelled or rejected in someway the Lord prior to birth in this world.

Whatever we did during the First World Age, it greatly influenced our election into this life. The fact that we find ourselves in the body is verification that we are not yet counted among the most elect angels of the Lord. He has with this life given us and most of the fallen ones renewed chance to redeem self as worthy of eternal life and the salvation promised to those who honor the Father/Son. I pray He find all of us worthy of a return to our first estate.

During the First World Age there were three groups of angels heralded by three different archangels. Michael was leader of the cherubim angels of the Lord, Gabriel the ophanim angels, and Lucifer the seraphim angels. War ensued in heaven when Lucifer and the Seraphim angels (one third) rebelled against Yahushuah's dominion and assumption of authority during the separation of light and darkness. Michael fought with and prevailed against Lucifer whose name became Satan the adversary. He and his hosts were cast out and banished to this lower earth on what Enoch said was the 2nd day of creation.

After he tricked Adam and Eve—causing their fall and later incarnation into the flesh—death, time, fate, and destiny would all come into being as repercussion of the 2nd world age. In this world age, the spirits of the 1st world age would be required to be born of the flesh and live on a planet where they/we would learn—through the experience of good and evil—to whom we wish to serve in our loyalties, thoughts, actions, and behaviors. In Job we are given the vision of a gathering of angels where Satan as accuser shows up before this heavenly council to challenge the loyalty of those who had incarnated into human form. In this occasion he is given authority by the Lord to subject Job to trials and tribulations that decimate his family wealth and status.

> Now there was a day when the sons of God came to present themselves before the LORD, and Satan came also among them. And the LORD said unto Satan, "Whence

comest thou?" Then Satan answered the LORD, and said, "From going to and fro in the earth, and from walking up and down in it."

Job 1 (KJV)

What we are not told in that particular story is that the Lord had gone to Job beforehand and warned him about impending persecution from Satan. If one studies a book called the Testament of Job, one will see that Job was busy smashing down the altars and groves that were established for the worship of Baal/Satan. This is the reason why Satan was angry with Job and desired to persecute him. Most believe that the Lord allowed Job to be oppressed and persecuted on a whim and at the discretion of Satan, but that is not the case. The Lord had forwarned Job and told him that should he accept this task that He would restore his family wealth and status more than twofold.

> And the archangel, said to me: "Thus speaketh the Lord: If thou undertakest to destroy and takest away the image of Satan, he will set himself with wrath to wage war against thee, and he will display against thee all his malice. He will bring upon thee many severe plagues, and take from thee all that thou hast. He will take away thine children, and will inflict many evils upon thee. Then thou must wrestle like an athlete and resist pain, sure of thy reward, overcome trials and afflictions.
>
> But when thou endurest, I shall make thy name renowned throughout all generations of the earth until to the end of the world. And I shall restore thee to all that thou hadst had, and the double part of what thou shalt lose will be given to thee in order that thou mayest know that God does not consider the person but giveth to each who deserveth the good. And also to thee shall it be given, and thou shalt put on a crown of amarant. And at the resurrection thou shalt awaken for eternal life. Then shalt thou know that the Lord is just, and true and mighty."

Whereupon, my children, I replied: "I shall from love of
God endure until death all that will come upon me, and
I shall not shrink back." Then the angel put his seal upon
me and left me.

Testament of Job

It's my opinion that when death came into being, Satan challenged
not only the Lord, but also all of the Ophanim angels, to a test—to
eat of the Tree of the Knowledge of Good and Evil. Flesh incarnation is that test, and we are those angels trapped in fallen bodies, lost
in a dual nature world of good and evil. Here we are given free will to
determine our own fate and destiny as to whether we could remain
righteous and true to the Lord and His commandments. Satan even
challenged Yahushuah to enter flesh form and sabbatical upon fhe
earth in his dominion for the short time allotted him.

The Lord rose up to his challenge and told him that not only
would he subject the other classes of angels to life in the flesh but
that He also at some point would adorn the flesh and incarnate as
Savior Messiah, or Jesus Christ. He would, by example, confirm to
the rulers and people of this world that the Father and the Son are
the arbiters of eternal life and forever death. As part of this fallen
world, we are being taught collectively just why we need Their
Sovereign rule in our lives, for without Them we would create nothing but chaos and evil. His life would become the example by which
the disciples and those that follow the law and commandments of
the Father can ascribe to, to hopefully have part in eternal life.

Moreover the Demiurge began to create a man according
to his image on the one hand and on the other according
to the likeness of those who exist from the first. It was this
sort of dwelling place that she used for the seeds, namely
[… separate …] God. When they […] in behalf of man,
since indeed the Devil is one of the divine beings. He
removed himself and seized the entire plaza of the gates

and he expelled his own root from that place in the body and carcasses of flesh, for he is enveloped by the man of God. And Adam sowed him.

The Valentinian Exposition

And he said to the authorities which attend him, 'Come, let us create a man according to the image of God and according to our likeness, that his image may become a light for us.' And they created by means of their respective powers in correspondence with the characteristics which were given. And each authority supplied a characteristic in the form of the image which he had seen in its natural (form). He created a being according to the likeness of the first, perfect Man. And they said, 'Let us call him Adam, that his name may become a power of light for us.'

And the powers began: the first one, goodness, created a bone-soul; and the second, foreknowledge, created a sinew-soul; the third, divinity, created a flesh-soul; and the fourth, the lordship, created a marrow-soul; the fifth, kingdom created a blood-soul; the sixth, envy, created a skin-soul; the seventh, understanding, created a hair-soul. And the multitude of the angels attended him and they received from the powers the seven substances of the natural (form) in order to create the proportions of the limbs and the proportion of the rump and the proper working together of each of the parts.

And the origin of the demons which are in the whole body is determined to be four: heat, cold, wetness, and dryness. And the mother of all of them is matter. And he who reigns over the heat (is) Phloxopha; and he who reigns over the cold is Oroorrothos; and he who reigns over what is dry (is) Erimacho; and he who reigns over the wetness (is) Athuro. And the mother of all of these, Onorthochrasaei, stands in their midst, since she is illimitable, and she mixes with all of them. And she is truly matter, for they are nourished by her.

The four chief demons are: Ephememphi, who belongs to pleasure, Yoko, who belongs to desire, Nenentophni, who belongs to grief, Blaomen, who belongs to fear. And the mother of them all is Aesthesis-Ouch-Epi-Ptoe. And from the four demons passions came forth. And from grief (came) envy, jealousy, distress, trouble, pain, callousness, anxiety, mourning, etc. And from pleasure much wickedness arises, and empty pride, and similar things. And from desire (comes) anger, wrath, and bitterness, and bitter passion, and unsatedness, and similar things. And from fear (comes) dread, fawning, agony, and shame. All of these are like useful things as well as evil things. But the insight into their true (character) is Anaro, who is the head of the material soul, for it belongs with the seven senses, Ouch-Epi-Ptoe. This is the number of the angels: together they are 365. They all worked on it until, limb for limb, the natural and the material body was completed by them. Now there are other ones in charge over the remaining passions whom I did not mention to you. But if you wish to know them, it is written in the book of Zoroaster. And all the angels and demons worked until they had constructed the natural body. And their product was completely inactive and motionless for a long time.

Apocryphon of John

After the eighth-day, fallen-dust Adam was molded into a form that could be utilized by the angels to incarnate into flesh his vessel was abandoned by Yaldaboath and the archons as they were fearful of a prophecy that warned of their condemnation and judgment to take place through the model form they had created. This form lay on the ground motionless for a period of time while the archons discoursed among themselves as to what next to do. While in deliberation, Yahushuah blew the breath of spirit into Adam, animating his form with life.

According to a Coptic tradition preserved in the Discourse on Abbatôn, the Angel of Death, by Timothy, Archbishop of Rakoti (Alexandria), the clay of which Adam was made was brought by the angel Mûrîêl from the Land of the East. When God had made his body He left it lying for forty days and forty nights without putting breath into it. At the request of our Lord, Who promised to become Adam's advocate and to go down into the world, God breathed into Adam's nostrils the breath of life three times, saying, "Live! Live! Live!" according to the type of My Divinity. Thereupon Adam rose up, and worshipped the Father, saying, My Lord and my God.

Cave of Treasures

Once Adam was animated with life, the archons would mold a female form to trap Zoe whom would come later as Eve to instruct Adam as to where he had fallen from and where he was now. Sophia-Zoe took residence in the female form that the archons had molded as Eve; she would be the one to awaken Adam to the reality of his situation. Finding her counseling Adam, the archons ravage her in foul ways attempting to soil the light within her so that the spirit inhabiting Eve as Zoe could not ascend back unto heaven. Amused by their futile attempt, Sophia-Zoe abandons Eve, leaving the modeled form empty while being violated by the rulers of darkness. The result of their actions led to the impregnation of the molded eighth-day dust Eve who would afterward birth Cain, the first hybrid and child of Satan upon the earth.

This story is echoed in the Kolbrin Bible, Book of Enoch, as well as countless other texts (see my fourth book, *Lucifer- Father of Cain*). Understanding that both the angels and the demons were involved in the creation of the eighth-day, fallen, earthly flesh Adam assists one to also explain why some believe that Satan, the ancient aliens, the Annunaki, or other extra-terrestrial beings had a part to play in the molding, but not creation, of humanity. Satan as the progenitor of death is depicted as forms of darkness such as the grim reaper because he is the lord of the dead, and Yahushuah our Lord is God of the living. Only the Father/Son can create imbuing life to matter, and the Elohim can only mold or form counterfeit replicas of things the Holy Trinity has already brought into being. Only the Holy Trinity can impart life and resurrect the dead.

Satan would like humanity to believe that he is our maker, but he had no hand in forming the sixth-day, immortal, angelic, androgynous Adam that fell from paradise. He only assisted in the creation of the eighth-day, fallen-dust Adam, and even then it was only after receiving instruction from the imperishable realms.

> The rulers laid plans and said, Come, let us create a man that will be soil from the earth. They modeled their creature as one wholly of the earth. Now the rulers [...] body [...] they have [...] female [...] is [...] with the face of a beast. They had taken some soil from the earth and modeled their man after their body and after the image of God that had appeared to them in the waters.
>
> They said, Come, let us lay hold of it by means of the form that we have modeled, so that it may see its male counterpart [...], and we may seize it with the form that we have modeled—not understanding the force of God, because of their powerlessness. And he breathed into his face; and the man came to have a soul (and remained) upon the ground many days. But they could not make him arise because of their powerlessness. Like storm winds they persisted (in blowing), that they might try to capture that image, which had appeared to them in the waters. And they did not know the identity of its power.
>
> The Hypostasis of the Archons

And when they had finished Adam, he abandoned him as an inanimate vessel, since he had taken form like an abortion, in that no spirit was in him. Regarding this thing, when the chief ruler remembered the saying of Pistis, he was afraid lest the true man enter his modelled form and become its lord. For this reason he left his modelled form forty days without soul, and he withdrew and abandoned it. Now on the fortieth day, Sophia Zoe sent her breath into Adam, who had no soul. He began to move upon the ground. And he could not stand up.

Then, when the seven rulers came, they saw him and were greatly disturbed. They went up to him and seized him. And he (viz., the chief ruler) said to the breath within him, "Who are you? And whence did you come hither?" It answered and said, "I have come from the force of the man for the destruction of your work." When they heard, they glorified him, since he gave them respite from the fear and the anxiety in which they found themselves. Then they called that day Rest, in as much as they had rested from toil. And when they saw that Adam could stand up, they were glad, and they took him and put him in Paradise. And they withdrew up to their heavens.

On the Origin of the World

It is important for the truth seeker to realize that this creation of Adam, though taking part on the seventh day—which is a day of rest or the Sabbath—is not inhabited by the fallen sixth-day Adam until the eighth day. Though very subtle, this distinction is very important in understanding how the story unfolded and that indeed there was not only a fall from grace, but also an elevation from darkness that took place once our ancestors were banished from Paradise.

> But the blessed One, the Mother-Father, the beneficent and merciful One, had mercy on the power of the mother which had been brought forth out of the chief archon, for they (the archons) might gain power over the natural and perceptible body. And he sent, through his beneficent Spirit and his great mercy, a helper to Adam, luminous Epinoia which comes out of him, who is called Life. And she assists the whole creature, by toiling with him and by restoring him to his fullness and by teaching him about the descent of his seed (and) by teaching him about the way of ascent, (which is) the way he came down. And the

luminous Epinoia was hidden in Adam, in order that the archons might not know her, but that the Epinoia might be a correction of the deficiency of the mother.

Apocryphon of John

After the day of rest, Sophia sent her daughter Zoe, being called Eve, as an instructor, in order that she might make Adam, who had no soul, arise, so that those whom he should engender might become containers of light. When Eve saw her male counterpart prostrate, she had pity upon him, and she said, Adam! Become alive! Arise upon the earth! Immediately her word became accomplished fact. For Adam, having arisen, suddenly opened his eyes. When he saw her, he said, "You shall be called 'Mother of the Living.' For it is you who have given me life." Then the authorities were informed that their modelled form was alive and had arisen, and they were greatly troubled. They sent seven archangels to see what had happened. They came to Adam.

When they saw Eve talking to him, they said to one another, What sort of thing is this luminous woman? For she resembles that likeness which appeared to us in the light. Now come, let us lay hold of her and cast her seed into her, so that when she becomes soiled she may not be able to ascend into her light. Rather, those whom she bears will be under our charge. But let us not tell Adam, for he is not one of us. Rather let us bring a deep sleep over him. And let us instruct him in his sleep to the effect that she came from his rib, in order that his wife may obey, and he may be lord over her.

On the Origin of the World

Now all these things came to pass by the will of the father of the entirety. Afterward, the spirit saw the soul-endowed man upon the ground. And the spirit came forth from the Adamantine Land; it descended and came to dwell within him, and that man became a living soul. It called his name

Adam, since he was found moving upon the ground. A voice came forth from incorruptibility for the assistance of Adam; and the rulers gathered together all the animals of the earth and all the birds of heaven and brought them in to Adam to see what Adam would call them, that he might give a name to each of the birds and all the beasts.

The Hypostasis of the Archons

I hope that you are beginning to understand the multiple creations of Adam and that we are also fallen angels imprisoned within the flesh for what is one lifetime in the immortal journey of soul. Unless one understands how the fall affects us each individually, one will not understand what Christ coming into the flesh truly means for each of us. There are two seed lines on the planet. One will inherit eternal life, the other condemned to death and nonexistence. One will be gathered and laid up into the barn during harvest, one bundled and consumed in the fire. One hears His voice, one doesn't. One are His sheep, the other slaughterers of His herd.

Unless one has a foundation for understanding that there are indeed two kinds of people on the planet—one dedicated to evil and the other dedicated to good—the entirety of what has happened up until now will not make sense. However, if one can open up to the possibility of entertaining truth this way, everything will click into place like pieces of a scattered puzzle.

The soul of Adam came into being by means of a breath. The partner of his soul is the spirit. His mother is the thing that was given to him. His soul was taken from him and replaced by a spirit. When he was united (to the spirit), he spoke words incomprehensible to the powers. They envied him […] spiritual partner […] hidden […] opportunity […] for themselves alone […] bridal chamber, so that […]… Adam came into being from two virgins, from the Spirit and from the virgin earth. Christ therefore, was born from a virgin to rectify the Fall which occurred in the beginning… There are two trees growing in Paradise. The one bears animals, the other bears men. Adam ate from the tree which bore animals. He became an animal and he brought forth animals.

The Gospel of Phillip

The Chaldaeans mention Adam and say that this person was the only one whom the earth produced. He lay without breath and motionless and immovable like a statue. He was an image of that human above, Adamas, and was made by many powers. The great human from above, from whom he and 'every family existing on earth and in the heavens' is derived, had to be completely submissive. Therefore he was given a soul, so that through the soul the enslaved creature of the great and most excellent and perfect human might suffer and be punished. They also ask what the soul is and where it originates and what its nature is, since it enters human beings and, by its movement, enslaves and punishes the creature of the perfect being on earth. They inquire not from the scriptures but from mystical doctrines. If you say that everything originated from one principal, you are wrong, but if you say it came from three, you are right and can prove the whole matter. There is one blessed nature of the blessed Adam from above, who is Adamas. There is one mortal nature below.

The Naassene Sermon

Without knowledge of the multiple creations of Adam and how one aspect of the story leads to the other, one would be hard pressed in trying to comprehend how the Genesis creation story fits in with the teachings of the apocryphal, pseudepigraphal, as well as newly discovered gnostic interpretations on creation and humanity's beginnings. Only with the knowledge I present here can one unravel the full picture of our total ancient history.

The rulers took counsel with one another and said, "Come, let us cause a deep sleep to fall upon Adam." And he slept.—Now the deep sleep that they caused to fall upon him, and he slept is Ignorance.—They opened his side like a living woman. And they built up his side with some flesh in place of her, and Adam came to be endowed only with soul. And the spirit-endowed woman came to him and spoke with him, saying, "Arise, Adam." And when he saw her, he said, "It is you who have given me life; you will be called 'mother of the living'.—For it is she who is my mother. It is she who is the physician, and the woman, and she who has given birth."

The Hypostasis of the Archons

The archons were only responsible in helping to form an appropriate receptacle for the incarnation of spirit into flesh. They were part of the process of bringing the eighth-day dust Adam into his fallen state, but they do not have the power or the authority to imbue matter with life. Only the forces of the imperishable realms have the power to imbue life, and that is only if it is the Father or Son's will. Satan is and has been setting up the notion that he and his angels are the true creators of modern humanity, but he was not.

He was, however, partially responsible for bringing free will to humanity though he desires humanity to use that free will only in condemning themselves to the same judgment that awaits him at the end of his temporary rule.

> And in that moment the rest of the powers became jealous, because he had come into being through all of them and they had given their power to the man, and his intelligence was greater than that of those who had made him, and greater than that of the chief archon. And when they recognized that he was luminous, and that he could think better than they, and that he was free from wickedness, they took him and threw him into the lowest region of all matter.

Since that time we learned about dead things, like men. Then we recognized the God who had created us. For we were not strangers to his powers. And we served him in fear and slavery. And after these events we became darkened in our hearts.

The Apocalypse of Adam

Then the Epinoia of the light hid herself in him (Adam). And the chief archon wanted to bring her out of his rib. But the Epinoia of the light cannot be grasped. Although darkness pursued her, it did not catch her. And he brought a part of his power out of him. And he made another creature, in the form of a woman, according to the likeness of the Epinoia which had appeared to him. And he brought the part which he had taken from the power of the man into the female creature, and not as Moses said, 'his ribbone.' And he (Adam) saw the woman beside him. And in that moment the luminous Epinoia appeared, and she lifted the veil which lay over his mind. And he became sober from the drunkenness of darkness. And he recognized his counter-image, and he said, 'This is indeed bone of my bones and flesh of my flesh.' Therefore the man will leave his father and his mother, and he will cleave to his wife, and they will both be one flesh. For they will send him his consort, and he will leave his father and his mother … (3 lines unreadable)

Apocryphon of John

The eighth-day dust Adam and Eve were clothed in flesh, not light like the sixth day Adam and Eve that were made in the image of the Word. These beings were initially nothing more than mere empty clay vessels devoid of life, consciousness, and movement that lay abandoned upon the ground after their molding. Yaldaboath's intent was to capture the image of the female sent to instruct Adam on where he had fallen.

In the place where I will eat all things is the Tree of Knowledge. That one killed Adam, but here the Tree of Knowledge made men alive. The law was the tree. It has power to give the knowledge of good and evil. It neither removed him from evil, nor did it set him in the good, but it created death for those who ate of it. For when he said, Eat this, do not eat that, it became the beginning of death.

The Gospel of Phillip

THE TREE OF GOOD AND ELEVATION OF CONSCIOUSNESS

It's important that one understands that the Lord knew Adam and Eve would succumb to temptation by Satan. He knew also the rebel angels would become unbridled in evil once Adam and Eve were transformed into the flesh bodies that the archons were given instructions on how to mold. Those modeled forms are the bodies that their spirits would wear while living out lifetime on this planet. It would be in these clothes of flesh that they would fulfill all of the promises of Genesis 3 as prophesied by the Lord before he banished them from upper Paradise and placed them on the lower earth.

Once Adam was transformed into his new fleshly body on the eighth day, Zoe was sent to wake him up as to where he had fallen from and how he got to be where he is now. She would take residence in the form of Eve while giving instruction to Adam. She ascends back up into heaven, leaving Adam and Eve to their new lives and fate when the archons rape the form of Eve, impregnating her with Cain. (While men slept, his enemy came and sowed tares)

Another theme that presents itself in the study of scripture is the veiled reference of angels having to drink from a cup of forgetfulness before incarnation into the flesh as humans. This cup of forgetfulness wipes remembrance clean so that, when born, the spirits enter flesh as a clean slate. The accumulation of memory begins anew with entrance into the womb and fusion with material form. Entering the flesh is much like putting on a suit of armor for the spirit. Bodies are only a temporary housing for what would be the duration of our existence in the Second World Age and third-dimensional timeline. The flesh is our second life and chance to redeem ourselves to the glory of what would be the Third World Age, which is an eternal age that has no end.

If we can just aspire to the required righteousness necessary to be counted among the Lord's most elect angels, maybe He will then count us worthy enough to have part in salvation and escape all those things that are coming upon the earth, for what is coming are horrors unimagined and not witnessed by humanity since the days of Noah.

Those abominations are tasked with decimating one third of humanity then left on the planet, or those not written into the Book of Life. Soon there will be a time when evil will be eradicated and allowed existence no more. I pray the Father Son bless us all with continuance and roles in their everlasting Kingdom.

For most it is difficult to consider life being about anything other than what is physical—succeeding in the material world, gaining a good education, securing a good job, providing for children, upholding the name and legacy of family; these are the things that people believe should drive the focus of human beings while living on the planet. It's difficult for people to grasp the bigger picture of life and being and to appreciate things on a more profound level, yet I believe that, more and more, people are starting to realize that those things, which they have worked their whole lives for, are falling short in their ability to deliver on the promises of joy and contentment—hence the search for new answers.

Continuing with the story, when Yaldaboath and the archons come upon the spirit of Zoe instructing Adam, she hides herself within his body. Attempting to retrieve her spirit, Yaldaboath paralyzes Adam in slumber, seeking to find where she had hidden herself within him, and removing a rib fashioned it into another molded form, this time of a woman. His hope was to capture Zoe in the form of Eve much as he had Adam who was now trapped in the flesh of their male-modeled form. If Zoe chose to inhabit its physicality, they thought they might then have chance to seize and soil her with their lust so that, being tainted, she would no longer have means to ascend again to the light.

This form becomes the eighth-day, fallen-dust Eve, the vessel by which she and Adam would fulfill all of the prophecies as laid out by the Lord in Genesis 3. On this planet and in their fallen forms they would lose their bright natures, suffer the ravages of thirst, hunger, childbirth, and as promised eventually succumb to death, which is the Tree of the Knowledge of Good and Evil, the flesh form.

When the archons attempt the rape of Zoe, she laughs at their futility, and hiding herself in the Tree of the Knowledge of Good, watches as they violate in foul ways the modeled form of the eighth-day, fallen-dust Eve. These rapes result in the birth of Cain and the seed line from which the Pharisees were born. This line is the synagogue of Satan, which says they are Jews, but are not.

> And the archons took him and placed him in paradise. And they said to him, 'Eat, that is at leisure,' for their luxury is bitter and their beauty is depraved. And their luxury is deception and their trees are godlessness and their fruit is deadly poison and their promise is death. And the tree of their life they had placed in the midst of paradise.
>
> And I shall teach you (pl.) what is the mystery of their life, which is the plan which they made together, which is the likeness of their spirit. The root of this (tree) is bitter and its branches are death, its shadow is hate and deception is in its leaves, and its blossom is the ointment of evil, and its fruit is death and desire is its seed, and it sprouts in darkness. The dwelling place of those who taste from it is Hades, and the darkness is their place of rest.
>
> Apocryphon of John

The Gospel of Phillip relates how the first tree leads to Adam, being under the authority of death, and how the second would in fact restore him to gnosis, wisdom, and knowledge that he is also a fallen angel trapped in flesh form. It's the Holy Spirit who would tempt them the second time to eat fruit from the Tree of Good, which expanded their minds, making them recognize that they were now naked to spiritual knowing and knowledge of their Maker.

> But what they call the tree of knowledge of good and evil, which is the Epinoia of the light, they stayed in front of it in order that he (Adam) might not look up to his fullness and recognize the nakedness of his shamefulness. But it was I who brought about that they ate.
>
> Apocryphon of John

The Apocryphon of John attributes Adam's awakening to Zoe the daughter of Sophia the daughter of Barbelo, who are representatives of the Holy Virgin Spirit. Zoe teaches Adam that the way of ascent is much the same as the way of descent and that in order to prepare the way for the restoration of the deficiency of the aeons, that it would take the Father sending the Son down to this planet and donning the flesh Himself, would then restore those righteous born of the flesh back to immortality and heavenly angelic form. Sophia's redemption would not be complete until Yahushuah/Jesus Christ was resurrected to life. When He returns the next time order will be restored and evil eradicated from the lower visible realms.

> And our sister Sophia (is) she who came down in innocence in order to rectify her deficiency. Therefore she was called Life, which is the mother of the living, by the foreknowledge of the sovereignty of heaven. And through her they have tasted the perfect Knowledge. I appeared in the form of an eagle on the tree of knowledge, which is the Epinoia from the foreknowledge of the pure light, that I might teach them and awaken them out of the depth of

sleep. For they were both in a fallen state, and they recognized their nakedness. The Epinoia appeared to them as a light; she awakened their thinking.

Apocryphon of John

They took Adam and put him in the garden, that he might cultivate it and keep watch over it. And the rulers issued a command to him, saying, "From every tree in the garden shall you eat; yet from the tree of recognizing good and evil do not eat, nor touch it; for the day you eat from it, with death you are going to die." They […] this. They do not understand what they have said to him; rather, by the father's will, they said this in such a way that he might (in fact) eat, and that Adam might <not> regard them as would a man of an exclusively material nature.

The Hypostasis of the Archons

Then the seven of them together laid plans. They came up to Adam and Eve timidly: they said to him, The fruit of all the trees created for you in Paradise shall be eaten; but as for the tree of knowledge, control yourselves and do not eat from it. If you eat, you will die. Having imparted great fear to them, they withdrew up to their authorities.

On the Origin of the World

Then the female spiritual principle came in the snake, the instructor; and it taught them, saying, "What did he say to you? Was it, 'From every tree in the garden shall you eat; yet—from the tree of recognizing good and evil do not eat?'" The carnal woman said, "Not only did he say 'Do not eat', but even 'Do not touch it; for the day you eat from it, with death you are going to die.'"

The Hypostasis of the Archons

THE TREE OF GOOD

And the snake, the instructor, said, "With death you shall not die; for it was out of jealousy that he said this to you. Rather your eyes shall open and you shall come to be like gods, recognizing evil and good." And the female instructing principle was taken away from the snake, and she left it behind, merely a thing of the earth. And the carnal woman took from the tree and ate; and she gave to her husband as well as herself; and these beings that possessed only a soul, ate. And their imperfection became apparent in their lack of knowledge; and they recognized that they were naked of the spiritual element, and took fig leaves and bound them upon their loins.

The Hypostasis of the Archons

And to I said to the savior, "Lord, was it not the serpent that taught Adam to eat?" The savior smiled and said, "The serpent taught them to eat from wickedness of begetting, lust, (and) destruction, that he (Adam) might be useful to him. And he (Adam) knew that he was disobedient to him (the chief archon) due to light of the Epinoia which is in him, which made him more correct in his thinking than the chief archon. And (the latter) wanted to bring about the power which he himself had given him. And he brought a forgetfulness over Adam."

Apocryphon of John

THE INSTRUCTOR AND THE FRUIT OF REDEMPTION

Then came the wisest of all creatures, who was called Beast. And when he saw the likeness of their mother Eve he said to her, What did God say to you? Was it 'Do not eat from the tree of knowledge'? She said, He said not only, 'Do not eat from it', but, 'Do not touch it, lest you die.' He said to her, Do not be afraid. In death you shall not die. For he knows that when you eat from it, your intellect will become sober and you will come to be like gods, recognizing the difference that obtains between evil men and good ones. Indeed, it was in jealousy that he said this to you, so that you would not eat from it.

Now Eve had confidence in the words of the instructor. She gazed at the tree and saw that it was beautiful and appetizing, and liked it; she took some of its fruit and ate it; and she gave some also to her husband, and he too ate it. Then their intellect became open. For when they had eaten, the light of knowledge had shone upon them. When they clothed themselves with shame, they knew that they were naked of knowledge. When they became sober, they saw that they were naked and became enamored of one another. When they saw that the ones who had modelled them had the form of beasts, they loathed them: they were very aware.

On the Origin of the World

Having been elevated in consciousness, Adam and Eve realize that they have now been transformed into flesh form, that they are in a fallen state, and that they live in a world full of demonic beings and dark authorities. They also recognize that they are different than the fallen rebel angels and that these dark angels are not friendly to their disposition. Having been instructed by Zoe as to where they had fallen from, they realize that they must uphold all the ordinances and laws of God if they are to be restored to eternal rest and salvation at the end of days.

And when Yaltabaoth noticed that they withdrew from him, he cursed his earth. He found the woman as she was preparing herself for her husband. He was lord over her, though he did not know the mystery which had come to pass through the holy decree. And they were afraid to blame him. And he showed his angels his ignorance which is in him. And he cast them out of paradise and he clothed them in gloomy darkness. And the chief archon saw the virgin who stood by

Adam, and that the luminous Epinoia of life had appeared in her. And Yaltabaoth was full of ignorance. And when the foreknowledge of the All noticed (it), she sent some and they snatched life out of Eve.

Apocryphon of John

And the man came forth because of the shadow of the light which is in him. And his thinking was superior to all those who had made him. When they looked up, they saw that his thinking was superior. And they took counsel with the whole array of archons and angels. They took fire and earth and water and mixed them together with the four fiery winds. And they wrought them together and caused a great disturbance. And they brought him (Adam) into the shadow of death, in order that they might form (him) again from earth and water and fire and the spirit which originates in matter, which is the ignorance of darkness and desire, and their counterfeit spirit. This is the tomb of the newly-formed body with which the robbers had clothed the man, the bond of forgetfulness; and he became a mortal man. This is the first one who came down, and the first separation. But the Epinoia of the light which was in him, she is the one who was to awaken his thinking.

Apocryphon of John

Then the authorities came up to their Adam. And when they saw his female counterpart speaking with him, they became agitated with great agitation; and they became enamored of her. They said to one another, "Come, let us sow our seed in her, and they pursued her." And she laughed at them for their witlessness and their blindness; and in their clutches she became a tree, and left before them her shadowy reflection resembling herself; and they defiled it foully.—And they defiled the stamp of her voice, so that by the form they had modeled, together with their (own) image, they made themselves liable to condemnation.

The Hypostasis of the Archons

THE RAPE OF EVE

What's important to understand about the next part of the story is that the prophecies stated in Genesis 3 would not be fulfilled until Adam and Eve had been transformed into bodies of flesh. This transformation did not take place until the eighth day. When Adam and Eve are transformed into flesh/dust form, then the prophecies as laid out in Genesis 3 are fulfilled one by one. Zoe, after instructing Adam, curses the archons for attempting to defile her in the molded form they created to trap her. This rape resulted in the birth of Cain, a fulfillment to, "Unto the woman he said, 'I will greatly multiply thy sorrow and thy conception; in sorrow thou shalt bring forth children; and thy desire shall be to thy husband, and he shall rule over thee'" (Genesis 3:15). The next passage is one of those hidden gems within the Word that verifies the dual seed line theory. For if there were not two blood lines and Satan did not have his own seed on this planet, why enmity between the seed of the serpent and seed of the woman? "And I will put enmity between thee and the woman, and between thy seed and her seed; it shall bruise thy head, and thou shalt bruise his heel," was fulfilled with the murder of Abel by his brother Cain, who as the firstborn son of the devil became the first murderer, liar, deceiver, and progenitor of evil on this planet.

Abel was the first casualty in the war between the bloodlines that would span the duration of the 7,000 years that would be the Second World Age. The Book of Enoch 22:7 states that, "This is the spirit which went forth from Abel, whom his brother Cain slew, and he makes his suit against him till his seed is destroyed from the face of the earth, and his seed is annihilated from amongst the seed of men." With the birth of his brother Seth, Adam would begin to work the soil to bring forth sustenance to feed his children a fulfillment of Genesis 3:17.

> Because thou hast hearkened unto the voice of thy wife, and hast eaten of the tree, of which I commanded thee, saying, Thou shalt not eat of it: cursed is the ground for thy sake; in sorrow shalt thou eat of it all the days of thy life; Thorns also and thistles shall it bring forth to thee; and thou shalt eat the herb of the field; In the sweat of thy face shalt thou eat bread, till thou return unto the ground; for out of it wast thou taken: for dust thou art, and unto dust shalt thou return.
>
> Genesis 3:17

It's important to understand that as the fall parallels the loss of immortality, bright nature, and their clothing of light, so, too, does the elevation of humanity parallel the restoration of intelligence, awakening from darkness and their realization as to whence they had fallen, being then trapped in the flesh in those forms which they then would fulfill the prophecies that were told to them by the Lord before He even banished them from Paradise.

It would be on this planet that the Second World Age began and angels born into the bodies of humanity would die the death of mortals. Lucifer is the prince that would be brought to the death mentioned in this passage, as well as Isaiah 14 and Ezekiel 28. Those two passages also acknowledge how Lucifer, as Satan, now occupies the form of a man, and how the Lord would force him to die the death of a man in sight of kings and queens, the seed of his progeny.

> God standeth in the congregation of the mighty; he judgeth among the gods. How long will ye judge unjustly, and accept the persons of the wicked? Selah.
>
> Defend the poor and fatherless: do justice to the afflicted and needy. Deliver the poor and needy: rid them

out of the hand of the wicked. They know not, neither will they understand; they walk on in darkness: all the foundations of the earth are out of course. I have said, "Ye are gods; and all of you are children of the most High. But ye shall die like men, and fall like one of the princes. Arise, O God, judge the earth: for thou shalt inherit all nations."

Psalms 82, KJV

Jesus answered them, "Is it not written in your law, I said, *Ye are gods?* If he called them gods, unto whom the word of God came, and the scripture cannot be broken; Say ye of him, whom the Father hath sanctified, and sent into the world, Thou blasphemest; because I said, I am the Son of God? If I do not the works of my Father, believe me not. But if I do, though ye believe not me, believe the works: that ye may know, and believe, that the Father is in me, and I in him."

John 10:34-38

Then Eve, being a force, laughed at their decision. She put mist into their eyes and secretly left her likeness with Adam. She entered the tree of knowledge and remained there. And they pursued her, and she revealed to them that she had gone into the tree and become a tree. Then, entering a great state of fear, the blind creatures fled.

Afterward, when they had recovered from the daze, they came to Adam; and seeing the likeness of this woman with him, they were greatly disturbed, thinking it was she that was the true Eve. And they acted rashly; they came up to her and seized her and cast their seed upon her. They did so wickedly, defiling not only in natural ways but also in foul ways, defiling first the seal of her voice—that had spoken with them, saying, What is it that exists before you?—intending to defile those who might say at the consummation (of the age) that they had been born of the true man through verbal expression. And they erred, not knowing that it was their own body that they had defiled: it was the likeness that the authorities and their angels defiled in every way.

On the Origin of the World

When we incarnate into this world we are stripped of our former memories. As part of the great mystery and fabric of creation we have rememberance that connects back to before the beginning, to the foundations of the world and universe when Yahweh/Yahushuah as part of self held all in being. We have been with the Father and Son since before the institution of time. The reason our memories are swept from us is so that we enter as a clean slate for renewed chance at redemption and salvation. What we do in this lifetime as angels, imprisoned within the flesh, determines our eternal fates and what we do in the life hereafter. Those who are blessed to be counted among the most elect will in fact judge angels and sit as jurors in the councils of the Lord to convict and condemn the rebel and fallen angels intended to be as gods themselves, forging a path of self service and vain personal glory.

"Do ye not know that the saints shall judge the world? and if the world shall be judged by you, are ye unworthy to judge the smallest matters? Know ye not that we shall judge angels? how much more things that pertain to this life?" 1 Corinthians 6:2-3, KJV.

There are only two paths we can follow in life, one as a foot-washer in service to one another or as tyrant king in service to self. One is the path of priesthood or the way of Abel, and the other of kingship and divine right to rule—or the way of Cain. Those who follow the Lord and adhere to His commandments become the priests, prophets, and apostles that are stood up by the Lord to serve the people. Those who are appointed by Satan to become kings, queens, rulers, presidents, and prime ministers in service of a New World Order are usually personas that serve his goal of world domination. These individuals believe in their divine right to rule over and decide the collective direction of the world. The fact that many of them gather yearly at Bohemian Grove to worship a 40-foot owl, in a mock ritual sacrifice of a human effigy, lets one know that something weird is still ongoing.

> He made a plan with his authorities, which are his powers, and they committed together adultery with Sophia, and bitter fate was begotten through them, which is the last of the changeable bonds. And it is of a sort that is interchangeable. And it is harder and stronger than she with whom the gods united, and the angels and the demons and all the generations until this day. For from that fate came forth every sin and injustice and blasphemy, and the chain of forgetfulness and ignorance and every severe command, and serious sins and great fears. And thus the whole creation was made blind, in order that they may not know God, who is above all of them. And because of the chain of forgetfulness, their sins were hidden. For they are bound with measures and times and moments, since it (fate) is lord over everything.
>
> Next, let me say that once the rulers had seen him and the female creature who was with him erring ignorantly like beasts, they were very glad. When they learned that the immortal man was not going to neglect them, rather that they would even have to fear the female creature that had turned into a tree, they were disturbed, and said, Perhaps this is the true man—this being who has brought a fog upon us and has taught us that she who was soiled is like him—and so we shall be conquered!
>
> On the Origin of the World

From that day, the authorities knew that truly there was something mightier than they: they recognized only that their commandments had not been kept. Great jealousy was brought into the world solely because of the immortal man. Now when the rulers saw that their Adam had entered into an alien state of knowledge, they desired to test him, and they gathered together all the domestic animals and the wild beasts of the earth and the birds of heaven and brought them to Adam to see what he would call them.

When he saw them, he gave names to their creatures. They became troubled because Adam had recovered from all the trials. They assembled and laid plans, and they said, Behold Adam! He has come to be like one of us, so that he knows the difference between the light and the darkness. Now perhaps he will be deceived, as in the case of the Tree of Knowledge, and also will come to the Tree of Life and eat from it, and become immortal, and become lord, and despise us and disdain us and all our glory! Then he will denounce us along with our universe. Come, let us expel him from Paradise, down to the land from which he was taken, so that henceforth he might not be able to recognize anything better than we can. And so they expelled Adam from Paradise, along with his wife. And this deed that they had done was not enough for them. Rather, they were afraid. They went in to the Tree of Life and surrounded it with great fearful things, fiery living creatures called Cheroubin, and they put a flaming sword in their midst, fearfully twirling at all times, so that no earthly being might ever enter that place.

On the Origin of the World

Having been granted authority over this fallen world for short time, Yaldaboath decided the best plan of action for he and his demon angels to assert their influence over the lives of those angels being born into the flesh as humanity was to make life so difficult that they/we wouldn't have time for seeking out the divine and coming to understand the larger questions for our reasons for being here on this planet and in this time.

The very reasons that this book was written—to wake you up to who you are, how you got here, and what this life is all about—these are the things that Satan does not want one to entertain and come to know. He wants people to focus only on those things that serve his purpose, vain distractions, and meaningless entertainment—things that do nothing as far as redeeming spirit for salvation of soul and succeed only in keeping one lost and wayward. This is a world of the blind leading the blind, of the lost leading the lost, and as such one must be careful in what one believes and whom one chooses to follow. Every decision we make is critical for determining individual, eternal fates and destinies. Use time wisely as none are guaranteed promise of future morrows, and truly any day could be our last.

Two other subtleties of variation to take notice of concerning the fall and elevation are that on day six the Lord asked Adam and Eve, "Where art thou?" not because He did not know where they were, but because they were trying to hide from Him, and after finding that they ate of the forbidden fruit the Lord does not curse Adam and Eve, but instead the serpent, placing enmity between the two seed lines and then the earth so that it would not grow freely in over-abundant bounty. Never does He curse humanity even though they would now be required to put forth effort in producing food from the ground whereas in the Garden of Paradise fruit gave of itself freely without necessary toil. When humanity returns to our first estate we will no longer have to work the ground to bring forth food.

On day eight when Adam and Eve eat of the fruit, Yaldaboath does not know where they are, verifying that he is limited in his cognitive capabilities unlike the Father and Son, who are omnipotent and all knowing. After finding that they ate of the fruit from the Tree of Good, Yaldaboath curses the instructor that beckoned them to eat—the earth—and both Adam and Eve before exiling them from his domain on the lower earth.

> Then Eve saw that the appearance of the fig-tree was beautiful, and that its smell was delightful; and she desired to eat of it and to become a goddess. So she stretched out her hand, and plucked, and ate, and gave also to her husband, and he likewise did eat.

And they were stripped of the fair glory and glorious light of purity wherewith they were clothed, when they saw not each other's nakedness. And their eyes were opened, and they saw their nakedness; and they took leaves of the fig-tree, and covered their nakedness for shame, and hid themselves beneath thick trees. Then God called Adam and said to him, 'Where art thou, Adam?'—not that He did not know where he was, but in a chiding manner—and Adam said, 'Lord, I heard Thy voice, and I hid myself because I am naked.' God said, 'Whence knowest thou that thou art naked? peradventure hast thou transgressed the law and command which I laid down for thee, and hast eaten of the tree of which I commanded thee not to eat?' Adam said, 'The woman whom thou gavest to be with me, she gave to me, and I did eat.' And God questioned Eve in like manner; and Eve said, 'The serpent beguiled me, and I did eat.' And God cursed the serpent, saying, 'Cursed art thou above all beasts upon the earth.' With the cursing of the serpent, who was the tool of Satan, Satan, who had instigated the serpent, was himself cursed; and immediately his legs were destroyed, and he crawled upon his belly, and instead of being an animal became a hissing reptile.

And God set enmity between the serpent and man, saying, 'He shall smite the heel of man, but man shall crush his head, and the food of the serpent shall be dust.' God said to Eve, 'In pain shalt thou bring forth children;' and to Adam He said, 'Cursed is the ground for thy sake, and in toil and the sweat of thy face shalt thou eat thy bread; for dust thou art, and unto dust shalt thou return.' And the earth, by reason of the curse which it had received, straightway brought forth thorns and thistles. And God drove them out from Paradise at the ninth hour of the same day in which they were created.

The Book of the Bee 16

Not having the power of foresight and omniscient abilities to comprehend the consequences of his actions, Yaldaboath, upon learning that Adam and Eve had in fact eaten of the Tree of Good and were endowed with a greater capacity to understand the secrets of the universe than even Satan and his fallen angels, was disgusted and banished them from his area of control upon the earth.

> Then the chief ruler came; and he said, Adam! Where are you?—for he did not understand what had happened. And Adam said, I heard your voice and was afraid because I was naked; and I hid. The ruler said, Why did you hide, unless it is because you have eaten from the tree from which alone I commanded you not to eat? And you have eaten! Adam said, The woman that you gave me, she gave to me and I ate. And the arrogant ruler cursed the woman.

> The Hypostasis of the Archons

> Then when the rulers knew that they had broken their commandments, they entered Paradise and came to Adam and Eve with earthquake and great threatening, to see the effect of the aid. Then Adam and Eve trembled greatly and hid under the trees in Paradise. Then the rulers did not know where they were and said, Adam, where are you? He said, I am here, for through fear of you I hid, being ashamed. And they said to him ignorantly, Who told you about the shame with which you clothed yourself?—unless you have eaten from that tree! He said, The woman whom you gave me—it is she that gave to me and I ate. Then they said to the latter, What is this that you have done? She answered and said, It is the instructor who urged me on, and I ate.

> On the Origin of the World

> The woman said, It was the snake that led me astray and I ate. They turned to the snake and cursed its shadowy reflection, [...] powerless, not comprehending that it was

a form they themselves had modeled. From that day, the snake came to be under the curse of the authorities; until the all-powerful man was to come, that curse fell upon the snake. They turned to their Adam and took him and expelled him from the garden along with his wife; for they have no blessing, since they too are beneath the curse. Moreover, they threw mankind into great distraction and into a life of toil, so that their mankind might be occupied by worldly affairs, and might not have the opportunity of being devoted to the Holy Spirit.

The Hypostasis of the Archons

Unless one understands and recognizes the subtle differences between the fall of humanity and the elevation of humanity, one would not be able to make sense of the sum total of not only the Gnostic teachings but also in how they fit into and confirm the work of the Old and New Testaments. Though the story of the fall and the elevation of humanity seem similar, they are very different tales that allude to differing time and place. We know that the Lord allows many major events to repeat in cycles; events that occurred in the past are often fated to transpire in the future. Just as Lucifer refused to bow before the dominion of Yahushuah on the second day, so, too, did Lucifer refuse to bow before the image of the Father and Son—or Adam, made on the sixth day. As we had an incursion of fallen angels and giants during the time of Jared and Enoch prior to the flood of Noah, so shall the same be repeated here in the last days as we approach the harvest and the separation of the wheat and the tares.

Understanding that indeed the Lord did have great part to play in the elevation of humanity once we found ourselves stricken to the planet in a fallen state will help one to unlock the teachings of the Nag Hammadi codices, Dead Sea scrolls, as well as other apocryphal and pseudipigraphal books, for without this insight, comprehension of these teachings, in my opinion, is just not possible. And because the stories were mixed, distorted, and changed during the evolution of humanity, the various characters that were the nephilim have become confused, and the context of their ancient interdiction into our ancestors' lives is lost.

> Then the rulers came up to the instructor. Their eyes became misty because of him, and they could not do anything to him. They cursed him, since they were powerless. Afterwards, they came up to the woman and cursed her and her offspring. After the woman, they cursed Adam, and the land because of him, and the crops; and all things they had created, they cursed. They have no blessing. Good cannot result from evil.
>
> On the Origin of the World

Notice that when Adam eats from the tree in Genesis it is Satan as the serpent that is cursed for seducing Eve into deceiving Adam, and that the Lord—upon finding that Satan had deceived his highest creatures—cursed him and stripped him of the beauty he once had. Satan, when cast from the heavens, was transformed into a dragon. Bereft of his glory, he and his seraphim angels are the reptilian class of angels mentioned as having had part to play in this planet's ancient past.

There is even one very interesting Gnostic tale told by the Lord that hint at His being the Instructor that came to elevate humanity from their/our darkened state. This particular story is very profound in that Yahushuah cited specifically that He came to this world in previous embodiment—prior to His incarnation and mission as Yahweh manifest in flesh—and that this previous embodiment was the one that awakened Adam and Eve as to where they had fallen. This story is further profound in that Yahushuah specifically cited a previous embodiment prior to His immaculate conception as Christ. In this text He seems to allude that He was the instructor—the one that awakened Adam and Eve as to where they had fallen and from whence.

Now I have come the second time in the likeness of a female, and have spoken with them. And I shall tell them of the coming end of the Aeon and teach them of the beginning of the Aeon to come, the one without change, the one in which our appearance will be changed. We shall be purified within those Aeons from which I revealed myself in the thought of the likeness of my masculinity. I settled among those who are worthy in the Thought of my changeless Aeon.

For I shall tell you a mystery of this particular Aeon, and tell you about the forces that are in it. The birth beckons; hour begets hour, day begets day. The months made known the month. Time has gone round succeeding time. This particular Aeon was completed in this fashion, and it was estimated, and it (was) short, for it was a finger that released a finger, and a joint that was separated from a joint. Then, when the great Authorities knew that the time of fulfillment had appeared—just as in the pangs of the parturient it (the time) has drawn near, so also had the destruction approached—all together the elements trembled, and the foundations of the underworld and the ceilings of Chaos shook, and a great fire shone within their midst, and the rocks and the earth were shaken like a reed shaken by the wind. And the lots of Fate and those who apportion the domiciles were greatly disturbed over a great thunder. And the thrones of the Powers were disturbed, since they were overturned, and their King was afraid. And those who pursue Fate paid their allotment of visits to the path, and they said to the Powers, What is this disturbance and this shaking that has come upon us through a Voice <belonging> to the exalted Speech? And our entire habitation has been shaken, and the entire circuit of the path of ascent has met with destruction, and the path upon which we go, which takes us up to the Archgenitor of our birth, has ceased to be established for us.

Then the Powers answered, saying, We too are at loss about it, since we did not know what was responsible for it.

But arise, let us go up to the Archgenitor and ask him. And the powers all gathered and went up to the Archgenitor. They said to him, Where is your boasting in which you boast? Did we not hear you say, I am God, and I am your Father, and it is I who begot you. and there is none beside me? Now behold, there has appeared a Voice belonging to that invisible Speech of the Aeon which we know not. And we ourselves did not recognize to whom we belong, for that Voice which we listened to is foreign to us, and we did not recognize it; we did not know whence it was.

It came and put fear in our midst and weakening in the members of our arms. So now let us weep and mourn most bitterly! As for the future, let us make our entire flight before we are imprisoned perforce, and taken down to the bosom of the underworld. For already the slackening of our bondage has approached, and the times are cut short, and the days have shortened, and our time has been fulfilled, and the weeping of our destruction has approached us, so that we may be taken to the place we recognize. For as for our tree from which we grew, a fruit of ignorance is what it has; and also its leaves, it is death that dwells in them, and darkness dwells under the shadow of its boughs. And it was in deceit and lust that we harvested it, this (tree) through which ignorant Chaos became for us a dwelling place. For behold, even he, the Archgenitor of our birth, about whom we boast, even he did not know this Speech.

So now, O sons of the Thought, listen to me, to the Speech of the Mother of your mercy, for you have become worthy of the mystery hidden from the Aeons, so that you might receive it. And the consummation of this particular Aeon and of the evil life has approached, and there dawns the beginning of the Aeon to come, which has no change forever.

Trimorphic Protennoia

The Second time I came in the Speech of my Voice. I gave shape to those who took shape, until their consummation. The Third time I revealed myself to them in their tents as

Word, and I revealed myself in the likeness of their shape. And I wore everyone's garment, and I hid myself within them, and they did not know the one who empowers me. For I dwell within all the Sovereignties and Powers, and within the angels, and in every movement that exists in all matter. And I hid myself within them until I revealed myself to my brethren. And none of them (the Powers) knew me, although it is I who work in them. Rather, they thought that the All was created by them, since they are ignorant, not knowing their root, the place in which they grew.

Trimorphic Protennoia

During the elevation of eighth-day Adam and Eve it would be the Christ as Holy Spirit that occupied the serpent as Instructor in form to tempt Adam and Eve to eat of the Tree of Good. This fruit would awaken them to the consequences of their fall from grace. Being a representative of the higher authorities, the archons have no power over the instructor and so curse the serpent (the form He was occupying) even though it was a creature of their own making. In the account of the fall, never did Yahweh/Yahushuah curse Adam or Eve, but Satan and the land only. Yaldaboath, in the account of the elevation, cursed the instructor, the serpent, Adam, Eve, and even the earth when he discovered both had eaten from the tree of the Knowledge of Good.

> And he was continuously in paradise, and the devil understood that I wanted to create another world, because Adam was lord on earth, to rule and control it. The devil is the evil spirit of the lower places, as a fugitive he made Sotona from the heavens as his name was Satanail, thus he became different from the angels, but his nature did not change his intelligence as far as his understanding of righteous and sinful things. And he understood his condemnation and the sin which he had sinned before, therefore he conceived thought against Adam, in such form he

entered and seduced Eva, but did not touch Adam. But I cursed ignorance, but what I had blessed previously, those I did not curse, I cursed not man, nor the earth, nor other creatures, but man's evil fruit, and his works.

Book of the The Secrets of Enoch, 31

Behold, see how greatly I have loved thee, for though I have cursed the earth for thy sake, yet have I withdrawn thee from the operation of the curse. As for the serpent, I have fettered his legs in his belly, and I have given him the dust of the earth for food; and Eve have I bound under the yoke of servitude.

The Cave of Treasures

Unless one understands that there literally is a seed line sired from and dedicated to Satan, and that this seed line is wholly dedicated to evil, one would not understand why the Lord attributes all sin to the rebel and fallen angels who brought all destruction and abomination into this world. Knowledge that we ourselves are fallen angels, imprisoned in flesh form, and that there are two individual blood lines on this planet, one wholly dedicated to evil and the formation of a New World Order and the other to righteousness and the rewards of salvation, can go a long way in deciphering where we are and what this life is all about. These discernments will bring much elucidation to the reading of scripture for those who are still hesitant to begin a serious study of Yahweh's Word and help one make sense of myriad teachings that otherwise would not make any kind of literal sense.

They turned to their Adam and took him and expelled him from the garden along with his wife; for they have no blessing, since they too are beneath the curse. Moreover, they threw mankind into great distraction and into a life of toil, so that their mankind might be occupied by worldly affairs, and might not have the opportunity of being devoted to the holy spirit. Now afterwards, she bore Cain, their son; and Cain cultivated the land. Thereupon he knew his wife; again becoming pregnant, she bore Abel; and Abel was a herdsman of sheep. Now Cain brought in from the crops of his field, but Abel brought in an offering (from) among his lambs. God looked upon the votive offerings of Abel; but he did not accept the votive offerings of Cain. And carnal Cain pursued Abel, his brother.

Hypostasis of the Archons

The next part of this story has to do with the fulfillment of those prophecies as laid out in Genesis 3. The Lord told them what would happen to them and their progeny once they ate from the forbidden fruit. Eating from the tree of the knowledge of good and evil would cause them to lose their bright natures and immortal status as angels, tending the garden of paradise in the third heaven where the new Jerusalem awaits us even now.

Paradise is also the place that the Lord said He went to prepare for us. Paradise is where we fell from and where we aspire to return to once again to embrace our first estate as restored sons of God.

> Let not your heart be troubled: ye believe in God, believe also in me. In my Father's house are many mansions: if it were not so, I would have told you. I go to prepare a place for you. And if I go and prepare a place for you, I will come again, and receive you unto myself; that where I am, there ye may be also. And whither I go ye know, and the way ye know. Thomas saith unto him, Lord, we know not whither thou goest; and how can we know the way? Jesus saith unto him, I am the way, the truth, and the life: no man cometh unto the Father, but by me. If ye had known me, ye should have known my Father also: and from henceforth ye know him, and have seen him. Philip saith unto him, Lord, shew us the Father, and it sufficeth us. Jesus saith unto him, Have I been so long time with you, and yet hast thou not known me, Philip? he that hath seen me hath

seen the Father; and how sayest thou then, Shew us the Father? Believest thou not that I am in the Father, and the Father in me? the words that I speak unto you I speak not of myself: but the Father that dwelleth in me, he doeth the works. Believe me that I am in the Father, and the Father in me: or else believe me for the very works' sake. Verily, verily, I say unto you, He that believeth on me, the works that I do shall he do also; and greater works than these shall he do; because I go unto my Father. And whatsoever ye shall ask in my name, that will I do, that the Father may be glorified in the Son.

John 14:1-13 (KJV)

Once Adam and Eve are transformed into the flesh on the eighth day, all of which was revealed in Genesis 3 would then transpire. It would be in these modelled forms that Eve would be raped and impregnated by the archons of the lower world. In one gnostic account about the daughter of Eve called Norea, the archons tell her that her mother had performed sexual favors for them and that she also must adhere to their lust.

> The rulers went to meet her, intending to lead her astray. Their supreme chief said to her, Your mother Eve came to us. But Norea turned to them and said to them, It is you who are the rulers of the darkness; you are accursed. And you did not know my mother; instead it was your female counterpart that you knew. For I am not your descendant; rather it is from the world above that I am come. The arrogant ruler turned, with all his might, and his countenance came to be like (a) black [...]; he said to her presumptuously, You must render service to us, as did also your mother Eve.

The Hypostasis of the Archons

Now that Adam and Eve were living in the Cave of treasures upon the lower wilderness of the fallen Earth, Eve would as prophesied give birth to Cain who, as the firstborn son of the devil, would murder his half-brother Abel who, as the firstborn son of Adam, became the first casualty in the enmity cited in chapter three verse fifteen. This enmity would play out between the two sides over the course of the next 7,000 thousand years that the second world age would be in existence. Not only would Adam have to work the ground to bring forth sustenance to feed himself and Eve, he would now also have to work to support the many children that would be born to them now that they were in the flesh. The final prophecy to be fulfilled would be there succumbing to death that the Lord told them would be the consequence for eating from the Tree of the Knowledge of Good and Evil.

This brings us to the part of the story that I published as my fourth book, *Lucifer—Father of Cain*. In that book I expound upon this topic with great detail, utilizing text from innumerable sources available from all over the world. The fact that Cain was not a child of Adam is only one of the many esoteric topics touched upon within the contents of that book. Over 300 pages long, it summarizes and ties together the loose ends of all topics, including mythology, religion, and secret lore that have until now never been brought together in such cohesive fashion.

It's my belief that the Lord allowed me to acquire a severe disability early in my life so that I would have the time and the focus necessary to study in-depth the vast amounts of wisdom in texts now available to us. Having read so much of them, He was able to show me the underlying truth connecting them all together. Most people do not have the time to study that wealth of information and so I consider my quadriplegia a blessing in that it aligned me with the intent of the Lord's will for my life. Like most, I was lost and wayward—wandering the broad path of destruction. That's the only thing that makes this work unique in comparison to others.

I pray that the Lord bless you and your family in protection and discernment so that you can utilize what time we do have left to prepare yourselves, loved ones, extended family members, and friends for those things that are coming quickly upon the earth. The Lord has warned us about this particular period of time for thousands of years through His many apostles and prophets that have—for millennia—told us of those things that we find now before us.